25 10 90

A.P.

**Edit**

| Undo | Alt Bksp |
|------|----------|
| Redo | |
| Repeat | ^R |
| Cut | ShiftDel |
| Copy | CtrlIns |
| Paste | ShiftIns |
| Clear | Del |
| Duplicate | ^D |
| Copy Style From... | |
| Edit Text... | ^T |
| Character Attributes... | |
| Select All | |

**COPY STYLE**

☐ Outline Pen
☐ Outline Color
☐ Fill
☐ Text Attributes

[ Cancel ] [ OK ]

After pressing OK, choose the object to copy from.

**TEXT**

Wombats in space

Alignment: ● Left ○ Center ○ Right ○ None

Avalon
Aardvark
Banff
Bangkok
Bodnoff
Brooklyn
Casablanca
Centurion_Old
Cupertino

Point Size: 24.0

● Normal
○ Bold
○ Italic
○ Bold-Italic

A

[ Spacing... ]    [ Cancel ] [ OK ]

**CHARACTER ATTRIBUTES**

Avalon
Aardvark
Banff
Bangkok
Bodnoff
Brooklyn
Casablanca
Centurion_Old
Cupertino

Point Size: 24.0

● Normal
○ Bold
○ Italic
○ Bold-Italic
○ Superscript
○ Subscript

A

Horizontal Shift: 0.00 ems
Vertical Shift: 0 % of Pt Size
Character Angle: 0 degrees

[ Cancel ]    [ OK ]

**ROTATE & SKEW**

Rotation Angle: 0 degrees
Skew Horizontally: 0 degrees
Skew Vertically: 0 degrees

```
        90°
180° —— 0°
       -90°
```

☐ Leave Original

[ Cancel ]    [ OK ]

**Transform**

Rotate & Skew...
Stretch & Mirror...
Clear Transformations

**STRETCH & MIRROR**

Stretch Horizontally: 100 %    [ Horz Mirror ]
Stretch Vertically: 100 %    [ Vert Mirror ]

☐ Leave Original

[ CANCEL ]    [ OK ]

*(continued on last page and inside back cover)*

# Mastering
# COREL DRAW!

# Mastering
# *COREL DRAW!*

*Steve Rimmer*

SYBEX®

San Francisco • Paris • Düsseldorf • Soest

385
R54
1990

Acquisitions Editor: Dianne King
Editor: Doug Robert
Technical Editor: Dan Brodnitz
Word Processors: Scott Campbell, Deborah Maizels
Series Designer: Julie Bilski
Chapter Art: Helen Bruno
Layout Artists: Helen Bruno and A. Eilene Carver
Screen Graphics: Jeff Giese
Typesetter: Elizabeth Newman
Proofreader: Patsy Owens
Indexer: Nancy Guenther
Cover Designer: Thomas Ingalls + Associates
Cover Photographer: Michael Lamotte

Library of Congress Card Number: 89-52199
ISBN: 0-89588-685-5
Manufactured in the United States of America
10 9 8 7 6 5 4 3 2 1

*For Sarah Jane Newman,*
*who discovered through experimentation*
*that publishers really do bleed non-repro blue.*

# *Acknowlegments*

**M**y thanks to Vivi Nichol at Corel, tech support extraordinaire, who answered all sorts of obscure questions.

Some of the details of "The History of Helvetica" in Chapter 9 came from Ed Cleary's excellent column on typography appearing in the May/June 1987 edition of *Studio* magazine.

Some of the ideas on logo design, as espoused in Chapter 10, are indebted to Tony Leighton's feature on "The Art and Science of Corporate Iconography" in the summer 1986 edition of *Applied Arts Quarterly*.

Jones the dog improved several of the figures and diagrams in this book by consuming the early—and very much inferior—drafts.

Delia Brown of SYBEX created the cow logo in Chapter 10.

And finally, acknowledgement should be given to John, King of England, Lord of Ireland, Duke of Normandy and Aquitaine, and Count of Anjou, whose great charter provided the civilization upon which this book is founded and, perhaps more importantly, several tens of kilobytes of wholly copyright-free text to use in some of the example designs.

# Contents at a Glance

# Table of
# Contents

## *appendices*

## A  *Hardware, Software, and Using Microsoft Windows*     *337*

# *Introduction*

The thickness of this book probably disguises one of the fundamental qualities of Corel Draw—namely, that it is easy to use. The actual mechanical processes of drawing lines, placing text, and printing files, among other things, can be mastered in a few hours. Having a pretty intuitive user interface, a well-thought-out structure which is very forgiving of mistakes, and a toolbox which does pretty much what you'd think it should do, many new Corel Draw users find they can produce gratifying results without ever cracking a manual.

In a sense, Corel Draw is a digital analog to pencils, rulers, rule tape, Rapidographs, french curves, Zip-a-Tone, and the other paraphernalia of drawing and design. With the possible exception of Rapidographs, which seem to require lengthy dissertations on their cleaning and maintenance, none of the aforementioned design tools require detailed instructions for their basic use. The mechanics of operating a pencil, for example, are pretty self-evident. Similarly, once you get over the initial problems of installing and becoming familiar with Corel Draw—perhaps analogous to locating the pointy end of a pencil—you'll find that you can start using it with relatively little instruction.

This doesn't explain, however, why this book is so thick.

As you probably know, getting truly satisfying results from your design tools is more than a matter of learning how to hold them or move them or otherwise make them go. Getting worthwhile results from your design software, likewise, is not just a matter of learning what all the menus and dialogs do. Aside from the comparatively easy task of mastering all the parts of Corel Draw, you must also come to terms with the elements of drawing, design, typography, and other bits of commercial art as they relate to the package.

The latter half of this book, accordingly, is a guide to designing with Corel Draw. Now, this is a rather tricky undertaking. This book certainly won't make you into the equivalent of a designer with four years of art college. It also won't teach you how to draw if you can't do so now. That is because original design—whether you're designing individual graphics, publication pages, or soup can labels—is an art, and art is something you can't learn from a book. Professional looking, well-executed, functional basic designs, on the other hand, are somewhat a mechanical process. There are guidelines you can apply to a design project, rules to follow, and so on. *Mastering COREL DRAW!* will help you to learn these rudiments of design.

## *VERSIONS USED*

If you have not yet acquired Corel Draw and you are looking at this book just to get an idea of whether you ought to, you should first be told that Corel Draw was created to operate on a PC under the Microsoft Windows operating environment.

This book covers Versions 1.0 through 1.11 of Corel Draw, using Version 2.0 of Microsoft Windows. In discussions of integrating Corel Draw with desktop publishing programs, the other programs and hardware referred to are those currently available or in common use. For example, discussions of Ventura Publisher refer in the main to Version 2.0 unless otherwise noted.

Appendix A deals with specific hardware, software, and memory requirements for using both Corel Draw and Microsoft Windows to their optimum capacities. If you have never used Windows before, or you have never used a large application such as Corel Draw, it might be best if you read Appendix A before trying out the program. The memory and operating tips contained there can save you a bit of frustration, and can guide you in making the right decisions concerning what kind of peripheral equipment you need to accomplish the sorts of projects you envision.

## *LEARNING COREL DRAW*

This book has been written to help you make Corel Draw into a workable extension of your fingers, to help you use it to realize your designs. In a less philosophical sense, it has been written to help you apply Corel Draw to the reality of commercial art—getting things out by deadline, having your graphics integrate with your page designs (or somebody else's), coming up with quick art to fill holes in a publication, and so on.

The best way to learn Corel Draw is to use it. The first part of this book consists of a series of exercises which you might want to work through to help you get a feel for the package and become familiar with how things are done. The rest of the book is the really important part, though. It will introduce you to using Corel Draw for design. It doesn't have any real exercises per se, although you might want to reproduce some of the examples to see how they were done. The exercises will be in the form of whatever designs your requirements confront you with.

You'll like Corel Draw. After a few hours of practice and some time with this book, you'll be amazed at the work it can produce.

The best thing about Corel Draw is perhaps not the results it can generate, but rather that it lets you generate them yourself. You can have graphics which really say what you want them to say, something that isn't always possible when you have to explain your requirements to someone else. You can also produce final results with less paperwork and expense, and, perhaps most important, in less time.

*part*

# I

# A Guide to Features and Applications

# chapter 1

## Learning the Basics

**B**EFORE YOU CAN WORK WITH COREL DRAW, YOU
have to understand what it is intended to do. This entails understanding how the program approaches the fundamental elements of
illustration and design, and it entails becoming familiar with the tools
the program provides.

This chapter will deal with these things. How much of this chapter
pertains to you will be a function of how much you already know
about computers and drawing packages, and about Microsoft Windows, the environment in which Corel Draw lives. The Windows
package, necessary to running Corel Draw, is very easy to work with,
and is actually rather intuitive once you have been introduced to its
essentials. If you are unfamiliar with Windows, the essentials are presented in Appendix A of this book.

As you read this chapter, bear in mind that its purpose is not to
serve as a tutorial on using Corel Draw. The remaining chapters will
do that. This chapter should serve to introduce the concepts, tools,
and vocabulary of Corel Draw so that you may learn more quickly
the techniques presented throughout the rest of the book.

## THE BASIS OF DRAWING

The simplicity of Corel Draw is deceptive. It shows fewer tools
than most paint programs, and far fewer than comparable drawing
packages. This is something you'll probably come to appreciate,
because Corel Draw is a great deal less complex to use as a result of its
small set of basic functions.

Before you can understand how to use Corel Draw, you should
understand what it does when it draws pictures. Most computer
users are at least passingly familiar with paint programs, such as PC
Paintbrush, and it often takes a bit of effort not to treat Corel Draw as
a peculiar sort of paint program. In fact, it's a very different application entirely, and therein lies its power. Corel Draw works with
*objects.* It's essential to understand the concept of objects in order to
really make the program perform for you.

## OBJECTS AND PATHS

The fundamental entity from which pictures are created under Corel Draw is called a *path*. For the moment a path may be thought of as a line—the distinction will become clear shortly. If you draw a line across the work space of Corel Draw, that line represents a path. A circle also represents a path. The letter A represents a path as well, or perhaps more correctly a number of paths joined together. Figure 1.1 illustrates some paths.

A path has rather intangible properties. For example, paths themselves are not actually visible. If you were to create a multitude of paths in the drawing area of Corel Draw and print the page, the sheet that would come out of your printer would be blank.

You make a path into a visible part of your drawing in two ways. If you want to have it appear as a line, you can *stroke* the path. This is

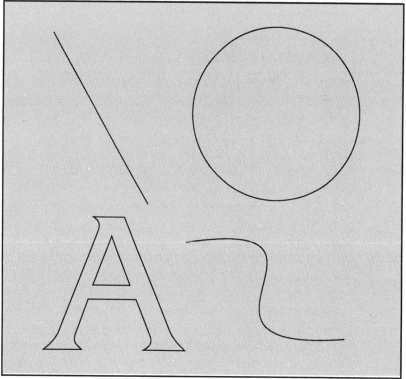

*Figure 1.1:* An example of paths under Corel Draw.

analogous to tracing the path with a pen, although you accomplish this simply by picking a path and entering a stroke command. If the path represents a closed figure, such as a rectangle or the letter A, you can *fill* the path, to make it solid.

In order to be filled, a path must be *closed;* that is, it must enclose an area with no ''leaks'' to the outside. If you have used a paint program and experimented with its fill functions, the idea of an enclosed area without leaks will be familiar. Under PC Paintbrush, for example, attempting to fill an area which is not closed results in the paint spilling out over the rest of your drawing. Under Corel Draw you would simply not be able to fill such an object.

When you consider one or more paths as constituting a complete entity, such as the letter A or a logical element of a drawing, that entity is called an *object*. Admittedly this term is a bit vague, because you can make any number of paths into an object to suit yourself. However, it is in dealing with collections of paths as objects that Corel Draw really gets up and dances.

## *MANAGING OBJECTS*

If you load a drawing file into Corel Draw, the picture will appear on your screen one object at a time, irrespective of the locations of the objects on the page. This is because of the way Corel Draw handles drawings. A drawing is really a list of objects arranged in a file.

If you draw a rectangle under Corel Draw, the software adds the definition of that rectangle to its current object list. All this means is that somewhere in memory there's a note to Corel Draw which says, in effect, ''place a one-by-two-inch rectangle three inches from the top of the page and two inches in from the left, stroke it with a thin line, and fill it with 50 percent gray.''

If you modify an object—for example, by moving it—Corel Draw looks through its object list until it finds the object you're working with and changes the appropriate parts of its notes to itself. Then when it needs to redraw the screen it does so according to the revised object list.

The two drawings in Figure 1.2 both started life as the same object. The only difference is that the second one appears to be flattened, or perhaps it's a reflection in a fun-house mirror. The fact

***Figure 1.2:*** A simple modification of an object.

that Corel Draw can make this transformation illustrates a very important aspect of objects: Objects are scalable.

Look closely at Figure 1.2. While the second drawing has been flattened, its lines are still smooth and there's no evidence of the sort of "crunching" that happens to paint-program images when you try something like this.

The top picture in Figure 1.2 might be thought of as a number of points with paths between them, and to make the discussion easy let's allow that all the points are positioned relative to the bottom of the page that the image was originally drawn on. In order to turn the top object into the bottom object, we might divide the vertical dimensions of all the points by a constant number—let's say three—and then have Corel Draw erase the screen and redraw the object.

In fact, I didn't have to do any of this sort of calculation. All I really did was grab the top of the object and drag it down until it looked suitably squashed. Corel Draw did all the figuring internally.

Because Corel Draw's objects are just paths between points, you can change the overall size of an object relative to the rest of a drawing, or you can adjust its dimensions anamorphically; that is, you can stretch it in one dimension more than in the other. As soon as you're finished adjusting an object Corel Draw will redraw it with clean lines.

It's not always easy to keep an eye on how paths are used in a complex drawing, but knowing how Corel Draw deals with its paths is fundamental in understanding the package and, thus, in making it do what you want it to. The example in Figure 1.3 serves to illustrate an important concept about the structure of objects. It is an elementary use of fitting text to paths.

This drawing began as the letter A in the American Typewriter typeface—what Corel Draw calls Memorandum—one of the many fonts which Corel supplies with its basic drawing package. Figure 1.4 illustrates the Corel Draw screen with the paths of the letter—expanded a bit. Each line between boxes represents one of the paths which make up the shape of this character in this font. (For the purposes of this exercise, I have chosen not to work with the enclosed interior paths of the character, that is, the interior triangle in the upper half of the A.)

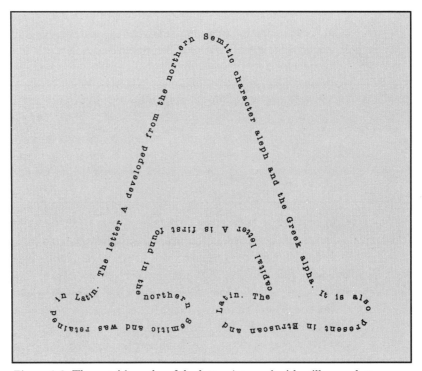

*Figure 1.3:* The outside paths of the letter A traced with still more letters.

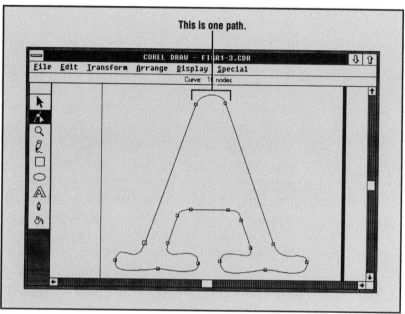

*Figure 1.4:* The letter A with its paths revealed.

When you place text on a Corel Draw page, it is drawn by default in relation to an invisible baseline. If you want to pick up the text and drag it to another location on the page, what you're really going to do is to move the baseline. The text, having been tied to the baseline, moves as well.

The baseline of the text is itself a path of sorts, although it isn't treated as such under Corel Draw. It needn't be a straight path, nor must it be a single path. I have chosen the series of paths constituting the exterior of a letter A.

While the math involved in drawing Figure 1.3 was pretty involved for the program itself, the principle is easy to understand if you have a good grip on the concept of paths. Drawing text this way need be no more involved than typing it along a straight baseline and issuing a few simple commands.

## OBJECT CHARACTERISTICS

When you add an object to a drawing, Corel Draw records all of its pertinent characteristics in its internal object list. Every one of these characteristics is available for later modification. Different sorts of objects have different characteristics.

- An *open path,* that is, a path that doesn't form an enclosed area, will have characteristics such as stroke thickness and color, location on the page, and the style of its ends. This latter characteristic allows you to specify lines which end in arrows, have rounded ends, and so on.

- A *closed path,* that is, a path that encloses an area with no ''leaks'' to the outside, will have some of the characteristics of an open path. It will also have a fill characteristic. You can fill a closed path with a particular color or pattern. Note that a closed path can have both a stroke characteristic and a fill characteristic. For example, consider a red rectangle with a black line around it.

- *Text* will have the characteristics just discussed plus a whole list of others. The characteristics of a text object determine its typeface, the size of the text, whether it's normal, bold, or italicized, the spacing between lines, and so on. Corel Draw has an unusually rich assortment of text effects.

Under Corel Draw you can alter any of the characteristics of an object, even after it has been added to a drawing. These alterations are called *transformations,* and they include moving objects and changing their dimensions. They also include a number of specialized functions, such as editing previously drawn text.

### Bezier Curves

Figure 1.5 is notable in that much of it involves the use of a drawing element which has not been discussed as yet. You will observe that quite a lot of the lines in it cannot be drawn with simple lines, circles, or rectangles. This picture represents a special sort of drawing element, that of Bezier complex curves.

Complex curved lines are difficult to manage in a drawing program. The math involved internally in having the computer draw such a curve is not too fierce, but there remains the problem of devising a way for users of the drawing application to manipulate the

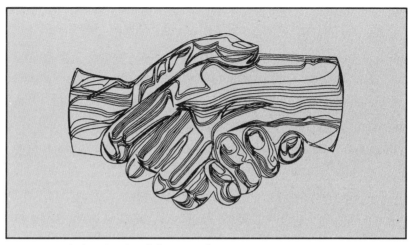

*Figure 1.5:* A drawing involving complex curves.

curves. Corel Draw has settled on a ''handle'' system, which works reasonably intuitively.

We will discuss the manipulation of curved lines in much greater detail later in this book, but for now you should be aware that Corel Draw allows for them. They have the same stroke characteristics as lines, but they have the additional characteristic of being able to be bent and shaped over complex outlines.

In addition to drawing single curves, you can also create several sorts of objects which are made up of multiple curved segments. The segments are combined automatically by Corel Draw when you draw with the freehand mode of the line tool and when you trace bit-mapped images.

### Fill Patterns

Another subject which will be treated in greater detail later in this book is that of fill patterns. Corel Draw features a rather generous assortment of ways to fill areas in a drawing, from simple gray shades through fountains and special PostScript fills.

The simplest form of fill patterns are shades of gray. Gray shades are expressed in terms of the amount of black in an area versus the amount of white. A 50 percent gray area has equal amounts of black and white. A 10 percent gray fill is almost white, while a 90 percent gray fill is nearly black. Gray shades actually pose some interesting problems for Corel Draw, as they don't behave as predictably as you might like. For example, in cartoons you might encounter a gray car with a perfectly uniform gray surface, but in real life the contours of the metal and variations of light on the surface of the car will make the surface appear to be a rainbow of various gray tones. This is one of those things our eyes do not bother telling us about unless we consciously make ourselves aware of it.

Figure 1.6 illustrates a solid object which has simply been filled with gray on the left and has had something rather more involved done to it on the right. The pop can on the left doesn't look very three-dimensional. In fact, it doesn't even look very interesting. The pop can on the right exhibits a reasonable simulation of natural light and depth. If you consider a real pop can for a moment you'll notice that it has similar variations in light intensity, as the sides of a cylinder don't reflect light as well as the part directly before your eyes.

*Figure 1.6:* Adding depth to a pop can.

The right pop can was filled with a variable gray fill called a *fountain*. In its simplest sense, a fountain is just a fill pattern in which the gray starts at some arbitrary percentage and changes smoothly to some other percentage over a defined distance. Fountains can also be *radial*. A radial fountain starts with a particular gray percentage in the center of an area and changes outward in all directions. Figure 1.7 illustrates a radial fountain being used to make a circle look spherical.

If you have a means of outputting your Corel Draw pictures to a color printer or other color device, areas of solid gray can be augmented with areas of solid color, a feature called ''spot'' color. Corel Draw has some first-class color facilities.

Additionally, Corel Draw provides you with a large assortment of PostScript fills. However, to use these fills you must output your drawing to a PostScript printer. A great deal more needs to be said about this before it will be completely clear, but suffice it to say here that in using PostScript fills you can fill an area with all sorts of predefined patterns, including bricks, broken glass, and so on. Figure 1.8 illustrates some PostScript fills.

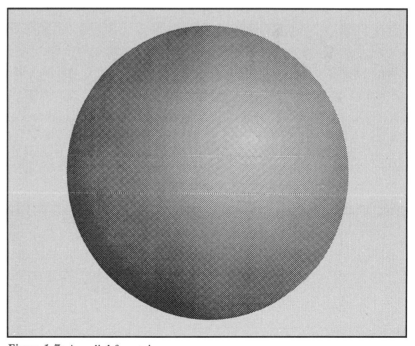

*Figure 1.7:* A radial fountain.

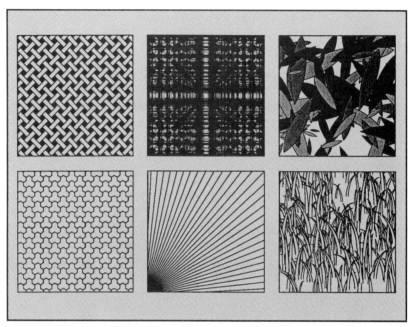

*Figure 1.8:* A few of the many PostScript pattern fills provided with Corel Draw.

### Transformations

Corel Draw allows you to transform an object or group of objects. A transformation changes the relationship of the points which define the paths of an object. In the example shown in Figure 1.2, flattening the Volkswagen was really a simple transformation, although this procedure is considered to be so basic to the capabilities of Corel Draw that it's hardly regarded as a transformation. More involved transformations have actual menu commands.

Most of the more interesting transformations involve having Corel Draw do some internal mathematics with the points of an object. For example, you can flip an object horizontally and vertically. You can skew it. Objects can be bent, stretched, and otherwise distorted. And all transformations can be repeated multiple times. Figure 1.9 illustrates the results of some transformations on a simple object.

Part of the usefulness of transformations is in the way they mimic the way the real world transforms our conception of what things look

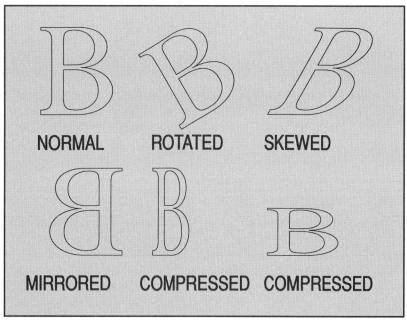

*Figure 1.9:* Some of the object transformations Corel Draw can do.

like. If you close this book for a moment and hold it before you, you will see a rectangle. If the angle is just right that's all you'll see—the sides of the book will be invisible. You can do this with all six faces of the book. All of them are rectangular.

When you hold the book so that it becomes visible as a three-dimensional solid, however, none of the faces of the book will appear as rectangles. They all will have been apparently transformed by the effect of moving some of the corners farther from your eye than others. In order to create a drawing of a three-dimensional book using a two-dimensional sheet of laser printer paper, Corel Draw must be able to effect the digital equivalent of these optical transformations. Once you get used to working with the transformations which Corel Draw offers you, you'll find that they do just that.

### Text As Objects

If you use Corel Draw to place the word ''Aardvark'' on a page, the letter ''A'' will automatically be combined with seven other letters to form a single object. If you wanted to move the word down the page, you could simply grab the whole thing as one entity and drag it.

Words and letters are a special case of objects under Corel Draw, inasmuch as they are text. Because ordinarily you would not want to get at the individual paths of text characters, text comes with its paths precombined.

There are times when you will want to deal with text as individual paths. Figure 1.3, the letter A with text wrapped around it, was an example of one of those times. Obviously, Corel Draw doesn't prohibit you from dealing with text at the path level, as, for example, Adobe Illustrator does. It does, however, insulate you from doing so when you don't really want to.

## *HOW DID YOU GET THOSE OBJECTS?*

The main reason for buying Corel Draw, for most of its potential users, is to turn out finished graphics. Corel Draw is a very flexible package, one which can be adapted to a surprising variety of requirements. It can be used to conjure up quick-and-nasty illustrations at a moment's notice, and it can be used to render stunning, visually exciting graphics with depth and meaning and all the other stuff they talk about at art college. Regrettably, the difference is more often a factor of the proximity of one's deadlines than of the skill in one's fingers.

### *Drawing*

The most obvious way in which objects can get into a drawing is for someone to draw them. This seems so simple as to barely need mentioning, but in fact there are several other ways to get an illustration together under Corel Draw. The basic drawing tools which are part of the package, however, are among its more shining features.

We've discussed Corel Draw's basic approach to drawing, and in a large sense this defines the drawing tools available. However, there are all sorts of enhancements to these. Some of the more important ones include

- Cut, Copy, Paste, and Replicate. Objects can be cut or copied to the clipboard, then pasted back into a drawing or replicated to produce extra copies of them.

- Snap to Grid. This allows you to force the endpoints of a path onto the nearest point of a grid. You can define the grid size. Grid snap can be toggled on and off.

- Object alignment. You can select several objects and have them aligned or centered, vertically, horizontally, or on a line of your choosing.

- Node editing. Having created a path, you can modify it—by moving its points, splitting and joining paths, modifying curves, transforming straight lines into curves, and so on.

As you will probably appreciate by now, just about anything can be drawn in Corel Draw. To be sure, drawing still takes time and a reasonable degree of talent. Fortunately, there are other ways to get a drawing together under Corel Draw besides actually drawing it.

*Tracing*

One of the more sophisticated abilities of Corel Draw is its *autotrace* feature. Under certain circumstances you can *import* a bitmapped drawing into Corel Draw and have Corel Draw automatically generate a line drawing based on the bitmapped picture. A bitmapped drawing is a picture from a paint program or a file from a scanner. If all goes well you will wind up with a really nice looking piece of line art and have done almost no work.

In practice, even under ideal circumstances traced bitmapped drawings can require a bit of hand-polishing after the fact.

The autotrace facility enables Corel Draw to accept pictures which have been scanned, downloaded from public-domain image file collections, or cooked up in PC Paintbrush and other art packages that can produce bitmaps. This means that images ranging from Victorian etchings to architectural blueprints can be imported into Corel Draw and given all the characteristics of object-oriented art.

This sounds almost too good to be true and, of course, it is.

Corel Draw does include a tracing facility for bitmapped images and it does work. In fact, it works better than any other bitmapped-image tracing function currently available for the PC. However, this does not mean that just any bitmapped image can be traced.

When you hand Corel Draw an image to be traced, it attempts to create paths around the dark areas of the picture, ultimately to form objects. This will work well if the picture has well-defined dark areas and dreadfully if it does not. Images which are suitably complex will confuse the autotrace algorithm into outlining the wrong areas.

Figure 1.10 illustrates a bitmapped image and the Corel Draw drawing which resulted from it using the autotrace function. This is the sort of bitmapped image which traces rather well, and the results shown are quite acceptable. There is no illustration here of a bit-mapped image which didn't trace well, because the results of a bad tracing are rarely even recognizable. There's very little middle ground between a good autotrace and a bad one. The results are either breathtaking or they're spaghetti.

If you're in a hurry to generate some art, autotracing a scanned image of some existing paper art may be a very good way indeed to get some quick results. The result of autotracing is a drawing formed of objects, so it's fairly easy to modify such a drawing once Corel Draw has finished tracing it. Thus, you can easily customize pictures gotten from another source.

While you will get a better feel for how the autotrace function works and what sort of original makes for good tracings as you play with it, there are a few basic guidelines. Pictures which have clean, defined edges tend to trace well. There is a limit to the number of

Traced and partially
filled bitmap

*Figure 1.10:* A bitmapped image, left, and Corel Draw's autotraced copy of
it, right.

paths that a drawing can have and still print properly (and even though the limit is pretty high, the autotrace function is capable of causing problems by exceeding it). Thus, pictures with countless details may not be suitable for tracing.

The techniques for successful autotracing will be discussed later in this book.

### Using Clip Art

It's amazing that small local newspapers, low-budget magazines, and junk-mail fliers often have professional-looking graphics. Sometimes they can't even get the type straight on their pages, but they'll have drawings that look like a professional artist has labored over them for hours.

In fact, a professional artist often did labor over the graphics, although usually not at the offices of the publishing company which produced the documents in question. Recognizing that pages often look a lot nicer with professional graphics on them—even if they're not quite appropriate graphics—many small publishers use ''clip art.'' Originally clip art was just what its name implies: professionally drawn pictures you could cut out and stick to a page, quickly and with little fuss.

Clip art has made the transition to computers. When you're in a hurry to generate a graphic it's a lot easier to pull one ready-made out of a file than to create your own from scratch. An additional attraction of this electronic form of clip art is the fact that, with Corel Draw, you can modify the picture somewhat to your own needs.

There is a growing industry of electronic clip art supply companies, some of which are the same companies which supply paper clip art to conventional publishers. The quality of electronic clip art has seen dramatic improvements over the past couple of years.

Corel Draw comes with a number of clip art samplers which offer something on the order of six megabytes of clip art files all ready to try out. Most of these are examples of the libraries of a number of the better clip art suppliers—they've been bundled with Corel Draw with the blessings of their owners in the hope that if you like the samples you'll buy more of the clip art. Figure 1.11 illustrates some of the many sample images which come with Corel Draw.

*Figure 1.11:* A tiny fraction of the sample clip art library provided with Corel Draw.

One of the features which makes Corel Draw so powerful is its ability to import files from many other applications: it is able to use clip art files from practically everywhere. A great deal more about importing and exporting foreign file formats will appear in Chapter 5.

*Clip Art and the Law*   If you haven't been involved in publishing, you might be wondering about the legal status of clip art. The drawings in some of the example files which come with Corel Draw look pretty sophisticated, and it might seem a bit questionable to find them thrown in for free. In fact, there are some restrictions on the use of clip art.

As a rule, you can use clip art for any purpose except to repackage it as clip art. For example, you can do anything you like with the electronic clip art samples which came with Corel Draw so long as the eventual audience of your pictures or publications can't use the art in an electronic form. Thus, you can print the pictures out and use them as part of a newsletter or magazine, but you can't give the original files—or any variations on them—to someone else as files.

There is a large body of paper clip art in the public domain. The existing copyright laws only date back to the turn of the century, and all sorts of commercial art predate them. There are books of Victorian line art, French advertising art, Baroque engravings, and so on which are all available with no strings attached. The most notable of these are the voluminous Dover books and the now rather rare Hart picture archives. If you have a scanner and a bit of time many of these images make first-rate input for Corel Draw's autotrace function.

With the exception of those pictures which predate the copyright laws, pretty well all pictures are owned by someone. This includes magazine advertisements and graphics, apparently anonymous image and drawing files found on computer bulletin boards and in public-domain software collections, and so on. Images are just as much the property of the artists who created them as books are the property of their authors. The difference is that usually images don't carry written copyright notices.

Corel Draw's powerful tracing and manipulation tools make it fairly easy to abuse the copyrights of artists. Before you use a graphic as clip art, make sure you know you have the right to do so. Aside from being a conscientious and decent thing to do, it can keep you out of court.

## THE PROGRAM AND ITS TOOLS

The rest of this chapter will be devoted to a quick look at the basic features and tools of Corel Draw itself. Once again, this is not intended to make you a master of the package in this short space, but rather to give you an overview of the geography of the program and the capabilities of the various tools and menus. A great deal more will be said throughout the rest of the book about the particular uses of these things.

Figure 1.12 illustrates Corel Draw at rest. It has had a drawing loaded into it. This is the default magnification for a drawing which has just been loaded—you can zoom in and out, as we'll see. In the

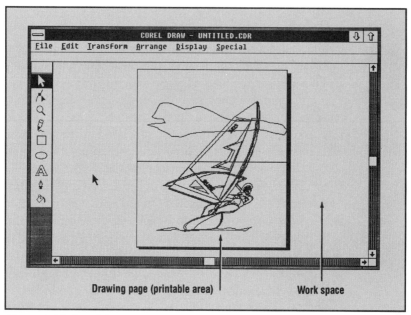

```
┌──────────────────────────────────────────────────────┐
│ ▭        COREL DRAW - UNTITLED.CDR              ⇩ ⇧   │
│ File  Edit  Transform  Arrange  Display  Special       │
│                                                         │
```

**Drawing page (printable area)**          **Work space**

*Figure 1.12:* Corel Draw just after booting up and loading a drawing.

center of the screen is the drawing page: the rectangle with a drop shadow behind it. You can draw anywhere on the screen you like, but only the drawing page will get printed.

It's very often useful to work in the space outside of the drawing page. For instance, you can work on something which is too big to fit on a page and then reduce it later, or work on a complex object all by itself and pull it into your drawing when it's done. The layout of Corel Draw's screen is very flexible in this respect.

If you've used a Windows-based application before, you will recognize the Windows-related elements of the Corel Draw screen: the menu bar, the minimize and maximize controls, and so on. You will also recognize the scroll bars along the right and bottom edges of the Corel Draw window, although their functions in this program might not be immediately apparent. In fact, the scroll bars serve to move around the drawing space when you've zoomed in to get a more detailed view of a section of your drawing. Should you be unfamiliar with these terms, Appendix A contains an introduction to Windows.

Figure 1.13 illustrates the most important part of the Corel Draw application window: the toolbox. If you've used a paint program, such as PC Paintbrush, the idea of a drawing toolbox may be familiar to you. The functions of the individual tools probably will not. Understanding Corel Draw is partially a matter of understanding its tools and what affects their use.

To select a particular tool all you need do is move your mouse cursor to the appropriate tool icon and click on it. The background of the newly selected tool will change color to remind you which tool you're currently using. In some cases, your cursor also will change.

Over the next few pages we'll have a really quick look at each of the Corel Draw tools. Don't worry if their functions still seem a bit vague at the end of this section—you'll be getting hands-on experience with them and more detailed explanations throughout the course of the book.

It's worth noting that, although you might not recognize them, the tool names used here do actually correspond to the documentation which accompanies Corel Draw. It's just that usually whenever the name of a tool is required in the text of the Corel Draw manual, its authors use instead a character which resembles the tool icon shown

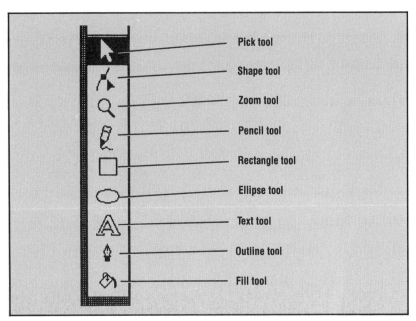

*Figure 1.13:* The Corel Draw toolbox.

on the screen. (Obviously someone at Corel likes creating special fonts with Z-Soft's Type Foundry or something similar). While a clever application of technology, this approach makes it a bit hard to write or speak about Corel Draw. One finds oneself speaking of the ''up-arrow tool,'' for example, or the ''wavy-line-with-box-in-the-middle tool,'' which is clumsy at best. For the purposes of writing this book, I will use the names Corel Draw has assigned but rarely uses. If you don't like these, of course, you can make up your own.

 ## THE PICK TOOL

The first tool is mainly used to select objects or groups of objects. For this reason it is called the ''pick'' (for ''select'') tool. (You might think it should be called the arrow tool, but there are enough arrows in Corel Draw that to call just one of them the arrow tool would be to invite confusion.)

After using the pick tool to select objects, you can duplicate them, delete them, cut and paste them, and drag them to a new location on the screen. You can also transform them—for example, you can rotate them, stretch them, mirror them, and so on.

Objects can be selected either explicitly or by area.

- *Selecting explicitly.* If you select the pick tool and then place the point of the arrow cursor over some path of an object on your screen and click, that object will be selected. When an object is selected, little black squares, or *selection marks,* appear at the corners and midpoints of the otherwise invisible sides of the smallest rectangle Corel Draw can enclose the object with. Figure 1.14 shows these selection marks around the back wheel of a bicycle.

- *Selecting by area.* If you select the pick tool and place the cursor to the upper left of a collection of objects, then hold the mouse button down and drag the cursor toward the lower right corner of the window of your screen, you will create a broken-line rectangle, with your cursor serving as the lower right corner. All the objects within the rectangular area so defined will be selected when you release the mouse button. Figure 1.15 shows the area that will be selected when the mouse button is released.

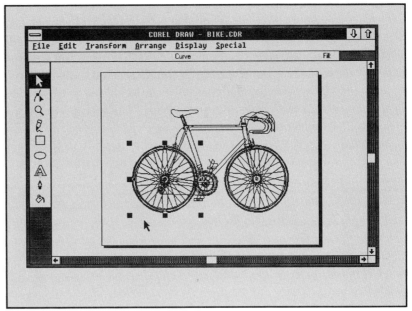

*Figure 1.14:* A selected object.

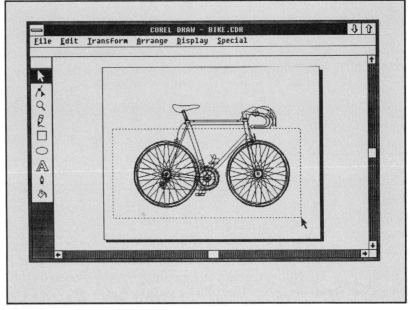

*Figure 1.15:* An area being selected.

When you select objects by area, the entire object must reside in the rectangular area defined by the mouse. The broken-line box indicating the area being selected is called a ''marquee'' by Corel Draw. The Macintosh has a more descriptive term for it: a ''rubber band box.'' This is the term I will use most often in the course of this book.

Having selected one or more objects, you can ''unselect'' them by simply clicking in an open space somewhere in the drawing page. The selection marks will vanish.

The pick tool is one of the most frequently used of the Corel Draw tools, especially when you're modifying a drawing.

##  THE SHAPE TOOL

The function of the shape tool will be a lot less obvious than that of the pick tool, and this section will not help all that much. In order to understand it you will have to know a lot more about how Corel Draw manages its objects.

All paths in a Corel Draw picture are defined as being *nodes* and something connecting them. For now, a node can be thought of as being a point along a path which has something to do with its position relative to the rest of the drawing. A straight line has two nodes, one at each end. A complex curve may have many nodes. If you move the nodes, you'll move the path or change its shape.

The shape tool allows you to do all sorts of things with nodes. For example, you can change the location of individual nodes, rather than whole objects. Figure 1.16 illustrates the effects of simply moving a few nodes around.

The shape tool also allows you to change the characteristics of the path which attaches to a node. For example, you can convert a straight path to a curved path and then manipulate the resulting curve to shape it the way you want it.

The shape tool can break a path, inserting nodes where there previously were none. Figure 1.17 illustrates the process of converting a circle to a pie chart—or to a Pacman character, if you prefer—with the shape tool.

A lot more remains to be said about the shape tool.

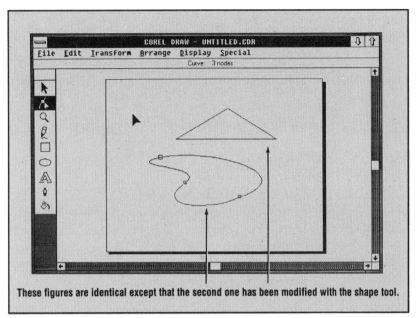

*Figure 1.16:* Using the shape tool.

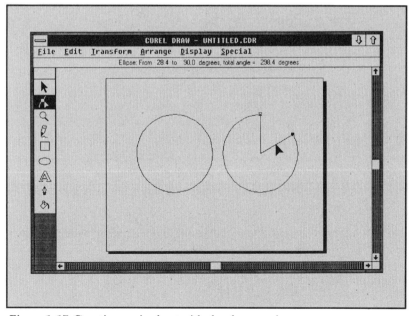

*Figure 1.17:* Creating a pie chart with the shape tool.

## Q  *THE ZOOM TOOL*

The function of the zoom tool is simple. It allows you to magnify sections of a drawing, so that you can work with details on a manageable scale. If you select the zoom tool the menu shown in Figure 1.18 will appear, allowing you to decide how you want the magnification to work. This sort of menu is described in the Corel Draw documentation as a "flyout" menu. The two most commonly used forms of magnification are zooming in, indicated by the magnifying glass with a plus sign in it, and zooming out, which predictably uses a magnifying glass with a minus sign in it.

In zooming in, the cursor will change to a magnifying glass. To zoom in on a particular area of a drawing you would do the following:

1. Select the zoom-in tool.

2. Place the cursor in the drawing page, in the upper left corner of the area you wish to magnify.

3. Click and hold the left mouse button.

4. Drag the mouse down and to the right so that the area you wish to zoom in on is enclosed.

5. Release the mouse button. The area you have defined with the zoom tool will replace the previous view.

You can use the zoom-in tool repeatedly to zoom in on sections within sections you have already zoomed in on.

Each time you zoom in, Corel Draw makes a note of what the view looked like before you clicked on the zoom tool. It keeps a "stack" of these notes, adding one note to the stack each time you zoom in. When you select the zoom-out tool it takes the most recent note off the stack and restores the view which it describes. Thus, you can step backwards through successive zoomings-in by using the zoom-out function.

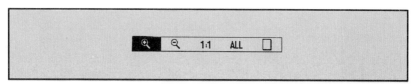

*Figure 1.18:* The zoom tool menu.

Having completed a zoom in either direction Corel Draw will automatically reselect whichever tool you were using before you selected the zoom tool.

The other zoom tool options will be discussed later as appropriate.

Should you discover that you've selected the zoom tool in error, clicking outside the zoom menu unselects the tool and banishes the menu without changing anything.

#  THE PENCIL TOOL

The pencil tool is used to draw lines. It can be used to draw straight lines or it can be used to draw freehand curves, which are in fact assemblages of complex curves.

### Drawing a Straight Line

1. Select the pencil tool.

2. Click the mouse at the point you want the line to start.

3. Move the mouse to the point you want the line to end. As you move the mouse, a straight line extends from the mouse to your starting point.

4. Click the mouse to anchor the free end of the line.

### Drawing Freehand Lines (Curves)

1. Select the pencil tool.

2. Place the mouse at the point you want the line to start.

3. Click and hold the left mouse button.

4. Move the mouse to form the line you want to draw. It's extremely difficult to get this to work out properly most of the time.

5. Release the mouse button to anchor the free end of the line and to stop drawing.

Freehand lines, once drawn, can be edited with the shape tool to clean them up and fix mistakes.

Until you go to draw something else, any line you have just drawn
will be automatically selected. As such, it need not be explicitly
selected again in order to change a characteristic of it, such as its line
width. This is true using any of the tools which actually draw objects.

## THE RECTANGLE AND ELLIPSE TOOLS

The rectangle and ellipse tools draw rectangles and ellipses respectively. You probably guessed that from their names. In fact, it's more
correct to say that they draw rectangular and elliptical objects. As
such, once drawn these objects can have their attributes changed.
You can meddle with their line weights, fill patterns and so on.

To draw a rectangle, simply select the rectangle tool and click and
hold the mouse where you want the upper left corner of your rectangle to be. Drag the mouse to where you want the lower right corner to
be and release it.

The ellipse tool works the same way. The rectangular area defined
by dragging the mouse specifies a box which encloses the ellipse being
drawn.

## THE TEXT TOOL

The text tool—also called the big A tool—is used for placing text in
a drawing. Corel Draw has unspeakably good text manipulation
facilities, far more sophisticated than can be spoken about in this
simple introduction. We'll cover the basic features here, with extensive elaboration to follow in Chapter 3 and elsewhere.

When you select the text tool, the cursor will change to a vertical
bar with ears at the top and bottom, this being the Corel Draw text-
insertion cursor. If you click it somewhere in the drawing area of the
Corel Draw window the Text dialog box will appear. This dialog is
shown in Figure 1.19.

The Text dialog box allows you to enter new text and to edit text
which you have previously created. If you click in the window at the
top of the dialog, a flashing cursor will appear on the first line, allowing you to type in some text.

The other items in this dialog box should be somewhat self-
explanatory. You can use the Alignment radio buttons to decide

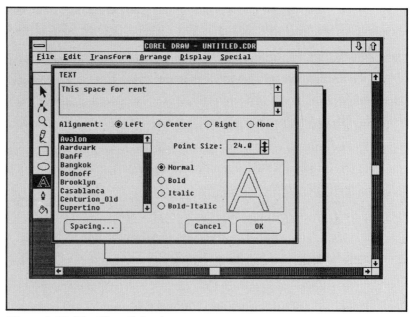

*Figure 1.19:* The Text dialog box.

whether the text you've typed in should be left-aligned, centered, right-aligned, or what. The typeface window displays, for your selection, the typefaces available. Below this is the Spacing options bar, which will call up a dialog window of its own. To the right are the Point Size entry box and buttons for selecting the typeface's font or weight. Below the Point Size box is a window which will display a sample character—the letter A by default—from the typeface you select.

There are also several other typographic controls available in Corel Draw.

If you're already well versed in the lore of type and typography, you might have glanced at the typeface window in Figure 1.19 with a moment of concern. Typefaces like Avalon and Bangkok may not sound like anything you've heard of before. The reason for this is that Corel Draw is not able to use the common names of the typefaces it includes. The names themselves are copyrighted. It uses contrived names instead. For example, the Helvetica typeface under Corel Draw is referred to as "Switzerland." In fact, all of the typefaces included with Corel Draw have other, more commonly used names.

Just because Corel can't ship fonts with their copyrighted names doesn't mean you can't use those names if they're more useful or familiar to you. Appendix B of this book discusses how to change the typeface names under Corel Draw so they're more in keeping with recognized typographic conventions.

## ♟ THE OUTLINE TOOL

The outline tool—also called the pen tool, the nib tool, and the "clogged Rapidograph tool" by experienced draftspeople—is one of the two tools which is used to modify the graphic attributes of selected objects. If you select an object in your drawing and then select this tool, a menu like the one in Figure 1.20 will appear at the bottom of your screen. This allows you to select the line weight and the line pattern or color for the object or objects you have selected. If you have selected multiple objects, all of them will be given the line characteristics you select.

The line widths and line shades shown in this menu represent a handy selection of commonly used values. Note that the HAIR (or "hairline") value is set by default to a quarter of a point, which is roughly equivalent to one dot on a 300-dots-per-inch printer.

If you need more control of widths and shades you can click on the pen or the paintbrush respectively at the left edge of this menu. These two tools will pop up precise-adjustment dialog boxes, as shown in Figure 1.21.

The Outline Pen dialog allows you to specify more line characteristics than you might have thought even existed, and widths in increments so precise that you'll never be able to afford an output device capable of making them that exact. The Outline Color dialog (invoked by selecting the paintbrush from the outline tool menu) allows you to define the shade or color of a line with great accuracy.

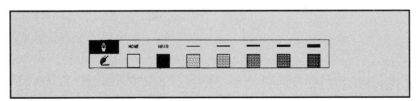

*Figure 1.20:* The outline tool menu.

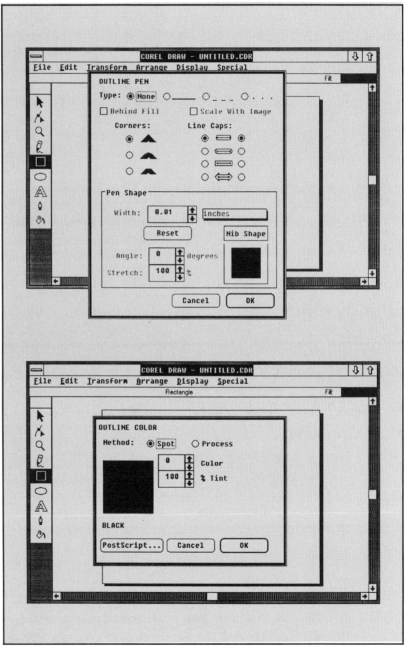

*Figure 1.21:* The precise-adjustment dialogs for the outline tool.

## *THE FILL TOOL*

The fill tool is used to set the fill color or pattern of selected objects. Obviously these would have to be objects which lend themselves to filling. You can't fill a line, for example. Specifically, for objects to be filled they must be defined with closed paths.

The fill tool's icon dates back to the early days of paint programs. Under a paint program, filling an area with a color or pattern is accomplished by the digital equivalent of pouring paint into it. The paint program literally starts with a point inside the area and paints all the pixels adjacent to it until it encounters a line. While the process is different under Corel Draw, the icon has remained.

Figure 1.22 illustrates the flyout menu which pops up when you select the fill tool. The rectangles in this menu represent some commonly used gray-level fills. As with the outline tool menu, the leftmost icon in the fill tool menu will pop up a precise-adjustment dialog.

The next to the rightmost icon is the fountain-fill icon. We've discussed fountains briefly earlier in this chapter. This icon pops up a fountain selection dialog.

The PS icon is used to select among the incredible library of Post-Script patterns which comes with Corel Draw. However, this icon will only be useful if you output your drawings to a PostScript printer.

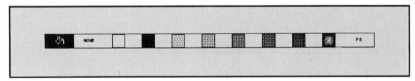

*Figure 1.22:* The fill tool menu.

## *COLOR AND COREL DRAW*

While color will be dealt with in detail in Chapter 11 and as appropriate throughout the course of this book, it deserves mention here as one of Corel Draw's more outstanding features.

Corel Draw supports drawing with an almost unlimited palette of colors. The representation of colored objects on your screen, however, will be handled by a "best guess" approximation of the colors you've selected, in keeping with the color facilities of your display card as well as what Windows will let Corel Draw get away with. As of this writing, Windows effectively limits color drawing to eight colors even if you have a super VGA display, for example, which allows for a larger palette.

Having created a color drawing with Corel Draw, you can output it to a color printer. Unfortunately, it takes a color PostScript printer to accurately reproduce the colors which Corel Draw can define, and these are severely expensive. However, there's a more useful purpose to which color drawings can be put under Corel Draw, that of generating color "separations."

The Corel Draw package is capable of outputting spot color and four-color separations. What this means is that you can use Corel Draw to sidestep one of the more expensive parts of color printing.

Color under Corel Draw can be specified in either of the two systems which printers use. The first of these is called process color and the second Pantone color. In defining a particular color as a process color, one specifies the percentages of cyan, magenta, yellow, and black inks required to represent the color in question. Pantone colors are specific colors of ink which are numbered in a color matching system widely accepted by the graphics industry. Thus, for example, one can specify the fill color of a certain area as being Pantone 525 and know precisely what color it will wind up when it's printed.

## *WRAPPING UP*

You can read about Corel Draw for hours and learn less about it than twenty minutes in front of a computer will teach you. It's a package of sufficient complexity as to really require a hands-on approach to using it. To this end, the rest of this book should properly be read not by the light of an incandescent lamp, but rather by the glow emitted by your monitor.

In learning Corel Draw you should bear in mind that you're really learning how to make it do the things you are particularly interested in. It's quite forgivable to ignore those of its features which have no application for your needs. It's also well in keeping with the spirit of the software itself to close this book partway through and simply mouse away at the package until you run up against something you don't understand. Corel Draw is very forgiving of users who make a few mistakes.

The rest of this book will go a long way toward making you into a Corel Draw artist instead of just a Corel Draw user. Behind its clever object-manipulation tools, its impressive library of typefaces, and its intuitive user interface is a tool for your imagination.

# chapter

# 2

## Creating
## Line Drawings

THE MOST BASIC LEVEL OF COREL DRAW IS DRAWING lines. If you have a good understanding of the line-drawing capabilities of Corel Draw you'll find that the rest of the package is pretty easy to understand.

As I noted in the introduction to this book, you can go at learning Corel Draw from the perspective of a designer or the perspective of someone simply following instructions. Both of these will give you a pretty clear understanding of what you're doing, but the latter will take a lot longer, and you will probably wind up with somebody else's idea of what you were trying to create.

This chapter will talk about drawing simple and some apparently not-so-simple figures using little other than lines. Complex fills and transformations, involved text manipulations, and other intermediate features and applications will be presented in later chapters.

In the spirit of the designer's approach, we'll be looking at a number of the Corel Draw tools, but this will be a drawing-oriented tutorial rather than a tool-oriented one. When you finish with this chapter and go for a Coke you will feel confident in your abilities to use the following:

- the pencil tool for drawing lines
- the pick tool for selecting them
- the shape tool for changing them into curves
- the rectangle and ellipse tools
- the zoom tool for looking at what you're doing
- the duplicate function
- the grouping function

You will also see how to print from Corel Draw, although this isn't much of an accomplishment. Corel Draw makes printing almost effortless.

Despite the apparent complexity of some of the things we'll be drawing in this chapter, you'll find that Corel Draw makes handling large drawings pretty painless. As with most large tasks—house building, for example—a large drawing under Corel Draw is really just a lot of small drawings stuck together. Corel Draw is particularly adept at letting you deal with drawings in this way. You can work on small sections, get them right, and then drag them into your main image. You can also reuse pieces of a drawing if they're applicable elsewhere, saving you the task of drawing the same or similar items over and over again.

## DRAWING LINES AND RECTANGLES: A ROOF AND WINDOWS

The first thing we'll be drawing is shown in Figure 2.1. It is a simple representation of the top section of a suburban house. Despite its apparent complexity, this drawing took only twenty minutes to complete. It has a number of elements which will help you to explore the basic line drawing facilities of Corel Draw. There are no fills and no tricky shading—applications we will present later in the book— but there are repetitive elements, mirrored curves (on the rain gutters), and various objects that entail measuring and moving.

*Figure 2.1:* The upper story of a house.

The most complex elements in this picture are the windows. They consist of numerous lines, all of which can be drawn in one way or another. You may notice that all of the windows are identical. This means you will actually have to draw only one of them, and only selected parts at that.

Another important aspect of this picture is that every line in it occurs at integral points on the page; that is, you could draw a grid such that all the end points of the lines in the picture would fall on points of the grid. This makes the accurate placement of objects in the picture a lot easier.

## *DRAWING WITH A GRID*

The Snap To Grid feature allows you to force Corel Draw to align all the nodes of the paths you draw to fixed grid points. While you'll never see the grid, you'll be able to observe its effects when it's active, as your lines and other drawn objects will snap to the nearest grid position.

Using a grid makes accurately positioning objects a lot easier. However, it does make positioning things by eye nearly impossible— you'll want to switch it off in instances which call for visual alignment rather than absolute accuracy.

Note that when you have the Snap To Grid feature active, the position and length values on the status line at the top of the work space also "snap" to the nearest grid value.

Let's make this grid do some of our work. Start by pulling down the Display menu. The two items of interest at the moment are Snap To Grid and Grid Size. Click on Grid Size. The dialog box in Figure 2.2 will appear.

The grid size dialog box allows you to specify the number of squares per unit of measure on the screen. The units of measure are also up to you—we'll use centimeters in this example. For various reasons, centimeters provide a generally useful number of increments across the screen. If your grid size dialog indicates units other than the ones you want to use, click on the unit name until it changes to the one you'd like.

The number of squares per unit of measure is entered by means of a special type of control which appears throughout Corel Draw

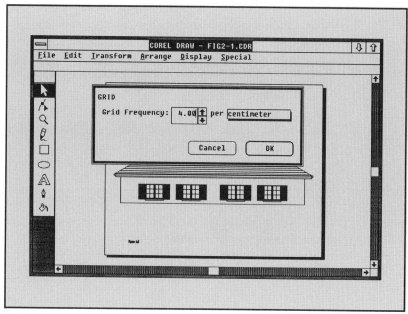

*Figure 2.2:* The grid size dialog.

whenever the need arises for entering numbers. This number-entry control allows you a choice of methods. You can click on the up or down arrows to the right of the number to increase or decrease the value by one, or you can click and hold one of the arrows to step through a succession of values. Alternatively, you can click on the number itself and then use the keyboard to enter the value you desire. This would be the method to use when you need a fractional value, a need that will arise more often than you might think. Recall that what you are deciding is not how many centimeters (or inches or whatever) wide your grid squares should be; rather, you are deciding how many grid squares you want to fit into the space of a centimeter (or inch or whatever). Thus, if you enter 4 in the grid size dialog box, you will be getting four boxes per centimeter, or one every quarter centimeter, which is the grid size we will be using throughout this house discussion. On the other hand, if you enter 0.25, you will get a quarter of a box in the space of a centimeter, or one box every four centimeters.

The Snap To Grid item in the Display menu is what is called a *toggle.* You can change its status between on and off as many times as you need by hitting the same button. If you select it when it is off, you're toggling it on, and a check mark appears beside it. Selecting it when it is on toggles it off, and the check mark disappears. Note that you can also toggle the Snap To Grid feature by simply pressing F6 on the keyboard. For the purposes of this drawing, toggle the Snap To Grid feature *on.*

Note that the actual grid is never visible in the work space. However, you can check the status of the Snap To Grid feature at any time by pulling down the Display menu—or by using the Alt-D keyboard equivalent—and then just not selecting anything. Your next move, clicking outside the menu or pressing Esc, will banish the menu, but it won't change the status of the toggle.

### Draw a Rectangle: The Window Glass

Figure 2.3 illustrates one of the double windows of the drawing. It's easiest to work from the inside of an object outward, so let's begin by drawing the glass panes of the windows.

The six panes of each window are actually six rectangles, each of which we could draw separately. However, it's easier to draw one large rectangle and then draw three lines through it. To draw the rectangle, you will be selecting the rectangle tool, which is easy, and

*Figure 2.3:* A double window.

drawing a rectangle five centimeters across by nine centimeters deep, which is not so easy in the default magnification of Corel Draw. Let's improve things a bit. First of all, use the Display menu to turn on the Ruler display if the rulers are not already visible. This will place rulers along the top and left sides of the work space of the Corel Draw window. Next, select the zoom tool and zoom in on the upper left corner of the work space—as described in Chapter 1—until the rulers are large enough to give you room to move the cursor within one-centimeter areas. You might have to use the scroll bars to position the work space so the the 0,0 intersection of the rulers becomes visible. If you overdo the magnification on your first try, select the zoom tool again and use the zoom-out function to return to your previous magnification level, then have another shot at it.

In drawing the rectangle, note that the position of your mouse cursor is reflected in the rulers by two faint lines. This makes it easy to line up the corners of the rectangle with the ruler graduations. Keep in mind that you only have to get the position close—with the Snap To Grid feature active the rectangle will snap to the nearest grid line.

This drawing does not use any fill patterns, but at the moment Corel Draw doesn't know this. Chances are the rectangle you've just drawn will have a fill associated with it (probably solid black) even though you can't see it at this time. Fills are never shown on the basic drawings which Corel Draw displays in its work space. However, you can check the fills and other visual characteristics of a drawing by looking at the preview window. You can toggle the preview window on and off by using the Show Preview item of the Display menu. However, it's a lot easier to use the keyboard shortcut for this one—just press F3 to show the preview and press it again to banish it. Figure 2.4 shows the rectangle with a preview.

You'll notice that the fill of a single selected object is also indicated in the status line at the top of the Corel Draw workspace. This is very useful when you're working with single objects; however, the status line cannot show you the fills of multiple grouped objects, the relative position of objects, the result of their fills, and other aspects of your drawing that can best be seen in the previous window. Using the preview window is thus a good habit to get into.

The Fill characteristic shown in Figure 2.4 is not what you need. In order to change it for this drawing, you need to select the pick tool

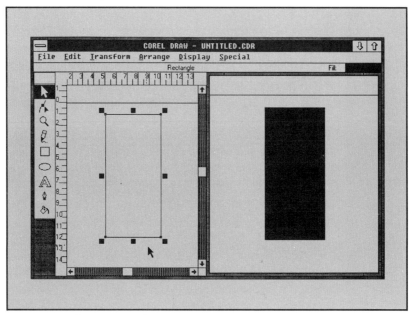

*Figure 2.4:* The preview window.

and then click on a line of the rectangle you've just drawn. Now select the fill tool. Click on NONE in the flyout menu.

While you're changing things, select the outline tool and click on the HAIR item to select the hairline width. When you're finished with the preview window, put it away by hitting F3. Because the preview window ties up screen and memory space and slows down your drawing as it updates itself, you should get in the habit of toggling it off when you don't need it.

Note that the preview window, like any other Windows window, can be moved and resized as described in Appendix A of this book.

### Draw Straight Lines: Divide the Window

To draw the separate lines which divide the window into six window panes, select the pencil tool. Move the pencil cursor so that it rests over the top of your rectangle midway between the two sides. As the rectangle is five centimeters across, this should be two and a half centimeters along.

To enable you to draw straight lines, Corel Draw offers a "constrain" feature. As long as you hold down the Ctrl key while drawing a line, the constrain feature will cause a line to be drawn straight. Part of the constraining nature of this feature is the fact that Corel Draw will force the line to lie along a path which is either horizontal or an even multiple of 15 degrees from horizontal. All you have to worry about is keeping your mouse within 15 degrees of the direction you want to go.

The procedure for drawing straight lines, then, is

1. Select the pencil tool and move the pencil cursor to the point you want to begin drawing the line.

2. Hold down the Ctrl key and click the mouse button once. This will start the line and anchor it.

3. Move the mouse cursor to extend the line in the direction you want.

4. When you've reached the point you want to end the line (the outside edge of your rectangle), click again. This anchors the other end of the line.

Repeat this procedure to draw the two horizontal lines. As the window is nine centimeters deep, these conveniently fall at three and six centimeters from the top. Your work space should now look like Figure 2.5.

## *FIXING MISTAKES*

If you get one of the lines wrong you'll have several options to correct it. One easy mistake to make in drawing lines under Corel Draw is to click and hold the mouse to anchor a line, rather than simply clicking and releasing it. This puts you in the freehand drawing mode, which will result in a very drunken looking window.

If you wind up with the wrong sort of line, you can delete it. This can be done by using the Clear item of the Edit menu or, even more simply, by pressing the Delete key—Del—on your keyboard. Both of these approaches will get rid of currently selected paths. Recalling that once drawn a path is automatically selected, you can use either of these methods to simply kill the path you have just drawn.

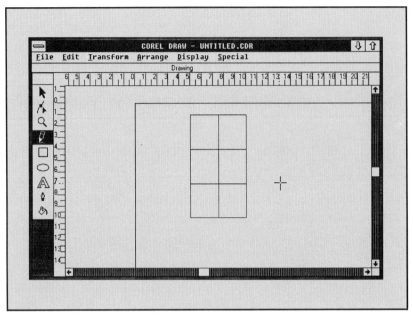

*Figure 2.5:* The window glass divided into panes.

You can also "undo" your mistake. If you select the Undo item of the Edit menu at any time under Corel Draw, your most recent action will be reversed and your drawing will immediately revert to the way it was one action ago. Holding down the Alt key while hitting the Backspace key will also undo your most recent change.

If you draw the right sort of line but you discover that it has come out a bit too long or a bit too short, you can simply resize it. Select the pick tool and click on the line. Selection marks like those in Figure 2.6 will appear. Grab the center selection mark from the group of marks at the end you want to adjust and then "pull" or "push" the line until it's the right length.

Looking back at the completed window (in Figure 2.3), you'll notice that there's a second rectangle around the glass, representing the wooden frame of the window. This is a quarter of a centimeter bigger than your first rectangle. Select the rectangle tool and draw this.

If you don't happen to get this rectangle quite right, you can adjust it just as you did the line above. Use the pick tool to select the offending rectangle by clicking on it. Selection marks will appear. If you

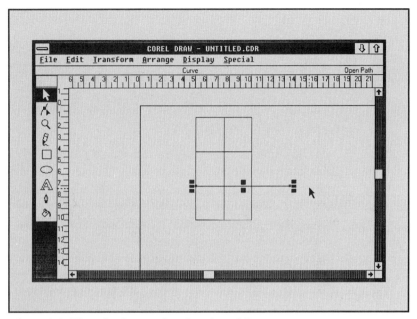

*Figure 2.6:* The selection marks of a selected line.

merely want to reposition the rectangle without changing its size, grab a line of the rectangle itself and drag it where you want it. The whole rectangle will move with it. If you have to resize the rectangle, grab a selection mark and drag that in or out until the rectangle is correctly sized. The selection marks of a rectangle, ellipse, or complex selected area allow you various automatic constraints depending upon which of the marks you choose to grab. If you grab a mark at one of the corners of the selected area, you'll be able to stretch the selected object in both directions. If you grab one that's in the middle of a side you'll only be able to stretch the object in one direction.

Resizing an object like this is a simple example of a *transformation*. Any object which is transformed retains its original dimensions and characteristics in the Corel Draw object list, as well as a record of all the transformations inflicted upon it. Thus, you can clear all of the transformations of an object and return it to its original state at any time, even three months and four hundred actions later, should you find yourself regretting having transformed the object in the first place.

Transformations and how to work with them will crop up in greater detail throughout the rest of this book.

Having drawn the complete glass part of the window, you might want to have a peek at it with the preview window to make sure that all the fills are correct, adjusting any that aren't.

## GROUPING OBJECTS

If everything is correct so far, you should not have to make any further changes to the individual paths that make up the glass part of the window. Because this part of the drawing will be used several times over, it's convenient to group the objects in this part of the drawing into a single object. You will do this by selecting the objects you want in your group and then selecting the Group item from the Arrange menu.

You can select items to be grouped in several ways. The most commonly used approach is to use the pick tool to draw a selection box around everything to be grouped. To do this with the window you have drawn thus far,

1. With the pick tool selected, place the point of the arrow cursor slightly above and to the left of the outer rectangle you've drawn.

2. Click and hold the mouse button.

3. Drag the mouse cursor down and to the right. A ''rubber band'' box will reel out behind it.

4. When the rubber band box encloses your entire drawing, release the mouse button.

Selection marks will appear around the rectangle. Everything inside the marks is now selected.

If a single rubber band box cannot include all the objects you want to select at one time, or if it would include objects you don't want selected, simply use the pick tool instead and click on each object you want while holding down the Shift key. This technique will prevent the first object you select from being unselected by the next one, and so on. Thus you can select several irregularly spaced objects—for grouping, transforming, deleting, and so on—by doing so one at a time.

Since the glass part of the window is the only thing you've drawn thus far, you could select it with an even easier technique: simply use the Select All item from the Edit menu. This will select every object in your drawing—which is just the glass and the window frame at the moment.

Once you have selected the items for your group, direct Corel Draw to group them, by clicking on Group from the Arrange menu.

With the objects selected and grouped, you can treat the glass part of your window as a single object. Anything which would affect a simple object can now be applied to this complex object. For example, you might want to make sure that all of the lines in this part of your drawing have the same line attribute. Using the pick tool, select the object— either drawing a rubber band box around it or simply clicking on any line in the object. Then select the outline tool, and click on a line attribute to apply to all the lines in the object.

A complex object *can* contain individual paths with different line widths and color attributes. If you had such an object in a drawing you could preserve the individual path characteristics by simply making sure you didn't do to it what you just did to the window pane object, that is, assign a single line characteristic to the whole object.

As long as they are in a group, paths are not accessible individually. You can't, for example, resize just one of the lines. However, grouped objects can be ungrouped at any time. Thus, you can always ungroup a complex object, alter one or more of its paths, and then regroup it.

(As you get more familiar with Corel Draw you may look back on this example and realize that the objects that make up your window pane should not have been grouped at all. They should have been *combined.* Combining objects is more involved than grouping them, and for this reason we'll leave it for later.)

## SAVING YOUR WORK

Before you go any further you should save your file. This will prevent you from losing all your work if your cat happens to trip over the power cord of your computer and pull it out of the wall. Another very good reason to save your file is that you can always revert to a previously saved file when you discover that you have mangled your drawing beyond the capabilities of the undo function to recover it.

Until you save a new drawing it is named UNTITLED.CDR. The *first* time you save any drawing you must select the Save As item from the File menu. This will pop up the dialog box shown in Figure 2.7.

With this box you should not need to change drives or directories when you save a file. Your current path should point to the directory called \WINDOWS\CORELDRW\CDRFILES, the default place to store Corel Draw drawing files. If this is the case, all you need do is type in a file name of up to eight letters and then press Enter or click on the Open control. You will notice that the Open control becomes active only after you have typed in at least one character for the file name.

Once you have assigned a file name to your file, the name will appear at the top of the Corel Draw window. This file will be unaffected by any changes you subsequently make to it on screen unless you decide to save it again. Then you have two choices.

- You can *update* the original file at any time, so that it includes your changes. Do this by selecting the Save item from the File menu (or by using the keyboard shortcut, Ctrl-S).

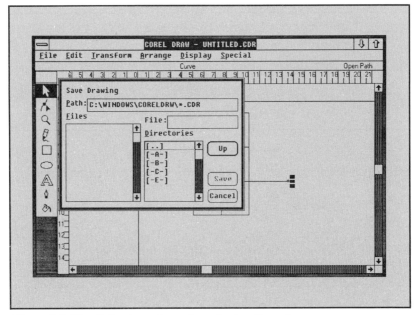

*Figure 2.7:* The dialog brought up by selecting Save As.

- You can *preserve* the original file, leaving it unchanged, by saving the changed file under a different name. Do this by using the Save As option from the File menu and entering a new file name.

If, in making changes to a file that has been saved, you do manage to mangle your drawing and decide you don't want to save any changes, preferring instead to revert to the previously saved version, select Open from the File menu. A dialog box will appear, asking if you want to save the changes you've made. Since the changes didn't quite work out, click on No. A file dialog box will then pop up. Select your file and click on Open.

When you open a file—whether because you're reverting to a previously saved version or because you just want to work with a drawing previously saved to disk—the name of that file becomes the default name of the drawing you're working with. Subsequently, if you select Save rather than Save As, any changes you have made will change the file. If you want to save your modified drawing but you also want the original to remain untouched, you must use Save As, which gives you the opportunity to choose a different file name for the modified drawing.

## *DUPLICATING AND MOVING OBJECTS*

Each double window consists of two sets of panes. There's no need to go through the work of drawing the second set by hand—you can just duplicate the first one and place it in the correct position.

Whenever you duplicate an object under Corel Draw, the new object is displaced from the original by a predetermined amount, which is zero by default. This is a very useful feature, as we'll see. The duplicate does not snap to the grid even if the Snap To Grid feature is on, however, which can make it difficult to place the duplicate precisely where you want it, especially if you're trying to keep objects in a straight line.

To avoid this—and to make placing duplicates easier—it's a good idea to change the displacement of duplicates to suit your needs at the moment. To do this,

1. Select the Preferences item from the Special menu. The Preferences box will pop up, as seen in Figure 2.8.

2. Change the Place Duplicate units of measure to coincide with the units of measure your grid is working with.

3. Change the Place Duplicate number values.

Once again, you can click on the unit name to step through the available units. The Place Duplicate values control the horizontal and vertical displacement respectively. Since we want the second window to appear to the right of the first one, we might as well make the vertical displacement zero. For horizontal displacement, let's choose one centimeter. This might look arbitrary, and it is. There is a good reason for this. If you're methodical you could figure out how far the second window has to be displaced in order to make it appear in the desired location without any further positioning and enter this for the horizontal displacement value. However, it's usually easier to drag it over once it has been duplicated.

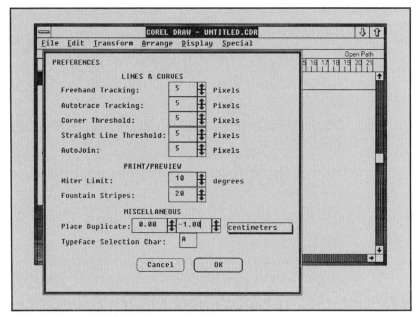

*Figure 2.8:* The Preferences dialog from the Special menu.

Note that if you change the units of measurement for a dialog such as this one, the numeric values associated with the units will be recalculated in the new units. Thus, if you had one inch of displacement and then changed to centimeters, you'd wind up with 2.54, which is the number of centimeters in an inch. Changing units usually involves entering new numbers as well.

Click on OK to accept the changes.

Now you can go about actually duplicating the window. Select the window pane with the pick tool. You can duplicate it either by using the Duplicate item from the File menu or by using the keyboard equivalent, Ctrl-D. This keyboard equivalent is well worth learning—you'll be using it repeatedly in a few minutes.

Once duplicated, the new object will automatically be selected by Corel Draw. Grab any line on the selected object and drag it to the right until there is half a centimeter between the windows.

It will be easier to check the exact positioning of the two windows if you zoom in on the space between them. Use the zoom tool to do this. Figure 2.9 illustrates the increased magnification used to align the window panes.

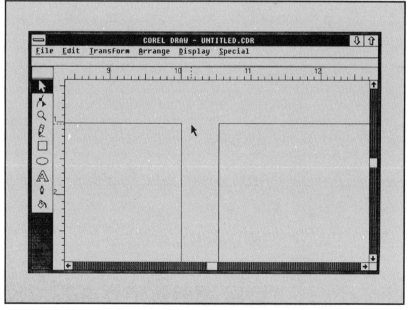

*Figure 2.9:* Zooming in to position the window panes.

Once you have the windows positioned, you will probably want to set the magnification so as to allow you to see both of them. Select the zoom tool again and then select ALL from the flyout menu. This will throw away any intermediate zoom steps and return you to the basic magnification level of Corel Draw so you can see the whole page. Now select the zoom-in tool and zoom in on the area which contains your window panes.

You will find that changing the magnification level of Corel Draw frequently greatly simplifies the execution of complex drawings.

### *Draw Adjoining Rectangles: The Window Frame*

The two window panes have a rectangle enclosing them both, again a quarter of a centimeter bigger than the area it encloses. You should draw this next, using the rectangle tool. Make sure the new rectangle has a hairline width and no fill. Again, you can use the Preview window to make sure that everything is as it should be.

Next, add the sill below the windows—it's half a centimeter deep—and the piece of wood below that. This latter rectangle is half a centimeter deep as well but it extends a quarter of a centimeter further out in each direction. Finally, add quarter-centimeter rectangles up each side, these being the boards that the shutters will be attached to.

Your work space should now look like Figure 2.10.

Also check the Preview window to make sure that everything looks right.

Once all the line widths and positions and such are correct, you should not have to change any of the individual paths in this part of the drawing again. Therefore, let's group everything we've done so far into a single object. Corel Draw allows you to include previously grouped objects into new groups, so you need not ungroup the individual panes before you create a new group with both of them. In fact, you can have as many layers of nested groups as you like under Corel Draw—within the bounds of available memory. Obviously, having an object buried sixteen levels deep in a group makes it very hard to get at if you want to ungroup it and change one of its component paths.

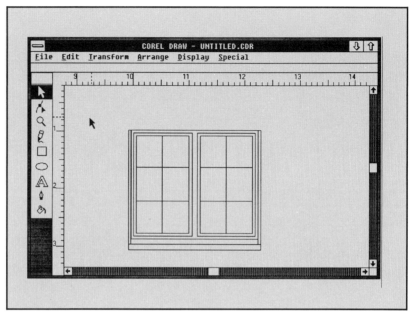

*Figure 2.10:* The window with all its woodwork in place.

To group everything in your drawing thus far, you can choose the Select All item from the File menu or select everything by area using the pick tool. Then go ahead and group them. Remember that the Group function is selected from the Arrange menu.

### *Draw Stacked Lines: The Shutter Slats*

The last elements of the window to be installed are the shutters. We'll create them in the same way we did the window panes, that is, by drawing one and then duplicating it. You might have to use the horizontal scroll bar to move the picture over slightly so you'll have enough room to draw the shutter.

The outer rectangle of the shutter is $4^{1}/_{4}$ by $10^{1}/_{2}$ centimeters. The inner rectangle is a quarter of a centimeter inside the outer one. Draw both of these using the rectangle tool. Your shutter should look like the one in Figure 2.11.

The slats on the shutter are just lines. However, there are a lot of lines, and it would be inconvenient to have to draw them all. Fortunately, Corel Draw offers ways around this problem.

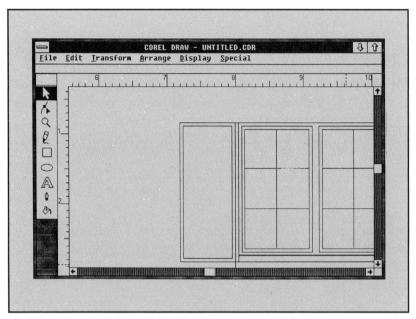

*Figure 2.11:* The shutter frame, ready for slats.

If we were using fills and knew that this drawing would be printed on a PostScript printer, we could simply fill the inner rectangle with a horizontal line pattern. For this example, however, we'll use real lines. One way to get all those lines in place is to draw one and then duplicate it many times. The lines will appear in the right locations if you set the displacement values in the Preferences box appropriately before you start. Open the Preferences box in the Special menu and set the horizontal displacement to 0 and the vertical displacement to – 0.25. The latter minus value will cause the duplicate to appear a quarter of a centimeter—or one of our grid units—*below* the original.

Now you are set to draw and duplicate the horizontal lines in the shutter. Start by zooming in so the shutter is fairly large. Then select the pencil tool and draw the top slat one quarter of a centimeter below the top inside line of the shutter frame. (Hold down the Ctrl key to constrain the line to be horizontal. Remember that you simply click the mouse button—don't hold it—and move the mouse so the line extends straight, then click it again when it touches the right inside line of the shutter frame.)

Now hit Ctrl-D. A second line should appear below the first one if you have set up the Preferences box properly. Press Ctrl-D repeatedly until you have created enough slats to fill the shutter. If you accidentally create too many you can just select them with the pick tool and blow them away with the Delete key.

Your work space should look like the one in Figure 2.12.

## *REGROUPING COMPLEX OBJECTS*

This double window is almost complete—it's only missing one shutter. You can add it by duplicating the shutter you've just created and dragging it to the other side of the window. To complete the window do the following:

1. Group all the elements of the shutter together. (Select them, then select Group from the Arrange menu.)

2. Set the displacement values (in the Preferences box of the Special menu) for no vertical displacement and let's say one centimeter of horizontal displacement.

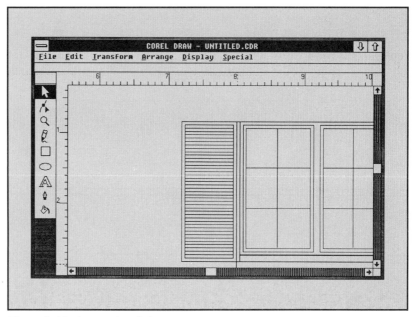

*Figure 2.12:* A completed shutter.

3. Hit Ctrl-D to duplicate the shutter.

4. Drag the duplicate over to the other side of the window and position it. You might need to zoom in on the area where it meets the window to see if it's properly aligned.

Now that you have a complete double window with shutters, you can select all the elements and group them. This will make the whole window behave as a single complex object, which will save some time in duplicating it and moving it around.

This would be a good time to save your work by pressing Ctrl-S.

There are four windows in the drawing, and by now you'll appreciate that Corel Draw will let you reuse all the work you've just done. Simply select the window object, duplicate it, and move the duplicate window to the right until it is positioned like the second window in the complete drawing in Figure 2.13.

In my version there are two groups of two windows, rather than four windows spaced equally. Having placed the second window I grouped the two windows together and duplicated the resulting group. The space between the right windows is thus the same as the space between the left, the right pair being a duplicate of the left pair. If you want the windows equally spaced just duplicate the one you've drawn twice more and move the copies into position.

The wall that the windows are set into is just a rectangle. Since none of the objects in this drawing have any fill patterns associated

*Figure 2.13:* What you're aiming at. How the drawing should look when it is completed.

with them, it doesn't matter whether the wall is drawn before or after the windows. In a drawing where fill patterns were being used we would have to make sure the wall was behind the windows as far as Corel Draw is concerned; otherwise the fill of the wall would obscure the windows.

Draw a suitable rectangle around the windows. This will probably extend outside the drawing page—don't worry about this for now. Once again you should probably use the preview window to check your drawing. If everything looks right hit Ctrl-S to save your drawing.

## DRAWING OBJECTS BEYOND THE WORK SPACE

Create the eaves by drawing some very shallow, long rectangles. If you look closely at the complete drawing you might be able to discern that there are three rectangles. The lowest one represents the wood of the roof itself. The next one is the rain gutter, and the upper one the lip of the roof. The upper one can be one quarter of a centimeter deep, with the others somewhat deeper. You can see a detail of these rectangles in Figure 2.14.

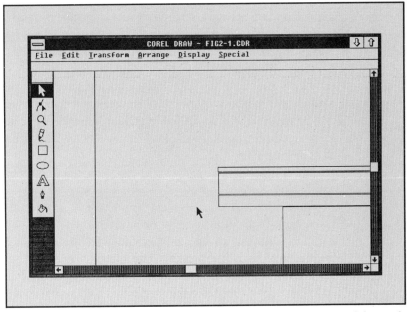

*Figure 2.14:* The eaves, which are too wide to draw in one section of the work space.

Because these rectangles will be so shallow relative to their widths, it can be extremely difficult to try to draw them in one easy motion. You will need to start each rectangle in a zoomed-in section of the drawing and extend it to the right edge of the work space, then use the scroll arrows or scroll ''thumb'' to move more of the drawing into the work space, such that the leading edge of the rectangle ends up on the left. By dragging this side of the rectangle with the pick tool, you can stretch the rectangle across the drawing section you have just scrolled into the work space. Repeat this scroll-and-stretch technique until you have extended the rectangle the appropriate distance beyond the other side of the front of the house.

## CURVING A STRAIGHT LINE

If you look closely at the extremes of the eaves you'll notice the curved profiles of the side gutters. Curves are something we have not yet discussed.

In drawing the side gutter you will draw two straight lines and convert one of them to a curve. You might conceptualize this as starting off with an art deco rain gutter which is triangular in cross-section and then hammering it out into a more familiar sort of gutter.

First, zoom in on the left edge of the eaves. Select the pencil tool, and click on the upper edge of the roof to anchor the first line. Use the constrain function—the Ctrl key—to get the line perfectly horizontal. Draw the line to the left a half of a centimeter or so and click again to anchor it. Click once more on the same place to start a second line, and bring that down to the lower edge of the roof. Do not use the constrain feature for this line. Your art deco gutter should now look like the one in Figure 2.15a.

One of the interesting features of the pencil tool is its propensity for combining paths if it thinks this will help you. If you click to start a new line within five screen pixels of the end of your previous line, Corel Draw will start the new line at the end point of the previous line and combine the paths automatically. In this case, the horizontal line and the diagonal one will wind up as a single object without your having to explicitly tell Corel Draw to make it so.

We are now going to convert the diagonal line into a curve. Select the shape tool and double-click on the end point of the diagonal line,

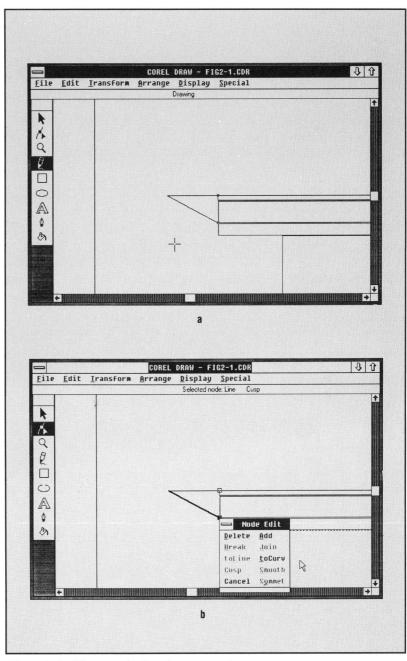

*Figure 2.15:* The steps in drawing a curved gutter.

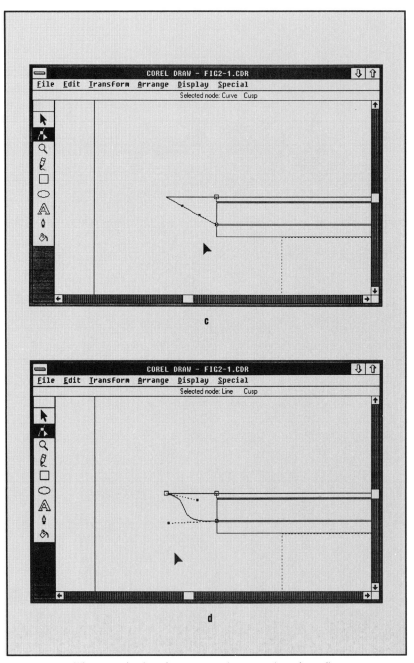

*Figure 2.15:* The steps in drawing a curved gutter. (continued)

where it meets the roof. The diagonal line will get thicker, and a menu like the one in Figure 2.15b should appear. Select toCurv from among the active options. The menu disappears and the line loses its thickness.

The diagonal line is now a diagonal curve. It happens to have no twist to it yet, but it now has all the properties of a Bezier curve rather than of a line. The most obvious manifestation of this is the appearance of two "handles," as shown in Figure 2.15c.

The curve handles are used to bend the curve and make it follow the contours you need. You will find that using them is largely an intuitive process. To begin with, grab one of them with your cursor and move it around to see what the line does.

Moving a curve handle alters the distance between the handle and its origin. You will have to adjust both handles to some extent to get the curve of the gutter to look right. When you're finished your work space should look something like the one in Figure 2.15d.

## CREATING MIRROR IMAGES

Having drawn one gutter, you must arrange to have another one with the same shape at the other end of the roof—or rather, you'll need a mirror image of it. Although you could just move over and draw it again, this would be both wasteful of time and a bit tricky, because drawing Bezier curves to match other Bezier curves is not an easy task. Fortunately, there's no need to attempt this.

Corel Draw allows you to duplicate the curve you've just drawn, flip it end for end, and move it to the other end of the roof.

1. Select the curve and the top of the gutter. (Because the curve began so close to the end of the top line, Corel Draw should already have combined these two paths into one object.)

2. Hit Ctrl-D to duplicate this object.

3. Use the Stretch & Mirror item of the Transform menu to flip the duplicated object horizontally. Click on Horz Mirror, then on OK in the Stretch & Mirror dialog box.

4. Zoom out so you can see at least a third of the roof, and drag the new object toward the far end of the roof. You will

probably have to drag it to the right edge of the work space, scroll the drawing, and drag it again. Plan on doing this several times.

5. When you have the new gutter roughly in place, zoom in and position it exactly.

This would be a good point to save your work again.

## *USING CONSTRAINT TO DRAW ANGLES*

The roof itself is a lot easier to draw than it would be to construct. It involves no complex line manipulation and very few objects. You will have to zoom out so as to be able to see the entire roof.

The sloping sides of the roof are 30 degrees from the horizontal. This slope was chosen because it provides the maximum utilization of materials for a climate-related design which is still in keeping with the aesthetics and functionality of the overall architectural criteria of the structure. Well, really it was chosen because Corel Draw can do 30-degree angles very easily. (It's worth noting here that although it's easier to draw angled lines using the constrain feature's 15-degree increments, Corel Draw is quite capable of producing lines at any angle you like.)

Select the pencil tool to draw the outlines of the roof. Constrain the lines to horizontal (top) and 30 degrees (sides) by using the Ctrl key while drawing. I placed the top line seven centimeters above the eaves, but you can choose any distance which looks good to you.

If you drew your top line before you drew your angled sides, chances are the horizontal line is the wrong length. Select the pick tool and click on the line. Selection marks will appear around it. Grab an end selection mark (the center one from either end's triplet of marks) and adjust the length of the line until it meets the angled lines of the sides. You might want to zoom in to make sure that everything matches perfectly.

The last task in completing the drawing is to fill the roof area with horizontal lines. Once again, except for the fact that we aren't using fills just yet, this could be done with a PostScript fill. In this case, we will fill it with individual lines.

Using the constrain feature and the pencil tool, draw a horizontal line a half a centimeter below the top of the roof. Use the Preferences item of the Special menu to set the horizontal displacement for duplicates to 0 and the vertical displacement to $-0.50$ centimeters. Now duplicate the line by pressing Ctrl-D as often as is required to fill the roof area.

Your work space should look like the one in Figure 2.16.

Unfortunately, there's no easy way to make the lines expand to meet the edges of the roof. You will have to select each one and drag it until it's long enough. This doesn't take very long—there aren't all that many lines.

Save your work—you're done.

## PRINTING LARGE DRAWINGS

At this point, the drawing of the roof is probably too large to print. If you zoom to ALL and you find that the image is bigger than the printable part of the work area, as shown in Figure 2.17, you will have to scale it down a bit.

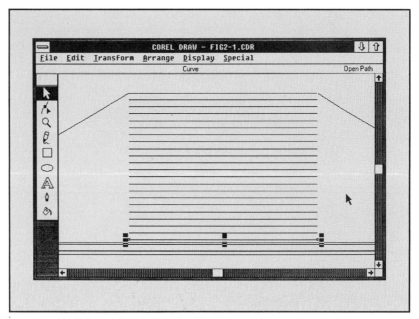

*Figure 2.16:* The roof with identical horizontal lines.

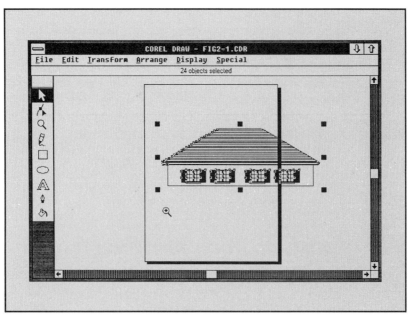

*Figure 2.17:* The picture larger than the page.

### Reducing the Picture

The easiest way to scale the picture down is to select the whole thing—either with the pick tool or by using the Select All item of the Edit menu—and then group it into a single object. Then use the Stretch & Mirror item of the Transform menu to resize this object. If you set both the Stretch Horizontally and Stretch Vertically values to 75, the drawing will be reduced—kind of the opposite of stretched—to 75 percent of its current size. This box is shown with the controls set up for this scale factor in Figure 2.18.

Now try printing the picture. Printing under Corel Draw is dead easy—all you have to do is select Print from the File menu. A dialog box with a lot of options will appear. Since you'll be printing exactly what appears in your drawing with no embellishments, you can ignore all of these. Just click on OK or hit Enter to accept the defaults. We'll be discussing most of these options later.

Depending on your printer and several other factors, you might not like the results that you get from your first attempt at printing the completed drawing. The lines which make up the shutter slats are

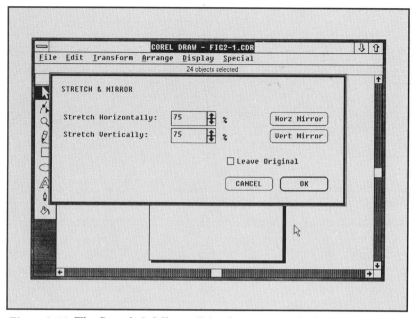

*Figure 2.18:* The Stretch & Mirror dialog box set to scale the image down to three quarters of its original size.

close enough that they might run together into solid black areas. Some of the other fine detail may also get lost. Remember that if you reduce the size of a drawing under Corel Draw the details are not lost in the picture itself, but thcy gct so fine as to be beyond the ability of your printer to manage them.

Another problem is the one illustrated in Figure 2.19. In this print, magnified to show the effect, the shutter slats are distinct lines, but they have become irregularly spaced. This has occurred because the printer has been told to print lines with greater positional accuracy than it could manage. The vertical positions of the lines have been "fudged" by the printer to the nearest increments of its own internal grid, with the result that they are no longer uniformly spaced.

When you're creating complex drawings under Corel Draw it's very important to keep in mind the characteristics of the output device which will ultimately reproduce your work. Inasmuch as this chapter started off with a picture of the complete drawing—and inasmuch as that drawing exhibited none of the problems we've just discussed—there's obviously a way around printer difficulties. The

*Figure 2.19:* A spacing problem.

solution is actually pretty simple: All of these print aberrations will vanish if the image being printed gets a little bigger.

### Rotating and Enlarging the Picture

As things stand, enlarging the drawing would cause it to spill off the paper. That's why we reduced it in the first place. However, since the sheet we're printing on *is* longer than it is wide, we could expand the image if it were to be printed lengthwise along the paper instead of across it. This is called printing in ''landscape mode.''

The first thing to do in making the drawing use more of the paper is to rotate it. You could do this with the Rotate & Skew item of the Transform menu, but it's probably more interesting at this point to use Corel Draw's free rotation marks.

### Using the Rotation and Skew Marks

If you select an object, such as a rectangle or a group of paths, the by-now familiar selection marks will appear around it. However, if you click again on one of the lines of the object—that is, if you select it while it's already selected—the selection marks will change to arrows, as shown in Figure 2.20. These arrows are called *rotation marks* for the ones at the corners of the selection rectangle and *skew marks* for those along the sides. You will also notice that a dot with a circle around it has appeared roughly in the center of the object. This is called the *pivot*.

If you're in a hurry to get to this rotate-and-skew mode you can just double-click on an object. Conversely, if you get to this mode by mistake, clicking on the object yet again will get you back to the normal selection mode.

Select the drawing—it should have been previously grouped into a single object. Click on the selected object to change the selection marks into rotation and skew marks. Move your cursor to one of the rotation marks. (Did you notice that your cursor changed into a cross?) Grab the rotation mark and turn the image until it's aligned with the long edge of the page. If you move slowly enough, you can read the current rotation angle displayed at the top of the window. You should be aiming for exactly 90 degrees.

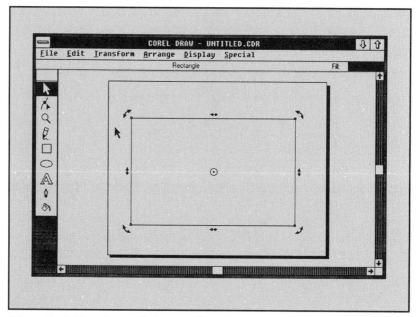

*Figure 2.20:* Rotation and skew marks.

When you stop rotating the image, your cursor will turn into a partial circle with upward pointing arrow heads. This indicates that Corel Draw is working on transforming all the paths in the object you've rotated so they will appear as you've positioned them. This may take a few moments.

With the drawing rotated you'll be able to increase its size to fill a lot more of the page. Click on the drawing to change the rotate and skew marks back to selection marks. Grab one of the corner marks and drag it to increase the size of the object. As long as you use a corner mark the drawing will expand in both dimensions equally. Adjust the drawing using whichever corner marks you need until it fairly fills the page.

There is a very important consideration in scaling the drawing up for printing. Laser printers do not print right to the edges of their paper. The exact amount of dead space varies from printer to printer, but it's not a bad idea to leave a quarter of an inch between the extremes of your drawing and the edge of the printable area of the Corel Draw workspace.

Try printing your drawing again. You should find some pretty respectable hard copy emerging from your printer.

It's worth noting that some of the things you've just done to the drawing to make it print—scaling it and such—can be handled by the printer driver itself without your having to actually change anything in your drawing. However, in doing it "the hard way," you've gotten to try out a number of Corel Draw tools and facilities.

## *A DIGRESSION ON COMPLEX DRAWINGS*

In drawing the upper story of a house, we did quite a few things in less than ideal ways for the sake of illustrating things about Corel Draw. These are things you would want to improve upon if you were confronted with really having to produce a complex architectural drawing or other intricate piece of art.

One of the things which seems to limit Corel Draw's ability to draw things like the upper story—and perhaps the whole house that it would be a part of—is the way the program bogs down when it's confronted with lots of objects. You might have noticed that it got a bit tedious when it was redrawing its screen after zooming out, and even when you were simply adding objects to the drawing toward the end of the session. This is partially the fault of the way we created the picture.

Corel Draw treats grouped objects as individual paths which just happen to have something to do with each other. Thus, if there are 385 objects in a drawing—this being the actual number of objects in my version of the second story—Corel Draw will have 385 entries in its object list to paw through every time you ask it to select an object or add something to the list.

*Combined* paths, however, are treated as single objects. This speeds up Corel Draw enormously, as well as reducing the amount of memory it uses to store its object list. In many situations, you should combine objects rather than group them. We'll discuss those situations in greater detail later.

Another drawback to handling big drawings with lots of paths is that when you work on part of a drawing, all the other parts must regenerate themselves to become visible. If we had drawn the entire house that this second story is part of, the whole house would have been redrawn to the screen each time you zoomed to ALL. This would have involved some intolerable waiting.

Corel Draw offers an easy way around this. You can draw complex pictures in sections, one section to a file. When all the sections are complete, Corel Draw lets you "import" them into a single file and combine them into a finished picture. This, too, will be discussed in greater detail later in this book.

There's a lot that can be done with Corel Draw when you're confronted with large images to manipulate. Much of what you can get together when you're running at the edges of Corel Draw's abilities will be determined by your understanding of the package itself and by a little common sense.

## DRAWING CIRCLES AND SECTIONS: A PIE CHART

The upper story of the house was a complex drawing, but a very simple exercise, as there were really no difficult drawing techniques used to execute it.

Corel Draw gurus will argue that nothing is really difficult. In a sense this is true—any drawing can be reduced to a series of simple

CH. 2

tasks. The drawing in Figure 2.21 may or may not look to you like a series of simple tasks. If you have ever tried to get professional looking business graphics created—or worse, tried to do them yourself with a software package designed for the task—you may well be daunted by the prospect of trying to make this pie chart.

This pie chart can be done in five or ten minutes if you're familiar with Corel Draw. By the time you've got this book under your belt, things like this will spring from your fingertips in less time than it takes most people to get a purchase order written up for a graphics house.

This drawing encompasses a number of elements which are not strictly speaking part of this chapter, most notably fills and text;

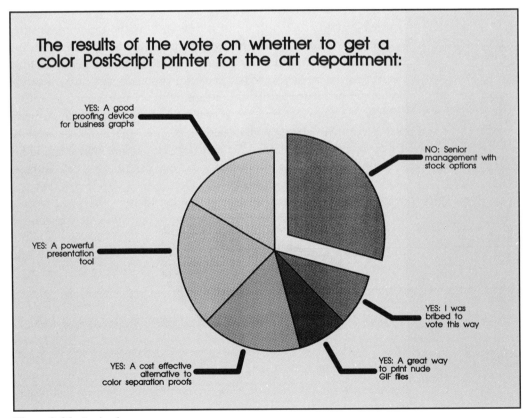

*Figure 2.21:* A pie chart.

however, we'll be making only light use of them here. You'll encounter the proper explanations of these facilities in the next two chapters.

There are a number of important things to note about the pie chart. It has lots of sections, each of which is filled with a different gray shade. All of them match up perfectly. There's an ''exploded'' section which also looks as if it would match perfectly. There's a drop shadow behind the chart to give it depth. There are smooth, angled lines pointing to the various sections.

The whole work appears professional, and if these guys ever had a chance of getting a color PostScript printer for their art department—which they don't, due to the nature of the exploded segment of the chart—this chart could do it for them.

The reason this chart was so easy to put together is largely tied up in the way the shape tool under Corel Draw works on ellipses. Because business graphics are very hot now, the authors of the package have gone to some length to make things like this work out easily.

To begin with, you will observe that this drawing lends itself to landscape orientation—it's wider than it is long. For this reason, we'll start by doing something we would have done with the house drawing had it been a real-world project. We'll change the orientation of the page in the work space.

Start with a blank work space by selecting New from the File menu. If you have not already exited Corel Draw since completing the previous drawing, this will wipe out any unsaved remnants of the house drawing which might be hanging around.

Select Page Setup from the File menu. A dialog box like the one in Figure 2.22 will appear. Change the Orientation item from portrait to landscape by clicking in the radio button next to Landscape. When you click on OK to accept this change, you will note that the printable part of the Corel Draw page is now oriented with its long dimension horizontal.

Select the ellipse tool. As with most of the tools that actually do any drawing, the ellipse tool can be constrained with the Ctrl key. If you constrain it you'll find that it draws perfect circles, rather than ellipses. Use it in this way to draw a circle 12 centimeters across. Actually, neither the size nor the units of measurement of the circle matter in this drawing. If you want to revert to inches or explore the as-yet unexplained world of picas and points you are free to do so.

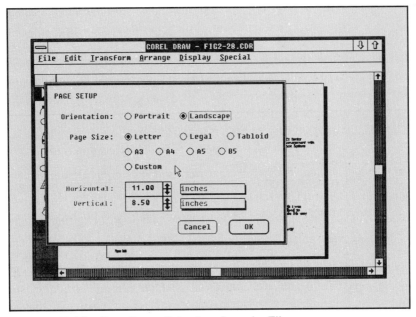

*Figure 2.22:* The Page Setup dialog box from the File menu.

Business graphics tend to get modified a lot. In this case, sufficient lobbying or threats by the art department could reduce the relative size of the exploded segment, in which case the chart would have to be redrawn. It's handy to have the original circle nearby to change or add segments later on.

We are going to make use of the work area outside the printable page in this drawing. Select the circle you've drawn and drag it off the drawing page into the work area. This will be your ''template'' for creating the various segments of the pie chart: it will be duplicated many times, but the original object will remain. Having the basic pie outside the printed area allows you to leave it in the drawing file without having it appear in your hard copy.

Your work space should look like the one in Figure 2.23.

## CREATING A SEGMENT

Let's create the segment of the chart which represents people who felt that a color PostScript printer would make a good proofing device for business graphs. Select your template circle and duplicate it by

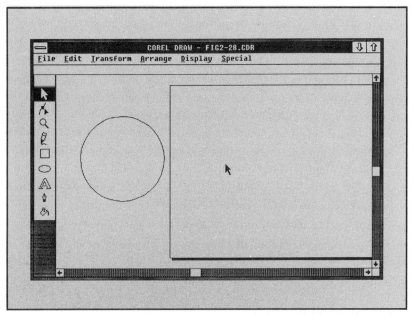

*Figure 2.23:* Corel Draw all ready to draw a pie chart. The basic pie is off to
the left.

hitting Ctrl-D. Drag the duplicate into the printable area. Select the
shape tool and select the circle you'll be working with.

Obviously you'll be splitting the circle into pie slices. If you hold
down the Ctrl key these slices will be constrained to multiples of
15 degrees. You don't have to constrain your segments in this way,
but it sure speeds things up a lot as it makes aligning the various segments dead easy. At least for the sake of this exercise, it's recom-
mended that you constain the angles. At such time as you come to
create a real pie chart you'll probably find that very few people can
quickly spot the difference anyway between, for example, a 15 degree
angle and a 17 degree angle.

When you select a circle or an ellipse with the shape tool, a single
node mark will appear either at the top or the bottom of the object. In
this case it should be at the top. Using the shape-tool cursor, grab the
node and drag it counterclockwise around the perimeter. If you keep
the cursor just inside the perimeter, the ends of the arc will automatically generate lines to the original center of the circle.

If you have a need for an arc without the lines, just move the shape tool cursor slightly outside the perimeter as you're dragging the node. The connecting lines will vanish.

When you began dragging the node around, you may have noticed that you left a second node behind. In splitting the circle into an arc, Corel Draw had to add a node to the object. Both nodes can be dragged, as we'll see in a moment.

When you have created a wedge which looks to be about right, release the node you've been dragging. Your work space should look like the one in Figure 2.24.

You will be adding the text and other regalia of the drawing later once the graph has been completed.

## ALIGNING ADDITIONAL SEGMENTS

Let's add the next segment to the graph. This is where Corel Draw proves to be very clever at this sort of drawing. As before, select the template circle, duplicate it, and drag the duplicate over to the printable area. Don't worry about positioning it exactly. Select it with the

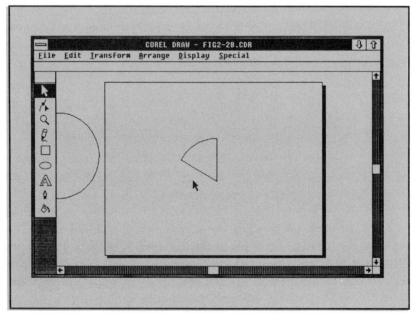

*Figure 2.24:* One segment of the pie chart in place.

shape tool and start dragging the node around, as before. Make sure you have the Ctrl key down while you're dragging the node.

In this case you will have to drag both nodes. Once you have moved the first one down to the far end of where the new segment will be, you'll have to release it and go drag the second one—the node Corel Draw added when you started dragging to form the first arc. This will form the other side of the wedge.

You might have to take several shots at getting the nodes positioned properly. Corel Draw allows you to go back and move them as often as you need to in order to arrive at the arc you're after.

Your work space should now look something like the one shown in Figure 2.25.

Chances are the second segment will not be positioned properly with respect to the first one. You can have Corel Draw move it automatically so the alignment is perfect. As far as Corel Draw is concerned, when you turn a circle into a wedge—a pie chart segment—the whole circle still remains as an object. You can see this if you select one of the segments you've drawn. The rectangle formed by the selection marks will be

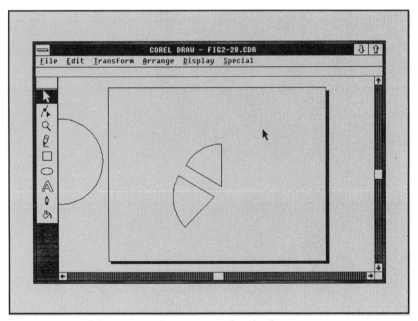

*Figure 2.25:* Adding a second segment to the pie chart.

the size of the original circle even though only a portion of the circle is displayed.

If you click on the selected circle to get the rotation and skew marks, you'll note that the pivot marking the center of the object is at the point of the wedge, that is, at the original center of the circle. In order to make the two segments fit together, you must get the centers of the two original circles to rest on the same point. Corel Draw will handle this for you. Use the pick tool to select both segments by drawing a rubber band box to encompass them both. You might notice that the text above the Corel Draw work space informs you that you have two objects selected. Now select Align from the Arrange menu. You will see a dialog box like the one in Figure 2.26.

Select the Center option for both the horizontal and vertical directions and click on OK. The two segments will be redrawn perfectly aligned.

Add the remaining segments to the pie chart by duplicating the template circle and making each duplicate into another wedge. You can align them as you go or all at once when you've completed all the ''Yes'' sections of the pie chart.

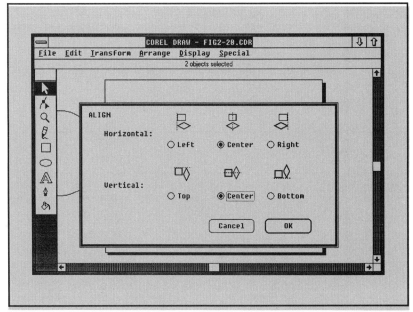

*Figure 2.26:* The Align dialog box from the Arrange menu.

The "No" portion of the chart then is obviously just a last segment which is not positioned to fit perfectly into the gap left in the chart.

If you hit F3 to pop up the preview window you should see the pie chart drawn in fine lines with no fill in any of the segments. Group together the objects you have created thus far.

## *USING FILLS FOR INTEREST*

In order to make the drop shadow appear as a shadow you will have to give it a fill. We haven't actually used fills for anything as yet, but at this level they're pretty easy. We will use numerical fill values for this drawing, rather than the basic default fills the fill-tool flyout menu offers us.

### *Adding a Drop Shadow*

The drop shadow behind the pie chart is very easy to manage, and will serve as a useful example of how Corel Draw deals with overlapping objects. Select the pie chart (you should already have grouped it into one object) and duplicate it. Place the duplicate slightly above and to the left of the original. If you want to keep an eye on what's happening during this process, open the preview window.

Select the duplicate pie chart, the one which is to become the drop shadow. You will notice in the completed example back in Figure 2.21 that the drop shadow has no rules around it. Therefore, you must make invisible the rules it inherited from its parent object, the real pie chart.

Select the outline tool. Click on NONE. While the outline of the drop shadow will still be visible in your work space, it should vanish from the preview window. It is now a white object against a white background with no outline.

With the drop shadow selected, click on the fill tool. When the flyout menu appears click on the leftmost item to pop up the fill precise adjustment box. It should look like Figure 2.27, except that the tint value will initially be set to 100, that is, fully black. Change it to 10 percent black, as shown in the figure, and click on OK.

If you look at the preview, you will notice that you have a slight problem. The drop shadow appears to be in front of the pie chart. This has happened because Corel Draw places objects on the screen in the order they're created unless it's told to do otherwise. With the

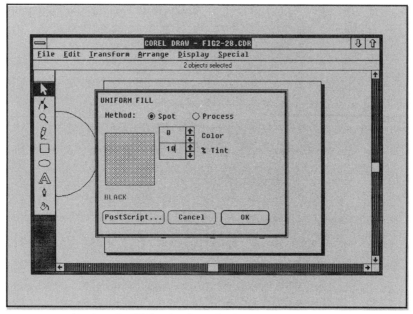

*Figure 2.27:* Setting the fill for the drop shadow.

drop shadow selected, use the To Back item in the Arrange menu to put it behind the pie chart object. Corel Draw will automatically "hide" the part of the back object the front object obscures.

You might have to click in the preview window to get it to redraw the pie chart. This is because in some situations the program hesitates to see if you're going to do something further before it decides you want an image redrawn. Clicking in the preview window overrides the hesitation.

### *Shading and Outlining the Segments*

There are two major tasks left in drawing the pie chart itself. The first involves setting the line thickness, or weight, of the outlines of the segments. As the segments of the pie chart have been grouped into a single object, it's very easy to set all the lines at the same time. Select the pie chart object with the pick tool—making sure you don't get the drop shadow by mistake—and then select the outline tool. Click on one of the middle line-thickness icons. This line weight will now be applied to all the lines in the selected object.

Note that the line colors will default to black, so you don't have to set the line color explicitly. The only time you'll need the lower level of icons in the outline tool's flyout menu is when a line is to be drawn in color or gray rather than solid black.

The next step of the drawing involves changing the fill patterns of the individual segments. You can't do this while the segments are grouped into a single object, so select the pie chart if it isn't currently selected and use the Ungroup item of the Arrange menu to return the segments to individual objects.

Select each segment in turn and use the fill tool's flyout menu to select a fill for it. In the case of a drawing like this one, it's probably preferable to use the precise adjustment box to set the gray levels, just as you did with the drop shadow.

Avoid the extremes of the gray levels. The lightest gray shade you use for a segment shouldn't be much below 20 percent black. The darkest probably shouldn't be above 70 percent black. This helps prevent the tone getting lost in the outlines. Try to arrange not to have two similar gray levels in adjacent segments.

When you've finished shading each segment, use the preview to see what you've drawn. Your work space should look like Figure 2.28. This would be a good time to use the Save As item in the File menu to assign a file name to your drawing and save your work to disk.

## USING TEXT: ADDING LABELS

Adding text to a drawing under Corel Draw is both one of the most effortless of its capabilities and ultimately one of the most fun when you get into the nuances of it. It will be dealt with in much greater detail later in this book, as it's one of the things which Corel Draw does best. We'll have a quick look at it here to see how to polish off the pie chart.

Zoom out as necessary so you can see the whole pie chart.

Select the text tool. Your cursor will change to a vertical bar with ears, the Corel Draw text insertion cursor. Click on your drawing somewhere close to where you think the text for the first segment should go—let's start with the ''Yes: A good proofing device for business graphs'' segment. Don't worry about exactly where the text is to go. You can position it accurately after it has been placed.

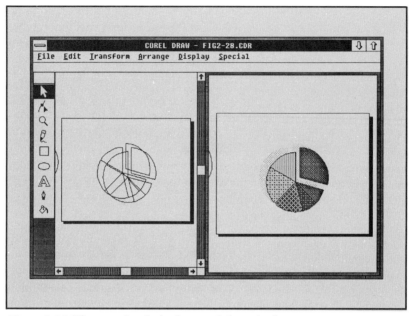

*Figure 2.28:* The completed pie chart and drop shadow.

A dialog box like the one in Figure 2.29 will appear, except the top box will be blank, the Alignment will be Left, and the default Point Size will be 24 points, which is entirely too big. Change this to 12 points. Then click in the box at the top of the dialog and type in the label text. Note that it's typed as three lines—you'll have to hit Enter at the appropriate places.

The text for the segments on the left should line up along the right margin of the areas they occupy. They are thus said to be right-aligned. The text on the other side of the chart is left-aligned. The text entry window defaults to left alignment. Select the Right alignment radio button located just below the text entry window.

Click on OK to accept your text.

If you discover after you've left the Text dialog that you've committed a few typographical errors in entering the text, or that you forgot to reduce the point size, for example, you'll be happy to know that you can edit any of the parameters of previously entered text. You can edit text under Corel Draw even after you've transformed it, twisted it, wrapped it into spirals, or pasted it onto the back of a royal ball python and sent it slithering off into the grass. Simply select

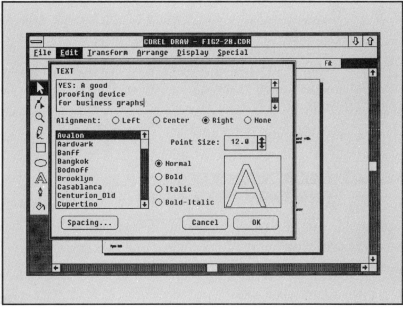

*Figure 2.29:* The Text dialog box with the label typed in.

the offending text with the pick tool and then use the Edit Text item of the Edit menu—or use the Ctrl-T keyboard shortcut—to return to the Text dialog box for another shot at it.

You can now position the text roughly where you think it should go in relation to the pie chart segment it describes. Simply select it with the pick tool and drag it like any other object. You might have to fine tune its location later on.

Add the rest of the text to the drawing in the same way, changing the alignment when you switch from one side of the chart to the other.

Now add the title of the chart: ''The results of the vote on whether to get a color PostScript printer for the art department.'' This is the same font in 24 points rather than in 12. The title text is left-aligned.

Just like the simpler objects we've seen thus far, text under Corel Draw has outline and fill attributes. These may not have defaulted to the most sensible values for the text you've just placed in your drawing. Rather than cranking up the preview and zooming in to check things out, you can just select all the text and set the outline and fill attributes of the whole lot at once.

To select all the text blocks at one time, click on the first one as you would normally do to select it. Having done this, hold down the Shift key while you proceed to click on all the others. As long as Shift is down you can add objects to the selected group. This will not actually group the objects together as the Group feature under the Arrange menu would; it will only select them long enough for you to change them all.

Use the outline tool's flyout menu to select a hairline rule for text and then the fill tool's flyout menu to select black fill.

## *DRAWING CONNECTING LINES FOR THE LABELS*

The last step in completing the pie chart is adding the heavy lines which run from the text to the segments. Except for the straight line associated with the ''Yes: A powerful presentation tool'' segment, each of these is made up of two line segments handled by Corel Draw as a single object.

Let's start with the line for the segment which represents the senior management with stock options. It will probably help if you zoom in on this area. To refresh your memory on how to draw this kind of object, the steps are listed here.

1.  Select the pencil tool.

2.  Place your mouse cursor to the left of the text.

3.  Hold down the Ctrl key throughout the rest of these steps to constrain the line.

4.  Click to anchor the line.

5.  Move the cursor left for about half the distance between the text and the pie chart segment.

6.  Click to anchor the end of the line.

7.  Click again in the same spot to start the second line. This will add it to the object formed by the first line, rather than starting a new object.

8.  Move the cursor further left and down. Because the Ctrl key is down—the constrain feature is active—the line will jump down by 15 degrees.

9. When you have the line where you want it, click to anchor its free end.

Having drawn the line you can set the line width and a few other attributes to make it look like the lines back in Figure 2.21. Use the pick tool to select the two-line object you've just created if it's not presently selected. Click on the outline tool and select the fattest line width, the one at the far right of the flyout menu. Then click on the outline tool again and click on the leftmost icon to pop up the precise-alignment box. Set the Line Caps and Corners as shown in Figure 2.30.

You might want to experiment with this dialog box to see what other sorts of lines you can come up with.

You can add the connecting lines to the rest of the segments in the same way. When you're finished, make sure you save your work.

If you print your pie chart it should look something like the one back in Figure 2.21.

The pie chart you've just created is a very versatile drawing. It can be exported as any one of a number of sorts of files, to pour into

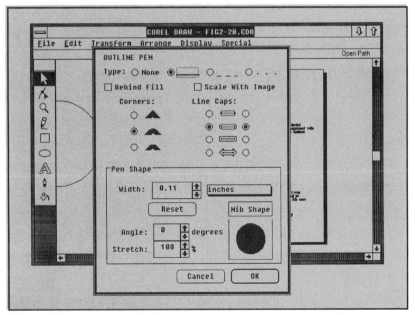

*Figure 2.30:* Setting up the line characteristics for a connecting line.

desktop published documents under Ventura Publisher or Page-Maker or into some of the higher-end word processors like Microsoft Word or WordPerfect. Assuming that your side of the argument lost in the discussion about getting a color PostScript printer, you could still change the fill patterns to colors and have the resulting file output by a graphics house that does have a color printer. There are companies which will take your Corel Draw files and make presentation quality slides from them. You can even have Corel Draw generate color separations for use with web or offset printing, which is how the color plates in this book were created.

If you consider how long it took you to draw this chart—and how much less it will take next time, now that you know what you're doing—you'll probably see why Corel Draw is such a powerful tool to have around.

## ▬▬ *DRAWING WITH CURVES AND MIRRORS: THE ART OF THE LUTE* ▬▬

The lute was a medieval instrument which was a precursor to the modern guitar—in much the same way that the Rolls Royce Silver Phantom IV was a precursor to the modern Honda Civic. Lutes were characterized by large, bowl-shaped bodies and short necks having a large number of doubled strings. The exact string count varied from lute to lute.

An aerial view of a typical lute can be seen in Figure 2.31. Actually, this is Corel Draw's interpretation of a lute. Two very important bits of lute lore are missing from this illustration. The first is any vestige of strings, which have been omitted for the sake of clarity. The other is the "rose." The sound hole of a lute is not simply an opening in the top, as is the case with a guitar. It is traditionally inlaid with a complex carved wooden disk, or rose. The rose has been omitted from this drawing because a lute rose is a very involved object, and quite the chore to draw. We will return to the topic of lute roses later in this book.

The drawing in Figure 2.31 is of a contemporary lute, from a design by Robert S. Cooper of Savannah, Georgia.

Inasmuch as the title of this book makes little mention of the construction or history of lutes, you might well ask what this one is doing here. In fact, lutes are representative of a large body of objects which

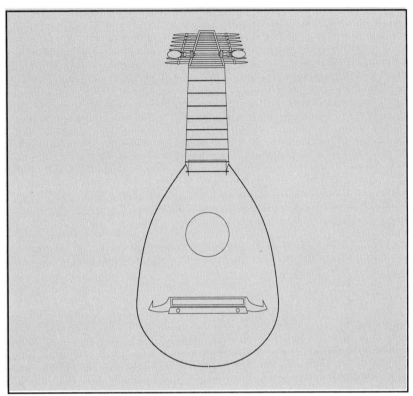

*Figure 2.31:* A lute as seen by Corel Draw.

get drawn using packages like Corel Draw. The important aspect of the lute from the point of view of this book is not so much its history as its symmetry: one half of a lute looks very much like the other half of a lute. For purposes of simplicity, we will ignore the fact that the tuning pegs on a real lute are not in fact arranged symmetrically. Figure 2.32 illustrates what you'll actually be drawing. When it's complete, you'll be able to create the whole lute by simply duplicating this collection of objects, mirroring it vertically and dragging the duplicate so it lines up with the original.

Corel Draw offers all sorts of ways to deal with complex, symmetrical drawings like this one. Whether you're designing a logo, a carburetor, or a better lute, being able to work with symmetrical drawings will save you at least half the time it would have taken to draw everything from scratch.

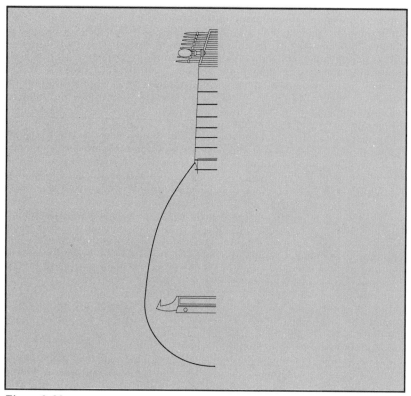

*Figure 2.32:* Half a lute.

Save your work periodically as you go through this drawing. There are a number of areas in which it's fairly easy to trash what you've done beyond easy repair. It's a great deal easier to simply revert to your most recently saved version when this happens than it is to try to pick through a tangle of paths and objects.

If your work space is still in landscape mode from the last drawing, return it to portrait mode with the Page Setup item of the File menu.

## DRAWING THE LUTE BODY

In drawing the lute, make sure the Snap To Grid feature, as found in the the Display menu, is off. There's too much tiny detail in this drawing to make the grid feature much use.

The first object to place in the drawing of the lute will ultimately not be there when the drawing is finally printed. Using the constrain function to assist you, draw a vertical line down the middle of the work space. This will serve as a guide and lets you know where your axis of symmetry lies. You might want to zoom out as far as possible in order to draw a really long line.

The outline of the lute body is created with two curves. The upper one is a straight path which has been converted to curves and bent using curve handles. The lower curve is a portion of an ellipse. You may recall using both of these capabilities earlier in this chapter. You will apply these techniques a bit differently in this instance.

There is a certain amount of freehand manipulation inherent in drawing a lute, and your drawing may not come out looking exactly like the one in Figure 2.31. This is quite acceptable—the relative shapes and dimensions of lutes varied a lot. No matter what your lute winds up looking like, chances are there used to be one just like it.

Start by drawing the lower part of the body. Select the ellipse tool and draw a large ellipse which is wider than it is high. You will not want to have the constrain feature active for this object—in other words, leave the Ctrl key alone—as you'll want an ellipse rather than a true circle. Select and drag the ellipse with the pick tool so it lies across the axis line of the drawing. When you mirror the lute half, the ''tails'' of the ellipses that extend across the center guide line can be moved to smooth out the curve.

Unless you plan to output this drawing on a pen plotter, slight overlaps in horizontal lines where the two halves of the lute join will not show on the final drawing. On the other hand, a gap between the two halves most certainly will be visible. Therefore, it's better to have the lines which touch the center line of the drawing a bit too long rather than a bit too short.

Using the shape tool, grab the node of the ellipse and turn the ellipse into an arc which runs from about six o'clock until a bit beyond nine o'clock. You may have to adjust the upper end of the arc a bit later on.

Make sure you keep the shape tool's cursor slightly outside the perimeter of the ellipse so you wind up simply with an arc rather than a wedge. When you're finished, zoom in on the lower end of the arc temporarily to make sure that it lies over the center line.

The upper part of the body involves bending curves, which is still more inexact but kind of pleasing to do. Select the pencil tool and draw a line from the upper end of the arc you've just created up to where you want the neck of the lute to start. This will be an approximation, of course. Use the shape tool to select the upper node of the line you've just drawn. The line should thicken to indicate that it has been selected. Click on the node again to pop up the node menu. Select toCurv. Handles should sprout from the ends of the line.

Grab the handles and manipulate the curve until it flows smoothly into the arc of the ellipse. When you think you have it about right, zoom in on the joint between the upper and lower curves. If the two lines don't quite meet, use the shape tool cursor to pull the end of the upper line to meet the top of the lower one. You might also have to adjust the end of the lower arc a bit.

Your work space should now look like the one in Figure 2.33.

If getting these curves to come out the way you want them seems a bit frustrating, bear in mind that it takes a week and a half to lay up the body of a real lute. You're getting off relatively easily.

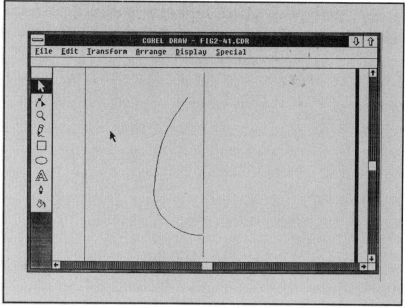

*Figure 2.33:* Drawing the body of the lute.

## DRAWING THE BRIDGE

The bridge of the lute is a fairly involved detail. You might want to zoom in a bit. The various elements can be seen in Figure 2.34.

The center part of the bridge—the functional bit which holds the strings—is made up of lines drawn with the pencil tool. Because you're actually going to draw only half the lute, the center of the bridge must be left open. That is why you can't use the rectangle tool for this task. Use the constrain feature to make sure your lines come out straight.

Draw the dowel in the lower part of the bridge with the circle tool (the ellipse tool constrained).

The horn that sticks out to the left of the bridge is somewhat ornamental. Draw it by approximating it with straight lines and then converting some of the lines to curves.

You could draw the circle for the sound hole of the lute at this time, but it would be very hard to position it accurately. Because it would overlap the center line of the drawing, there would be two of them when the first half of the lute was duplicated and flipped. It's a lot easier to add the circle when the two halves have been assembled.

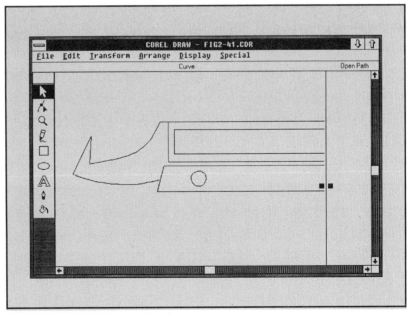

*Figure 2.34:* The bridge of the lute.

## *DRAWING THE NECK*
## *AND MEASURING FRET DISTANCES*

The neck of the lute is fairly easy to draw. The hook where it meets the body is formed by drawing straight lines with the pencil tool and then converting the appropriate one to a curve with the shape tool. Once again, it's important to zoom in on the place where the horizontal line meets the center line of the drawing and make sure that it just overlaps the center line.

The frets of a lute consisted of strings made of animal gut tied around the neck at suitable intervals. To create a fret, draw a line anywhere across the neck with the pencil tool, using the constrain feature. Next, set the vertical duplicate displacement values in the preference box to result in duplicates being placed very slightly below the original. Something on the order of $-0.050$ to $-0.100$ centimeters is about right. Select the line and duplicate it.

The rounded end of the fret is drawn by using the ellipse tool. Zoom in and use the shape tool to make the ellipse into an arc running from six o'clock to twelve o'clock. Then select and grab it with the pick tool, and drag it to the edge of the fret, as shown in Figure 2.35.

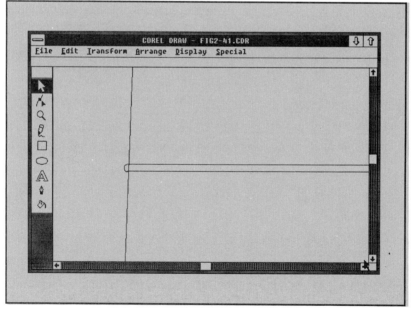

*Figure 2.35:* Fretting the lute.

The positioning of the frets on the neck of a lute can be handled in one of two ways. You can just stick them down where they look about right, inasmuch as this is only a drawing and not a real lute. Alternately, you can place them where a proper lutanist would have placed them using the "rule of eighteen," to be discussed momentarily. The rule of eighteen actually turned out to be the rule of 17.835 when pocket calculators came along, but eighteen will be accurate enough for this drawing.

If you bought this book with more interest in learning Corel Draw than in building a lute of your own—I understand that people like this do exist—you might well wonder about the rationale behind this digression into fret theory. In fact, it points up a very important problem under Corel Draw and the solution thereof.

If you attempt to locate the frets using the rule of eighteen you will discover that short of hunting for the plastic ruler that comes with the package and holding it up to your monitor, Corel Draw offers you no obvious way to measure the distance between two objects in a drawing. Knowing how to position the frets would thus seem to be of very little use.

In fact, there is a fairly convenient way to measure distance under Corel Draw—it's just not explained anywhere. If you select the pencil tool and draw a line with it, the length of the line will be displayed up on the status line above the work space. In order to measure the distance between two objects, simply draw a line between them and see how long the line is. When you no longer need the line, hit the Delete key to blow it away.

In the case of working out the fret positions, make sure to use the constrain feature and draw a vertical measurement line, as any other line will be slightly longer than a vertical one covering the same distance.

Figure 2.36 shows the status line illustrating the distance measurement. Note that this will not be visible if you have disabled the status line using the Show Status Line item of the display menu. If you can't see the measurement values, select this item to toggle the display back on.

To place the first fret on the neck of the lute, measure the distance between the end of the neck and the top of the bridge. Divide this value by eighteen. (Unfortunately, Corel Draw does not provide its own calculator.) The resulting value is the distance between the top

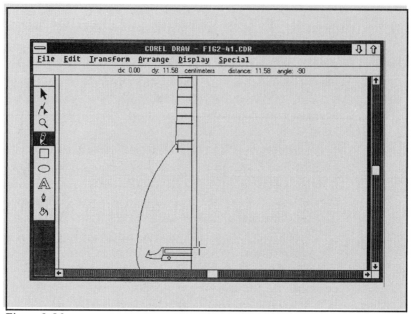

*Figure 2.36:* Measuring distance with the pencil tool.

of the neck and the first fret. Select the fret you have drawn and move it to the desired location.

To locate the next fret divide the distance between the previous fret and the top of the bridge by eighteen. The resulting value will be the distance between that fret and the next fret. Duplicate the first fret line and move it into place. Repeat this process until you run out of neck. Note that the line just below the point where the neck joins the body is also a fret. It was usually made of hardwood or bone glued to the top of the lute.

## DRAWING THE TUNING PEGS

The peghead is the most involved detail of the lute. By now you will appreciate that it will be nowhere near as hard as it looks, because most of the details are simply objects (tuning pegs) which have been duplicated several times.

For largely aesthetic reasons, the peghead tapers. Over the course of the history of the lute, the number of strings grew, and it eventually became impractical to contain all the tuning pegs within the peghead. The ones at the far end of the box would have had to be so short as to be unusable. For this reason, toward the latter part of its evolution, the lute began to sprout secondary flying pegs, such as the ones shown in our example. Each extra peg rests in a scroll which sits above the peghead.

You will be drawing the basic peghead peg shown in Figure 2.37 using the pencil tool for the shaft and the handle, and separate lines for the continuation of each shaft through the peghead. The lines of the handle are converted to curves with the shape tool and bent slightly. You will be drawing the knob-like object in the middle with the rectangle tool. You may have noticed that the middle bit appears to be not a rectangle so much as a lozenge. In fact, it's a rectangle with its corners rounded.

If you draw a rectangle and then grab one of its corners with the shape tool, you'll find that all the corners begin to get round. The further you drag the corner toward the center of the rectangle, the greater the rounding will become. If you drag it far enough, you can turn the rectangle into a circle or a lozenge, depending on its original proportions.

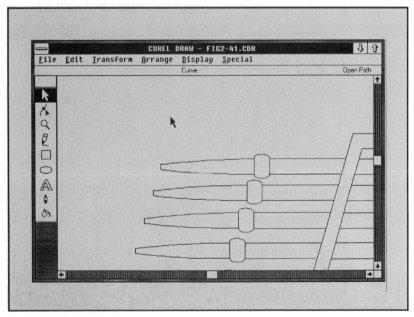

*Figure 2.37:* Peghead pegs up close.

Once you have drawn one peg, group all its elements together into a single object and duplicate it down the length of the peghead. There is no fixed number of strings on a lute, so you can simply add enough pegs to make the peghead look full.

The flying peg shown in Figure 2.38 is not much more difficult to draw. The handle is an ellipse. The rounded lines joining it to the shaft are straight lines drawn with the pencil tool and bent into shape with the shape tool. In order to make them both look the same, it's best to draw one, bend it to fit, and then duplicate and mirror it to form the other line. The capstan—the thing the string winds on at the right end of the peg—is just a rectangle with rounded corners and two lines drawn through it. There's a half circle stuck on the end of it to represent the end of the peg.

When you've finished drawing this peg, group all its elements into a single object and drag it into position on the peghead.

On a real lute, the flying peg is placed above the other pegs. To simulate this on your drawing you can just select the flying peg object and give it a white fill. This will have the effect of obscuring the lines

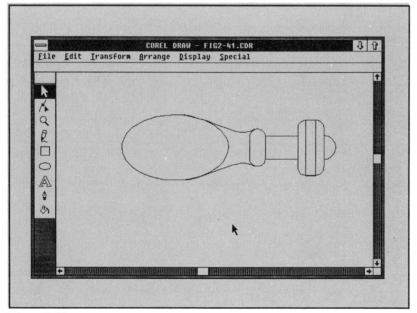

*Figure 2.38:* A flying peg.

below it. This might be thought of as the most primitive form of hidden line removal. CAD packages such as AutoCAD can take nine hours to remove hidden lines from a complex drawing, although admittedly the process is a lot more involved.

## *FINISHING THE LUTE*

At this point you should have half a lute in your work space. The rest of the drawing is so easy as to be almost effortless. Select all the objects in the left half of the lute—you can use the Select All item of the Edit menu for this, since there's nothing else in your drawing—and group them together.

When you want to mirror an object, that is, create a copy of it which is flipped along one axis, you could simply use the Stretch & Mirror box from the Transform menu and select Horz or Vert Mirror. However, your real objective here is not simply to mirror what you have drawn, but to align your mirror image with your original drawing. This entails making a mirror-image copy while leaving an original, unflipped image with which to join.

You can handle the process in more than one way. One is to duplicate the object in question using Ctrl-D and then use the Horz Mirror in the Stretch & Mirror box to flip the duplicate. Another is to go straight to the Stretch & Mirror box and click on the Leave Original option before selecting Horz Mirror. The results are no different from what you'd have arrived at had you duplicated the left half of the lute explicitly and then flipped it.

This option will crop up again in other contexts. It's often important in creating multiple copies of an object with progressive changes in position or other characteristics.

Align the two halves of the lute by zooming in on a fairly detailed area of the joint—the bridge or the peghead will do—and grab the right half. Drag it toward the left half until the center lines overlap and the horizontal lines meet.

Next, zoom out until you can see the entire drawing. Select and ungroup both halves. Select the center vertical line of each half and remove it by hitting the Delete key. Remember that since you duplicated the lute half you also duplicated the center lines—there are two of them to dispose of.

You might want to zoom in again to make sure that there are no gaps in any of the horizontal lines between the two halves of the lute. If there are, use the shape tool to stretch the lines a bit.

Draw yourself a circle in the middle of the body, using the ellipse tool with the constrain feature. Your work space should now contain one basically complete lute.

No mention has been made thus far about the line thickness attributes of the objects which make up the lute. Corel Draw will probably have defaulted to using 1-point lines, which are a bit thick for this sort of picture. Hairlines would look better, especially if you'll be outputting the lute on a 300-dot-per-inch laser printer. You can quickly give all the lines in the drawing a hairline attribute.

Select all the objects of the lute with the Select All item of the Edit menu. Select the outline tool and click on HAIR.

In my version of the lute I gave the outline of the body a slightly thicker line. You might want to do this as well, although it's not really essential.

## *PRINTING THE LUTE*

If you've drawn your lute according to the preceding guidelines, chances are it's a bit too big to be printed. This happens a lot under Corel Draw. You could group all the objects and scale the drawing so it would fit within the printable area of the Corel Draw work space. However, there's an easier way. You can make the printer driver of Corel Draw handle the scaling for you while it's printing, so that your drawing need not be modified.

Select the Print item of the file menu. The printing dialog box will appear, as in Figure 2.39.

The upper right corner of the printing dialog box contains two items which deal with scaling a large drawing to fit a small sheet of paper. The first one lets you specify the amount by which you want to scale the drawing down. You could also scale it up using this feature if you had a reason to. The second item allows you to have Corel Draw scale your drawing to fit the available paper. Actually, this feature is a bit erratic on many PostScript printers. PostScript tends to deal with objects at the edge of its printing area somewhat unpredictably. If you use this option you might find that parts of your drawing do not

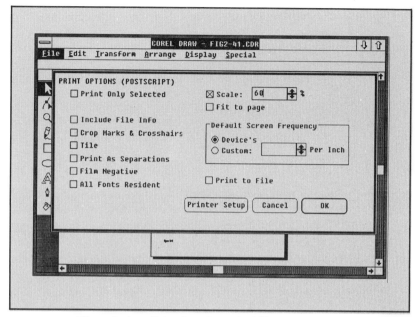

*Figure 2.39:* The printing dialog box from the File menu.

print. When you've selected one of these options click on OK to begin printing.

## WRAPPING UP

This chapter should have given you a pretty good handle on the basic line-drawing facilities of Corel Draw. If you've succeeded in getting the example drawings to work out you should not encounter difficulties with any line-based objects, no matter how complex they get.

There is more to be said about drawing lines under Corel Draw, especially about some of the more involved node and path manipulations. Seeing as it is the basis for just about everything that Corel Draw can produce, we'll be coming up against line drawing throughout this book.

# chapter

# 3

## Manipulating
## Type and Text

IT WOULD PROBABLY BE PRESUMPTUOUS TO SUGGEST that its type facilities are Corel Draw's best feature. However, if you work with text you'll probably be staggered by what it can do with type—as well as by all the type it offers you. Users of desktop publishing software will unquestionably find Corel Draw to be useful in this respect. You can pop into Corel Draw and generate headlines in almost 40 typefaces—plus a few symbol faces—and save them into files suitable for importing into desktop publishing documents.

Aside from just setting type, Corel Draw allows you to manipulate the characters of your text just as you would any other drawing objects. Unless your requirements call for you to thoroughly mangle the objects which make up your text, you can have Corel Draw deal with them in both ways: as text when it's convenient to do so, and as objects the rest of the time.

Text effects are among the most attractive of object-oriented art. People are used to seeing type as being fairly plain. It's easy to catch one's eye with type that is otherwise. Figure 3.1 illustrates a tiny fraction of the effects Corel Draw is capable of producing. As with all its other facilities, the full scope of what it can do with text is limited only by your imagination.

## _UNDERSTANDING TYPE AND TYPOGRAPHY_

Before you can begin to work with type intelligently, it's important to understand some of the art—and a bit of the tradition—which lurks behind it. Type is very much an art form, if a rather esoteric one. Before the advent of laser printers and the gradual flow of typographic terms and ideas into microcomputer software, type lore was almost exclusively the province of typesetters.

The simplest form of type is the text generated by a typewriter. Typewriter text is very primitive by type standards. It is _monospaced,_ for one thing. All the characters on a line occupy the same amount of

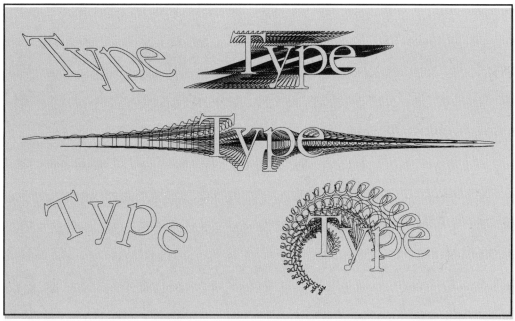

*Figure 3.1:* Some example text effects.

space, even though some, such as the letter M, are a great deal fatter than others, such as the letter i. Typewriter text is also incapable of changing size, expressing emphasis with italics or boldface, and displaying most of the other niceties we expect to see in typeset text.

Typeset text is generally *proportionally spaced*; that is, each character on a line occupies only as much space as it needs. This makes the text look more attractive, generally makes it easier to read unless you choose a particularly ornate font, and allows a great deal more text to fit on a page. To be sure, monospaced fonts do exist for typesetters, but these tend to be used as special effects or in those rare cases where you want to imitate monospacing, as in typesetting computer program listings.

The earliest typesetting was, of course, done by hand. Late in the nineteenth century several manufacturers began to create mechanical typesetting machines, of which the Linotype is probably the best known. These machines set type by forming each character from molten lead and assembling the lead slugs into trays of type, or *galleys*. Metal type after it has been used and stored somewhere is referred to as *cold type*.

Metal type was used until quite recently in some circles, and a few Linotype typesetting machines are probably still functioning somewhere. The Linotype company now makes laser typesetters—including several very high resolution PostScript typesetters suitable for outputting Corel Draw files to. You can usually see one of their old hot metal machines at printers' trade shows.

Many of the things which make up modern typography are derived from the traditions of hand-set text and hot metal type. For example, the *serifs,* the little points on the corners of the characters of many typefaces—including the one you're reading at the moment—were originally put there back in the days of hand-set type to keep the corners of the characters from wearing down and getting rounded too quickly.

Many of the typefaces we now use with laser printers and programs like Corel Draw date back to the heyday of hot metal type. Times Roman and Helvetica, perhaps the most widely used typefaces, were both born around the turn of the century. In dealing with typesetters, printers, and other parties well versed in type lore, certain typefaces are well known. For example, something set in Helvetica will be the same no matter where you get the work done.

The commonly used typefaces are commonly used because back at the beginning of this century the type *foundries,* the companies who employed type designers and produced the dies—and often the machines—for hot metal typesetting, were very aggressive about selling their typefaces. In its own circles, marketing type remains as much of a battle as marketing colas or political candidates.

## TYPOGRAPHIC TERMS

The fundamental unit of type measurement is the *point.* There are 72 of them in an inch. Type which is one inch high would be referred to as 72-point type. One typically measures the capital letter E in the normal style for that typeface in order to determine the point size for the entire set of fonts and weights available with that typeface.

Space on a line of text is measured in *picas.* A pica is 12 points long, and there are 6 picas to the inch. Under Corel Draw, as we've seen, you're free to measure things in any units you like, so you need not deal with picas and points if you don't want to, except in specifying type size.

When you do use picas and points, you will find that they're expressed as the number of picas followed by the number of points with a comma between them. If you specify a number higher than 12 in the points part of this value, Corel Draw will automatically convert it to the correct number of *picas* and points. Thus, entering 6,13 is incorrect, but Corel Draw corrects it to 7,1. Corel Draw comes with a plastic ruler which, among other things, features a pica scale for measuring things and a type gauge for determining how big printed type is.

### Leading

The origin of the term for space between lines of type, *leading,* is another bit of obscurae from the days of hot metal. Originally the space was formed by placing strips of lead between the rows of characters. Leading is expressed in points. Most text is set with one or two points of leading beyond the size of the text. Nine-point type would normally be set with ten-point leading, or ''set nine on ten'' in typesetters' terms. Text which is set nine on nine would run the risk of having the *descenders* of one line occasionally touching the *ascenders* of the next.

Traditional capital letters do not have descenders, so it's quite forgivable to set text which is all in capitals with less leading than you could get away with in lowercase type.

Figure 3.2 illustrates the effect of leading using Corel Draw's interline spacing control.

### Ems and Ens

On a typewriter, the space bar produces a character which is of a fixed and predictable width. So does the dash key. Neither of these is true in setting type. As with most typeset material, this book is set in what is called *justified* text, that is, with the right as well as the left margins of the columns of text even. The typesetting system which produced this book managed this by padding out short lines with additional space between the words. Corel Draw will not automatically justify text, but it gives you tools to do it yourself.

There are calls for specific sizes of fixed spaces and fixed dashes. These are measured using still more arcane typesetting terminology. A very fat dash—such as the one you just encountered—is defined as being the width of the letter M in whatever typeface you're using at

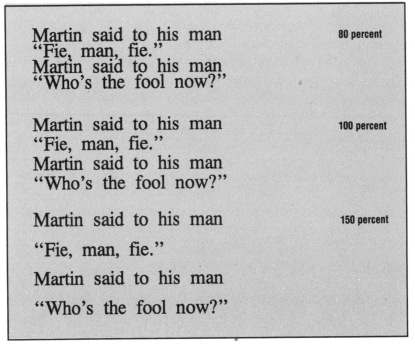

*Figure 3.2:* Different leading.

the moment. This space is called one *em,* so the dashes you just saw were *em dashes.* There are also slightly smaller dashes called *en* dashes—originally the width of the letter N, now typically one half the width of the em dash.

We'll discuss how to produce these characters under Corel Draw a little later on.

### Kerning

It is quite common in using proportionally spaced type to find letters which appear to have too much space between them—not because the typeface has been badly designed, but simply because the letters themselves seem as if they should fit together more neatly. For example, the letters A and W often look this way if they're set together.

In some cases, these two letters would automatically be moved close together to overcome this effect. This is called *kerning,* and if these two letters required kerning to make them look right in a particular font, they'd be referred to as a *kerning pair*. Desktop publishing packages such as Ventura Publisher can automatically kern text based on kerning pairs.

Figure 3.3 illustrates the effects of kerning.

Corel Draw does not kern text automatically but it does allow you to kern letters manually when necessary.

## *TYPES OF TYPE*

Typefaces can be broadly classified in a number of ways. The first—and perhaps the most important under Corel Draw—is the distinction between *display* and *body* faces.

Display faces are designed to be used in large point sizes, primarily as headlines. Body faces are designed for use in body text, such as that which you are reading now. Few faces are suited for both. Display faces are usually either too ''pudgy'' or too ornate to be easily readable when they're reduced to 9 or 10 points and used to set body copy. Body faces look spindly and anorexic if they're expanded out to 72 points and used to set headlines.

There are exceptions to this. One frequently finds Helvetica used in both cases, although heavy versions of Helvetica exist which are more suited for use as display faces.

The typefaces which come with Corel Draw are, for the most part, ones which have been designed and fine-tuned for use as display faces. Corel Draw is not intended for use in setting body copy.

Typefaces are also often described as being either *serif* or *sans serif*. Serifs are the pointy bits at the corners of the characters of typefaces

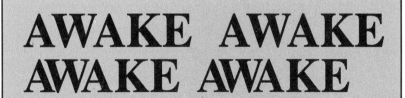

*Figure 3.3:* Kerning some text.

such as Times Roman. Helvetica is a typical sans serif face; that is, it has no serifs. For largely traditional reasons most people have gotten used to seeing serif faces as body copy.

Type is usually specified in a specific *weight,* that is, how bold it is. The weight of type is a somewhat subjective quantity, and much of what defines particular type as being bold or extrabold dates back into the prehistory of typesetting.

Normal type—such as the text you're reading—is called medium weight, and darker text is called bold. These are the weights which Corel Draw supports.

Type weights at the extremes of these—light, and extrabold, ultra-bold, or heavy—really require slightly different versions of the type-faces in question. This is how Corel Draw treats them. For example, Helvetica is available in Helvetica and Helvetica Black, the latter being the extrabold version.

Not all typefaces are available in all weights under Corel Draw.

### *Typeface Names*

Although the terms "typeface" and "font" often appear to be used interchangeably, *typeface* is used most often when referring to uniquely named type style, such as New Baskerville, which will appear to be the same style even when you are comparing different versions of it, such as italic or boldface. The term *font* is used to refer to the basic styles generally available within a named typeface—for example, most text typefaces come with an italic font. Font is also used somewhat inclusively to identify any complete collection of a certain style of type; thus you will often see "font" where "typeface" would be equally correct.

It's in dealing with specific typefaces by name that things really start getting confusing. You almost need a program and a score card some of the time.

The name Helvetica, when it's applied to type, is a copyrighted trademark of the International Type Corporation, or ITC. ITC was recently purchased by Letraset, the press-on letters company—you can decide who really owns the name now.

Anyone can produce a typeface which looks pretty much like Helvetica, and similar faces abound. One could not, however, call it Helvetica without the permission of ITC.

For this reason, desktop publishing software which comes with a typeface compatible with Helvetica usually calls it something else, frequently ''Swiss'' or, as in the case of Corel Draw, ''Switzerland.'' The origin of this pseudonym is a bit obtuse—the Helvetii were an ancient celtic race which inhabited part of Switzerland about two thousand years ago.

Prior to the advent of laser printers, typesetting companies which sought to compete with ITC faced a similar problem and came up with similar results. Thus, you might encounter Compugraphic typefaces called Helios and English Times which look pretty much like ITC Helvetica and Times Roman. Both are available for use with microcomputers and laser printers.

When Adobe, the creator of the PostScript laser printer language, set out to design its software, it negotiated a license with ITC rather than attempting to knock off copies of ITC typefaces. As a result, they were able to use the ITC names in their language. If you use Ventura Publisher, for example, you may have noticed that Helvetica is specified as Helvetica if you're printing to a PostScript printer and as Swiss if you're not.

In dealing with body text, the distinction between ''real'' faces and copies of those faces becomes fairly important. For example, the minute differences in character widths between real Helvetica and a knockoff called Swiss will frequently cause one to occupy a significantly different amount of space than the other over three or four pages of text. Because Corel Draw is not intended to set text in amounts that great, this is not usually a concern under Corel Draw.

When Adobe created PostScript with its authentic ITC fonts, it allowed for other, non-ITC fonts to be used as well, but it encrypted the real ITC fonts it sold to prevent other companies from using them in their own products. They also crippled PostScript to prevent someone from writing a PostScript program which would unravel their font protection. This has also served to cripple several PostScript-related applications from Adobe, such as Adobe Illustrator. One of the reasons Corel Draw is able to do a lot of things Illustrator cannot is that Corel Draw uses its own fonts.

For legal reasons, Corel Draw is not able to ship its software with the real names for its typefaces, even though many of them correspond exactly to real commercial fonts. However, the font names are stored in an easily accessible place—the Windows WIN.INI file—and can easily be changed by users of Corel Draw. If you have not already done so, consult Appendix B of this book to see how this is done.

I strongly recommend that you make this simple change to Corel Draw. If you're going to learn about type you might as well learn the generally accepted names for typefaces. The lack of standardization among laser printer typefaces has frequently led to confusion in terms of the same or similar names being applied to different typefaces. For example, Corel Draw calls its version of Times Roman ''Toronto.'' This name is also used in other circumstances for a typeface which is called Stymie by Compugraphic, and Rockwell by ITC and Adobe.

Figure 3.4 illustrates the text typefaces which come with Corel Draw. I've used the generally accepted names of those faces where they're applicable, with the names as they're shipped with Corel Draw in small print beside them. This list excludes the several symbol faces which also come with Corel Draw.

Bear in mind that while it may well be in violation of copyright for Corel Draw to be shipped with the ITC names, you're free to call the fonts that you've paid for in buying your copy of the package anything you like.

You can add faces to this list to suit your own requirements. The Corel Draw font-conversion program WFNBOSS is able to import entire fonts from other sources, and it can even read Adobe's encrypted font files, should you wish to add more Adobe fonts to Corel Draw. WFNBOSS will be discussed in Appendix B.

### Symbols and Dingbats

In addition to the text fonts supplied with Corel Draw, there are several fonts consisting entirely of symbols or ornaments. These fonts are extremely useful, especially for creating unusual graphics in a hurry. The fonts include Greek/Math Symbols, equivalent to the Symbols font in other applications, a music notation font which is similar to the PostScript Sonata font, and Dixieland, which is equivalent to the widely used Zapf Dingbat font.

Dingbats are usually entered as numerical codes. The procedure for this will be described later in this chapter.

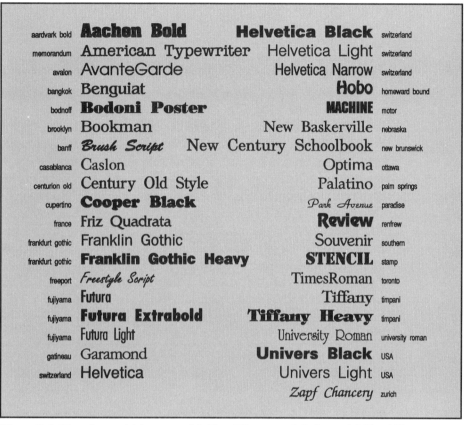

*Figure 3.4:* Typefaces which come with Corel Draw, and their special Corel Draw names (small print).

### Type as Objects

Under Corel Draw, text characters are drawn on the screen just like other objects are. However, text is stored in Corel Draw's object list differently than, say, the object which defines a rectangle. Corel Draw's note to itself for a line of text defines its location on the screen; transformations which have been applied to it; the font; the point size and other typographic qualities of the text; and, most important, the text itself.

Corel Draw always attempts to hold onto the original text as you entered it. It's only forced to abandon the text and deal with the resulting drawing strictly as paths when you explicitly convert the text to objects. Each letter is defined as a collection of paths which traces the outline of the character such that if the paths are placed on a Corel Draw page and filled, the result will be text. Text of this sort can be scaled and stretched any way you like without any loss in the quality of the type.

The fonts in a PostScript printer are also object-oriented in this way, and offer similar opportunities for scaling. However, Corel Draw does not always use the fonts in a PostScript printer—for reasons we've discussed: it cannot control them to the same degree that it can its own fonts. If you attempt to print basic text to a PostScript printer from Corel Draw using the Helvetica typeface, for example, the internal Helvetica font in the printer will be used. If you've manipulated the text, however, chances are Corel Draw will use its own Switzerland outline font. When it prints to a PostScript output device with its own fonts, it simply sends down the paths of its drawings, some of which might define text.

Appendix B discusses how to tell Corel Draw which fonts your PostScript printer actually has.

In thinking up new things to do with type under Corel Draw you should always keep in mind that it can be treated in this way.

## *UNDERSTANDING THE TEXT DIALOG BOX*

The basis of the Corel Draw text mode is the Text dialog box. This can also be thought of as the text-editing or even the text-entry dialog box since Corel Draw regards entering text for the first time as essentially editing an empty text string.

The Text dialog box pops up when you select the text tool—the big A on the left side of the Corel Draw window—and then click anywhere in the work space. Figure 3.5 illustrates the dialog with all its features. You have encountered it briefly in the previous chapter.

Text created by means of the Text dialog will be drawn starting with where your cursor was when you clicked your mouse button. If the Snap To Grid feature was on when you called for the dialog, the text will begin at the nearest grid point. However, because it's an object, you will be able to move the text with the pick tool if it doesn't wind up exactly where you want it.

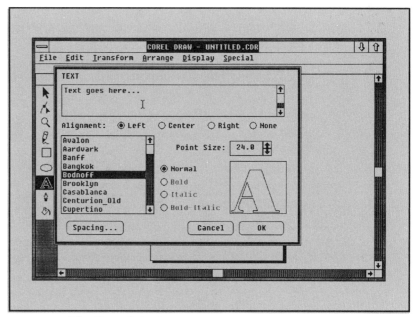

*Figure 3.5:* The Text dialog box.

## *ENTERING TEXT*

Each time you click the text cursor to open the Text dialog box, Corel Draw starts up a new text string. A text string can contain up to 250 characters.

You can think of the text entry window at the top of the dialog as being a tiny word processor, although there are many areas where it doesn't behave exactly like one. For example, unlike a word processor, Corel Draw does not automatically end each line for you. You can thus type up to 250 characters on a single line. The text wrapped around the big A back in Chapter 1, for example, consisted of one long line of text. You can, however, type multiple lines by hitting Enter where you want each line to end.

The text you enter will always be displayed in the text entry window using the Microsoft Windows system screen font, which is pretty uninteresting. However, when it is drawn by Corel Draw it will be drawn in the actual font you choose.

There are a number of things you should know about entering text which may serve to make the text you include in your Corel Draw documents a bit more professional looking.

- Avoid double spaces. These wind up looking like large gaps in the text, and are rarely needed.

- Avoid using the usual double quote symbol, the one which is usually found over the single closing quote or apostrophe key on a PC keyboard. Instead, use two single opening quotes (usually found on the same key as the tilde character), and two single closing quotes. These look a lot better in most proportionally spaced fonts.

- Avoid using the minus sign as a dash, as it's usually very small. Longer dashes are provided in most Corel Draw fonts.

Each text string can be entered in a single typeface only. If you want to have text in multiple faces or in one face with multiple weights, you would have to enter all the text in a single face and then change the attributes of characters you want to be different using the shape tool. This will be discussed shortly.

If you want to enter text which takes up more than the three lines which are visible at any one time in the text entry window, just keep on typing. (But remember there is a 250 character maximum.) Your previously entered text will scroll up past the top of the window but it will still remain in the text string you're entering.

The small scroll bar control to the right of the text entry window will allow you to scroll through a multiple line text string if you have to edit it.

### Entering Special Characters

In addition to the keyboard characters which can be entered directly into the text entry window, most fonts support additional ''high order'' characters. These are so called because they reside in the ASCII character numbers above 128, that is, above the usual range of printable characters.

Appendix B of this book lists special symbols and corresponding numbers for Corel Draw's fonts and for fonts from several other sources. However, there is no real standard for high-order characters. If you add fonts to Corel Draw you might have to experiment a bit to find out what extra symbols you've acquired.

The Windows screen font which is used to represent text in the text window of the dialog box also has a set of high-order special characters. Unfortunately, they do not correspond to the ones included in the Corel Draw fonts in all that many cases for characters above 128. For those cases where there is no corresponding Windows character, you'll see a black box in the text entry window. The symbol, however, will be drawn in your text string when it actually appears in the Corel Draw workspace. Figure 3.6 illustrates some special characters which have been entered into the text entry window and what they

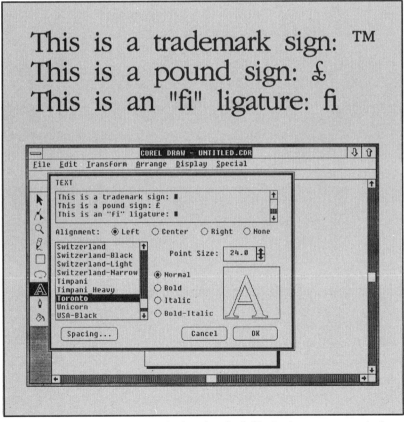

*Figure 3.6:* Special symbols and what they look like in the text entry window.

resulted in when Corel Draw actually got to place them on a page. You have to trust the software in this case—what you see isn't really what you get.

In order to type a character into a text string for which you know the numerical code, you must do the following:

1. Hold down the Alt key of your keyboard.

2. Type in the character's three- or four-digit code. (If the first digit is not zero, add a zero in front of the number.) You will need to use the number keys on the numeric keypad of your keyboard to do this. The number keys on the top row of the alphabetic part of your keyboard will not work.

3. Release the Alt key. A character—with any luck the one you were after—will appear in the text entry window.

This procedure is also used to enter Dingbats and other symbols.

### Editing Text

The editing facilities of the text entry window are actually quite sophisticated for such a tiny amount of text. You will find them useful for entering text both initially and later on should you have to recall the Text dialog box to edit your text.

Most of the text editing facilities are pretty intuitive and you should not experience any difficulties in learning how to deal with them. If you've used a word processor at all you probably already know how most of them operate.

When you type text it always appears at the current *insertion point*, which would normally be at the end of the string of text you're typing. This is indicated by the flashing bar cursor in the text entry window. However, you can move this around in a number of ways.

If you move your mouse cursor to some place in the existing text and click, the insertion point will appear between the nearest two characters. Anything you type subsequently will appear at this point, pushing the text in front of it along. You can also position the cursor using the left and right arrow keys of your keyboard. These are usually found on the numeric keypad.

In addition, the Home and End keys will position the insertion point cursor at the beginning and end of the text string respectively. The PgUp and PgDn keys will move it up and down by two lines. The Backspace key will delete the character immediately to the left of the cursor, pulling any text to the right of the cursor back by one space. The Delete key will delete the character to the right of the cursor.

If you place your mouse cursor to the left of some text and click and drag it, the text which it passes over will be selected and highlighted. If you then hold down the Shift key and hit Delete the selected text will be removed from the text window and placed in the Windows clipboard. If you hold down the Ctrl key and hit Insert the text will be copied to the clipboard but left in the text window. (If you hit the Delete key by itself the highlighted text will be removed without being placed in the clipboard.)

If you hold down the Shift key and hit Insert, text previously cut or copied to the clipboard will be pasted into the text entry window at the current insertion point as if it had been typed there. By using Cut and Paste you can move pieces of a string around within the text entry window.

The clipboard will be discussed in greater detail in the next section.

### Importing Text

In addition to typing text into the text window directly, you can also "paste" it in from the Windows clipboard. The clipboard is the repository of anything which is cut or copied from a document in any Windows application. This can be text, pictures, Corel Draw objects, and so on. The text entry window is smart enough to know if it's being fed something other than text and it will refuse to accept inappropriate clipboard contents.

If you open the Text dialog box by clicking in the Corel Draw work space with the text tool, you can paste the current contents of the Windows clipboard into the text entry window by holding down the Shift key and hitting the Insert key. If there is nothing in the clipboard, if the nature of the current clipboard contents are indigestible by the text window, or if there are more than 250 characters of text in the clipboard, the dialog box will beep and nothing will happen.

You might want to try importing some text from Windows Write into Corel Draw in this way. Write is the free word processor which comes with Microsoft Windows. Bear in mind that Windows Write and Corel Draw can be running at the same time if your Corel Draw document isn't too complex and if you have started Corel Draw from Windows, not from the command line.

Here's how it's done.

1. Select no more than 250 characters of text from a Windows Write document. Spaces count as characters and the end of each line counts as 2 characters.

2. Cut or copy this text into the Windows clipboard with the appropriate items of Write's Edit menu. You can use the Windows Clipboard application to make sure that your text is really in the clipboard.

3. Boot up Corel Draw, or click it into the foreground of your screen if it's already running.

4. Select the text tool and click in the Corel Draw work space to pop up the Text dialog box.

5. Hold down the Shift key and hit Insert.

The contents of the clipboard should appear in the text entry window as if you'd typed them there directly. Figure 3.7 illustrates the steps involved in importing text from Write into Corel Draw.

## UNDERSTANDING TEXT ATTRIBUTES

You can set the attributes—the weight, the size, and so on—of an entire string of text from within the Text dialog box. You can also change the attributes of selected characters of a string with the shape tool long after the string has been drawn in the work space.

Note that the text attributes will remain as you last used them within the same Corel Draw session. If you have several labels to add to a drawing—as was the case with the pie chart in the previous chapter—setting the various controls once will suffice for all of them.

### Alignment

Directly below the text entry window is a series of radio buttons which set the text alignment. The effects of left, center, and right alignment are shown in Figure 3.8.

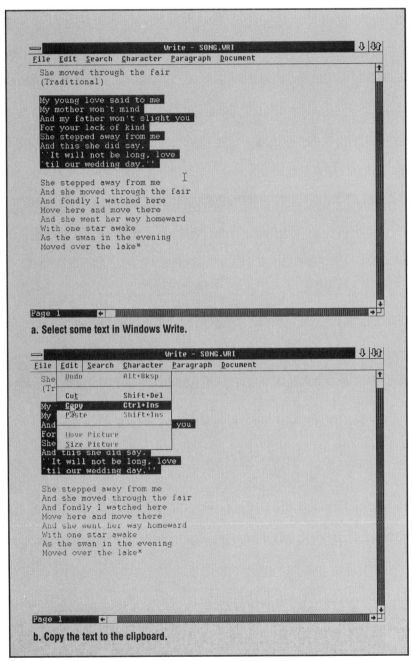

*Figure 3.7:* Importing text from Windows Write into Corel Draw.

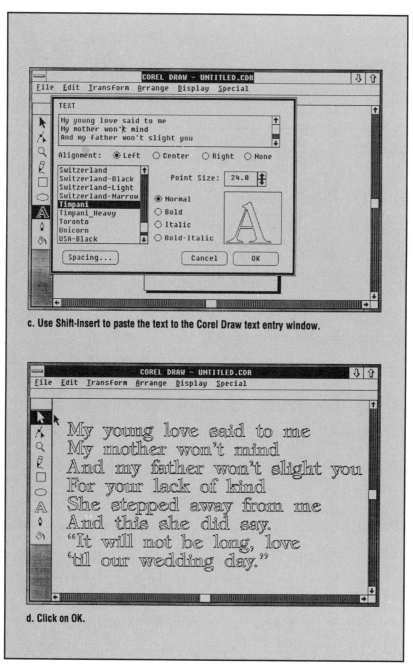

c. Use Shift-Insert to paste the text to the Corel Draw text entry window.

d. Click on OK.

*Figure 3.7:* Importing text from Windows Write into Corel Draw. (continued)

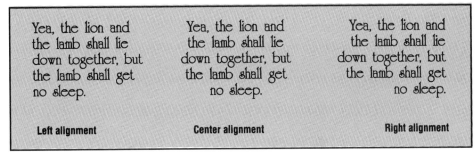

*Figure 3.8:* Text alignment.

The text will initially be drawn in the work space relative to the place where you clicked to pop up the dialog box. If you select Left alignment, all the text will be drawn to the right of where you clicked. If you select Right alignment it will be drawn to the left of where you clicked. Center alignment will cause it to be centered horizontally on the point where you clicked.

None is the alignment you would select to keep Corel Draw from imposing alignment on text that you have effectively aligned by hand by means of kerning individual characters using the shape tool. Kerning will be discussed in greater detail shortly.

### Typeface Selection

The typeface selection box will display the names of all the available faces. You can use the scroll bar to the right of the box to scroll through the list. Clicking on one of the names will select it as the current typeface for the text you have entered or are about to enter.

The sample window will show you one character of the typeface you've selected. This will be the letter A by default, but you can select any character through the Preferences item in the Special menu. These samples are approximations of what your text will look like, and often not terribly good ones. The chart in Figure 3.4 gave a better representation of what your text will look like.

Note that not all typefaces have a complete set of characters. The Motor face which comes with Corel Draw, for example, lacks lowercase letters. Unfortunately, the text window will allow you to enter letters which the typeface you've selected doesn't have, with the result that some characters may be drawn as meaningless rectangles. If this happens, go back and either select a different typeface or edit your text to remove the unavailable characters. In the case of text to be set in Motor, simply make sure the caps lock is on when you enter it.

### *Point Size*

The Point Size item in the Text dialog box works like all the other numeric controls in Corel Draw dialogs. You can click on the arrow heads to change the point size in increments of one point. You can also type in the number to specify any point size directly. Corel Draw allows you to specify point sizes from 1 to 999.9 points in increments of one tenth of a point.

Type smaller than 6-point is very nearly unreadable on a 300-dot-per-inch laser printer, and you should not hurt people's eyes in this way if you can avoid it.

You should also know that laser printer typefaces often do not print as nicely at small point sizes as they do at larger ones, because as the characters decrease in size the printer dots start to represent a significant amount of area in relation to the area represented by the character as a whole. The algorithm which fills the outline for a 6-point font is frequently confronted with the question of how to handle half dots, that is, places where a dot would be half in the character and half outside it. Because the algorithm isn't smart enough to be able to consider the aesthetics of the characters it's creating, it can be assumed to guess wrong half the time. The results are occasionally crunchy looking small characters.

One of the things which real Adobe fonts have and Corel Draw's lack is a feature called "hinting." Hinting provides the fill algorithm, which creates text from outlines, with suggestions about how to handle half dots at small point sizes. This being the case, if you must print small text, use a PostScript printer and try to print in a font which the printer has resident—such as Helvetica—so that the printer can use its hinting. Keep in mind also that small type usually looks better in sans serif faces.

Note that when Corel Draw's font-management utility program WFNBOSS converts Adobe downloadable fonts for use with Corel Draw, it throws the hinting away.

*Weight and Font*

The four radio buttons to the right of the typeface selection window select the weight and font. Not all of these will be active for all typefaces. Many of the more specialized typefaces, such as Zurich (or Zapf Chancery) come in only one font, in this case in italic.

Note that bold text will usually take up more space horizontally than normal text, all other things being equal.

*Spacing*

If you click on the button marked Spacing below the typeface selection window you'll see a new dialog box, as shown in Figure 3.9.

This dialog allows you to adjust the amount of space between the characters in your text string. There are three sorts of space.

- Interword space is the amount of space between words. Corel Draw measures this in ems.

- Intercharacter space is the amount of space between characters. Corel Draw also measures this in ems.

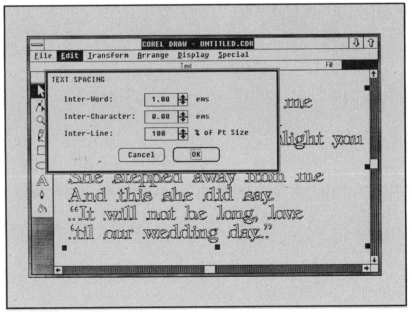

*Figure 3.9:* The Text Spacing dialog box.

- Interline space, or leading, is the space between lines of text in the same string. Corel Draw defines this as being a percentage of the point size of the type.

As will be discussed later in this chapter, you can use these controls to great effect in creating special effects with text. The simplest changes can improve the aesthetics tremendously. For example, headlines often look better with less than the usual space between their characters. Conversely, you can feather text out to completely fill an area by interactively adjusting the interword and intercharacter spacing to make it fit.

## *EDITING EXISTING TEXT*

Once you have placed text on a drawing you can edit it using the same dialog box you used to enter it. Thus you can not only change the text itself, but also any of the attributes we've just discussed.

To edit a text string, select it with the pick tool. Select Edit Text from the Edit menu or use the keyboard shortcut Ctrl-T. The Text dialog box will pop up with your selected text in the text window and all the text attributes set up as you last chose them for that string.

You cannot edit text which has been converted into curves, a procedure to be discussed later in this chapter. Such text loses its identity as text, becoming instead pure drawing objects.

Corel Draw does not permit you to select several text strings and use the text edit feature on them all at once. You must edit text strings individually.

## —— *GRAPHICS OPERATIONS ON TEXT* ——

Once Corel Draw has placed a string of text in its drawing space, you're free to manipulate it. Corel Draw allows you to transform text in much the same way that you transform other objects. The problem in creating visually interesting text effects is often more a question of what to do than how to do it.

It's quite easy to manipulate text beyond the point of recognizability under Corel Draw. While this isn't always bad—thoroughly mutated text can produce very interesting abstract graphics—you should make sure that what you produce does not *need* to be read, before you really lay on the special effects. Figure 3.10 illustrates text effects taken (perhaps) to extremes.

Attractive text effects are not merely a matter of clicking on some menu options until your text looks sufficiently strange. You really do have to understand what you're doing. In the process of exploring how to manipulate text, you'll also learn a lot about manipulating objects in general under Corel Draw.

## USING TEXT AS GRAPHICS

As with any object under Corel Draw, text has basic graphic attributes. It consists of paths which can be stroked, and, because text paths are always closed, filled as well.

You might want to boot up Corel Draw and follow along with this portion of the book to see if you can reproduce the effects which we discuss. Note that if you're printing your results as you go, you'll find that it takes longer to print the more complex examples in this chapter. Down towards the end you might find that you have to wait for several minutes before some output deigns to emerge from your printer.

When you first place a text string in the work space, it will probably be stroked with a one-point rule. This is quite a lot fatter than is usually required for text operations. You might want to change this to a hairline, or even no stroke at all if your text is to be filled with a solid color.

*Figure 3.10:* Manipulating text to extremes.

One of the common "uglies" that happens on first printing a drawing is having your text stroked with a rule that's thicker than you might have wanted. Figure 3.11 illustrates the effect of varying rule thicknesses on text.

Just about every unwanted effect has its potential uses under Corel Draw, and fat, pudgy strokes applied accidentally to text do too. For instance, one common problem in complex drawings is arranging to have text stand out from its background. One way to deal with this problem is to stroke a duplicate of the text with a thicker line and a contrasting color and place the duplicate behind the original text. This serves to outline the original text, as shown in Figure 3.12.

Outlining text by stacking it on a copy of itself is managed very easily under Corel Draw. Try it for yourself by writing some text into the work space and then following these steps. First, select and duplicate the text. Stroke the rearward text with a fat rule and make its stroke color white. You might want to set the fill color to white as well.

Next, position the second text directly over the first and set its stroke and fill attributes normally. You will probably have to open the preview window to see if this has worked out properly.

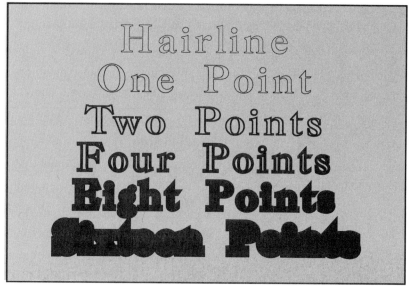

*Figure 3.11:* Increasing the stroke weight for text.

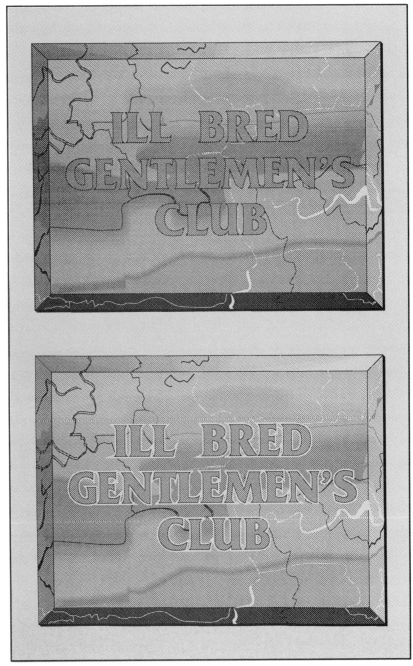

*Figure 3.12:* Keeping text from being engulfed by its background.

It's a lot easier to position text if you use the grid-snap feature.

Quite a number of the more interesting text effects involve using multiple copies of the same bit of type, as we'll see. For example, a drop shadow is particularly easy to do if you use two copies of the same text slightly displaced. A different kind of effect can be created by duplicating the same text multiple times and changing the stroke width and stroke density with each new iteration. The results can be seen in Figure 3.13. The two precise-adjustment boxes of the pen tool control the stroke qualities—we'll discuss them in detail in a moment.

The first or backmost object was set with a stroke width of 2 picas—a very fat line—and a stroke density of 10 percent. This object was then duplicated and the duplicate was given a slightly narrower width—1 pica 10 points—with a slightly denser stroke of 15 percent. This was repeated until the stroke width reached 1 point and the density reached 70 percent.

This whole process is a great deal easier if you set the duplicate displacement values in the Preferences dialog box to zero so the duplicates are automatically placed directly on the original without the need for any adjustment by hand.

If you'll ultimately be printing to a color output device or if you'll be having Corel Draw create color separations for you, you can do all sorts of interesting things with these basic text attributes.

*Figure 3.13:* Adding a glow to text with multiple iterations.

The fill attributes of text also offer a lot of interesting possibilities—as well as a few pitfalls. We'll discuss fills in greater detail in the next chapter.

### Fine-Tuning Outlines

In choosing the stroke weight for your text you can, of course, use the default values displayed in the outline tool's flyout menu. However, considerably more control can be had through the use of the precise-adjustment boxes, available through the leftmost icons in this menu. Figure 3.14 illustrates the Outline Pen box with a few as-yet undiscussed items.

The set of radio buttons at the top of this box tells Corel Draw how to stroke the line which will trace the paths of your text. There are four options. If you select None, the path won't be stroked at all. If the fill of the character is the same as that of the background of your drawing—white on white, for example—your text will be invisible. If you select a solid line, your text will be stroked with the stroke color or tint you select in the Outline Color precise-adjustment box. The other two options are broken lines, which can look quite interesting.

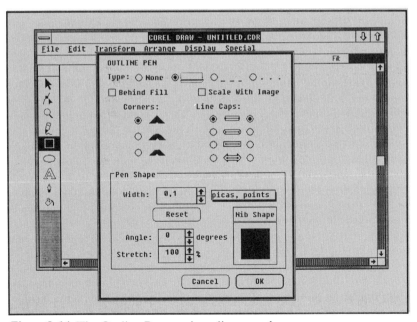

*Figure 3.14:* The Outline Pen precise-adjustment box.

The two check boxes below these radio buttons are particularly applicable to text. The Behind Fill box tells Corel Draw to fill your text before stroking it. By selecting this box, the stroke will appear on top of the fill.

The Scale With Image box tells Corel Draw what to do with the stroke width of your text should you decide to stretch the text. If it's selected, the width of the rule used to stroke your text will expand in the direction you stretch the text. You should use this feature if you plan to change the size of your text by transforming it, especially if the text you have in mind involves a fat rule.

Changing the corner and line cap settings for the stroke of your text will have decided effects on its appearance if you're stroking it with a heavy rule, and you should experiment with these settings to see what happens. Likewise, play with the Pen Shape box as well. Figure 3.15 illustrates the effects of some variations on these values.

## TRANSFORMING TEXT

The transformations which Corel Draw can apply to text are particularly effective. They range from simply changing how it lies on your page to really making a serious mess of it.

*Figure 3.15:* Changing the outline pen characteristics for stroking text. The last effect uses the Pen Shape controls of the Outline Pen dialog.

If you select a text string with the pick tool, you will find that you can stretch it just as you can other objects. If you grab one of the corner selection marks you can stretch it while preserving its aspect ratio. If you grab a center selection mark you can stretch it more in one direction than in the other.

This sort of transformation does not cause Corel Draw to stop dealing with the text as text. If after stretching the text you hit Ctrl-T to pop up the Text dialog box, you will notice that not only has the point size changed to reflect the new, stretched size of the text, but the text is still editable.

If you select the Clear Transformations item from the Transform menu the text will return to its original size and aspect ratio, exactly as it was before you started meddling with it.

You can rotate text just as you have rotated simple objects. Select a bit of text, then click on the selected text with the pick tool and grab one of the rotation marks. The text will freely rotate about the pivot. Likewise, if you grab one of the skew marks you can bend the text along one dimension. Figure 3.16 illustrates these basic transformations.

### Using the Transform Menu

Rotating and skewing text using the pick tool is great for matching it to the rest of a drawing by eye, but not quite as useful if you want to

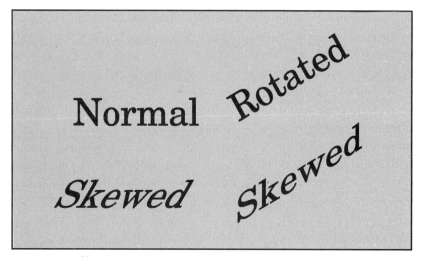

*Figure 3.16:* Simple transformations.

manipulate it by a specified number of degrees. Fortunately, the same rotation and skew effects can be handled through the Rotate & Skew item of the Transform menu. This dialog box was discussed previously in Chapter 2.

A lot of very interesting text effects can be achieved by using this box along with the Repeat item of the Edit menu (or the Ctrl-R keyboard shortcut). Bearing in mind that the act of applying a transformation, like rotating or skewing a bit of text, automatically selects the *result* of the transformation, you will understand why you need to ''leave an original'' in the drawing if you want to create iterations of a progressive transformation by using the Repeat function several times.

For example, if you tell Corel Draw to skew some text by 10 degrees and repeat this several times, you'll wind up with something which looks like Figure 3.17.

Actually, this isn't quite true. There's one more step involved. As you will recall, as objects are added to a drawing they're placed, by default, forward of the existing objects. You might imagine each object to have been drawn on a sheet of clear acetate and placed atop a pile of earlier objects. Thus, the original text in the example of Figure 3.17 was actually behind all the copies, rather than in front of them. This was easy to correct using the following procedure.

1. Select all the objects in this effect with the pick tool by drawing a rubber band box around them.

2. Select the Reverse Order item from the Arrange menu.

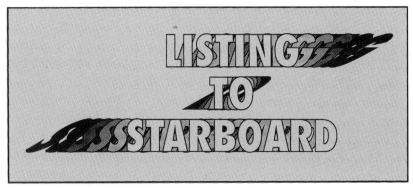

*Figure 3.17:* Progressive skewing.

The progressively darker gray fills of the duplicated text did not happen automatically either. Each one was selected and a particular fill level was applied to it.

The Stretch & Mirror item of the Transform menu offers similar possibilities for special effects. The mirror functions allow you to flip an object either horizontally or vertically. (You would have to use this function twice to flip it in both dimensions.) The stretch functions allow you to expand or contract an object in both dimensions by specified amounts.

As with the previous example, you can invoke this function several times using the Repeat function. Figure 3.18 illustrates an effect created using the stretch function. These objects, too, were created in the wrong order and had to be reversed before they appeared like this.

You can probably dream up a number of effects which entail using several transformations on a single object for each stage of the effect. This could get a little tedious because Corel Draw allows you to repeat only the last thing you did. For example, if you wanted to create a text effect which involved rotating *and* reducing each duplicated object, the repeat function would be of no use.

There is a way around this. It involves the use of the Corel Draw macro facility.

## USING MACROS

Like most of the transformations and other tools discussed in this chapter, macros can be applied to all sorts of operations, not just text effects. They save buckets of time, allow you to make the program do things with greater precision than you probably could on your own, and allow you to store frequently used special effects—such as drop

*Figure 3.18:* A text effect using progressive stretching.

shadows—so that you can apply them to any object with just a few mouse clicks.

A macro under Corel Draw is any series of steps which might affect a selected object. These can be either menu selections or keyboard shortcuts. Corel Draw allows you record macros ''on the fly'' as you perform the procedures you want to store.

Once completed, a macro can be saved to disk and recalled at a later time. Once used, all the steps stored in a macro can be repeated using the Repeat function.

Figure 3.19 is an example of a text effect made possible through the use of macros. You should have no difficulty in understanding what has been done here. The initial text string was selected and rotated 6 degrees with the Stretch & Mirror item of the Transform menu, using the Leave Original option to force the creation of a duplicate. The duplicate was then automatically selected by Corel Draw. The Stretch & Mirror item was used to scale the duplicate down to 94 percent of its original size, this time with the Leave Original feature not selected. This entire procedure was repeated twenty or thirty times by hitting Ctrl-R over and over again. The resulting collection of objects was subsequently selected and had its order reversed so the original text appeared at the front of the stack.

Watching these objects redraw after a preview is extremely interesting—they seem to spiral out of the screen at you.

In order to arrange the two transformations so they are both repeated, you need to place them in a macro. The procedures for creating the macro and calling it into play are outlined below. First of all, however, you need to create an appropriate text string in a large

*Figure 3.19:* Repetitive rotation made possible with a macro.

point size. Ornate fonts create lots of detail for this sort of effect and look best. I've used University Roman (or Unicorn) in this example.

*Create the macro*

1. Select the text with the pick tool.

2. Select the Record Macro item of the Special menu.

3. Select the Rotate & Skew item of the Transform menu and arrange to have the selected object rotated by six degrees. Select Leave Original.

4. Select the Stretch & Mirror item of the Transform menu. Scale the selected object down to 94 percent in each dimension.

5. Select the Finish Macro item of the Special menu. A file box will pop up allowing you to save and name your macro.

*Use the macro*

6. Select the Play Macro item from the Special menu. A file dialog box will appear, allowing you to load your macro. This will create a new iteration of your selected object.

7. Hit Ctrl-R repeatedly until there are enough objects in your drawing to look like it took hours to create.

Now select all the objects. Select the Reverse Order item from the Arrange menu to place the first iteration at the front of the heap. You might want to use the outline and fill tools to give the objects a hairline stroke and white fill. Also, it's not a bad idea to group all the objects together.

You can apply this macro to any other object which strikes you as being a good subject for this sort of effect. This can include very complex ones, such as entire drawings.

There are, obviously, a lot of variations on this type of effect. There are also a lot of other uses for macros.

Figure 3.20 illustrates the same effect with the pivot of the initial object moved up against the leftmost stem of the letter N. This version has 64 duplicates of the original text.

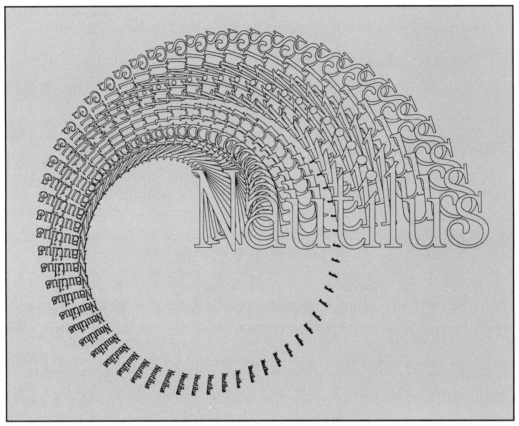

*Figure 3.20:* One of many possible variations on the original spiral.

## CONVERTING TEXT TO CURVES

The most radical text effects available under Corel Draw involve manipulating the paths which make up the individual characters of your text. At this level the text ceases to be text as such and reverts to being basic objects. Once you have reduced text to its component parts it can never be turned back into text objects. It will no longer be possible to edit or change the text attributes of such text with the Text dialog or the Character Attribute dialog.

While converting text into paths prohibits you from dealing with it as text any longer, it does open up a whole world of new possibilities in dealing with it as graphics. If you plan ahead and perform all the text-related modifications to your text objects before you convert them to graphic objects, this shouldn't be a problem.

In order to convert a text object into a purely graphic object, select the text object or objects with the pick tool and then select the Convert to Curves item from the Arrange menu. The resulting object will display all the Bezier curves used to outline the selected text. The curves will all be combined together. If you plan to manipulate some of the curves you should subsequently select the Break Apart item from the Arrange menu. (You can use the Combine item after you've changed these paths. This will make all the paths into a single object again.)

The ''Bigfoot'' graphic in Figure 3.21 is an example of text which has been converted to curves and worked over.

The top line is simply text which has been set normally. This is the New Century Schoolbook font, or what Corel Draw calls New Brunswick. It's a good choice for this graphic as it has big, chunky serifs at the bottom of its uppercase characters, suitable for expansion into big feet.

If you convert this text into curves, node marks will appear at strategic locations around the text. As you will be working in this example

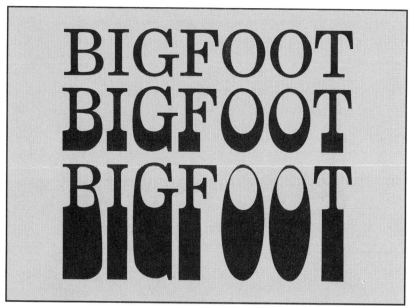

*Figure 3.21:* Text converted to curves.

with all the characters at once, there's no need to break them apart. You can select the curves which represent the bottoms of all the characters by using the shape tool to draw a rubber band box that encompasses just the bottoms of the characters. That way, when you grab just one of the selected nodes and drag it down, all the nodes will follow. Use this technique to expand the bases of the characters to give them feet of any proportions you like.

Some final touching up may be necessary. The lower curves on the B and the G didn't expand all that well initially, and it was necessary to manually pull those nodes down a bit.

You can create some eye-catching graphics by playing with the component parts of text. It's possible to make parts of your characters into other sorts of graphics, to fuse text and other objects, and so on. Figure 3.22 is some text in University Roman and one of the clip art images which comes with Corel Draw.

In creating graphics which use text converted to curves, bear in mind that there are lots of ways to mangle such a collection of objects. Most of the time the results of making a mistake are complex at best to untangle. It's a good idea to save your file frequently while you're working on graphics of this sort, so you can revert to your most recently saved version if things go amiss.

It's also worth noting that when you save a file under Corel Draw, your previous version is renamed rather than deleted, just as most word processors do with their documents. If your drawing is called BRASS.CDR, your previous version will be called BRASS.BAK. If you were to save your drawing and then realize it was mangled—or in some way your file was damaged—you could rename the

*Figure 3.22:* Brass and horn, fused objects.

appropriate .BAK file to a .CDR file and effectively take up where you were two revisions ago.

You can rename files by quitting Corel Draw and using the DOS rename function, or you can use the Windows renaming facilities. See your Windows manual for directions on doing this.

## *THE JOY OF DINGBATS*

In addition to the text typefaces which came with Corel Draw, you will have received several symbol sets. These include a music notation typeface, a greek and math symbol set, and something which Corel Draw calls Dixieland but the rest of the world knows as Zapf Dingbats.

Dingbats is a peculiar little typeface. It's intended for use as ornaments, bullets, and other typographic regalia which appear in text from time to time. Figure 3.23 illustrates some of the many denizens of the Dingbats font.

The most obvious use of Dingbats is to set the odd dingbat in your text. Depending on how off the wall you can allow your text to get, you can work in quite a few of them.

*Figure 3.23:* Some dingbats.

It's not hard to use dingbats. For example, to add a giant exclamation mark to a line of text, you would do the following:

1.  Use the text tool to open the Text dialog box and prepare to set the text normally in any typeface you like. Dingbats seem to go well with serif faces.

2.  Begin typing. However, instead of entering an exclamation mark when you get to the place where it should go, hold down the Alt key on your keyboard and enter 0162 on your numeric keypad. A cent symbol will appear in the text at this point. This is largely meaningless, and can be ignored.

3.  Release the Alt key and enter the rest of the text. Click on OK to accept the text and display it in the work space.

4.  Using the *shape* tool, select your text. Locate the node that corresponds to the cent symbol—it will appear to its lower left—and double-click on it to get the Character Attribute dialog box. Change the typeface to Zapf Dingbats or Dixieland, then click on OK.

When Corel Draw redraws your text, the cent sign will have been replaced with the appropriate dingbat.

You can also add dingbats after the fact by editing your text and replacing conventional characters with the character codes for dingbats. Having done this, use the shape tool to select the new characters and change their fonts.

In some cases it's desirable to make dingbats bigger than the text they're part of. Their natural sizes tend to make them look a bit diminutive.

Dingbats are also useful as graphics which don't have anything much to do with text. If you blow up a dingbat so it looks like a graphic you can use it for all sorts of things. The heart-shaped leaf object in Figure 3.24 is actually a dingbat.

## FITTING TEXT TO PATHS

Text is normally drawn with respect to a baseline. The baseline is, by default, straight. You do not actually move text when you drag it around. You move the baseline, and the text which is tied to it moves

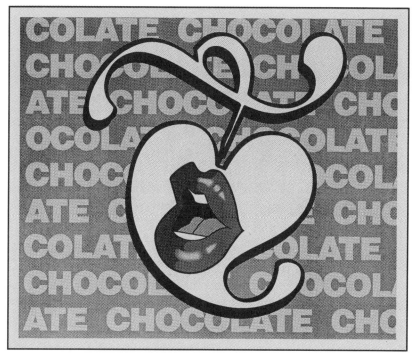

*Figure 3.24:* A dingbat, some clip art, and two thousand calories.

with it. If you change the shape of the baseline the shape of the text string will also be altered.

Corel Draw does not allow you to manipulate the baseline as you would a true path. Instead, it provides a facility for fitting the baseline—hence the text—to a real path. This Fit Text to Path function (in the Arrange menu) is the genesis of countless text effects.

Let's start with a simple example. The upper screen in Figure 3.25 illustrates a text string and an ellipse. If you select them both—either with the pick tool or by using the Select All item of the Edit menu—and then select the Fit Text to Path item of the Arrange menu, the result should look like the lower screen.

This actually depends upon a number of things. If you try this example you might not get exactly the same result. Therefore, you should probably be familiar with another item in the Arrange menu, Straighten Text. If you select this when you have selected a bent text

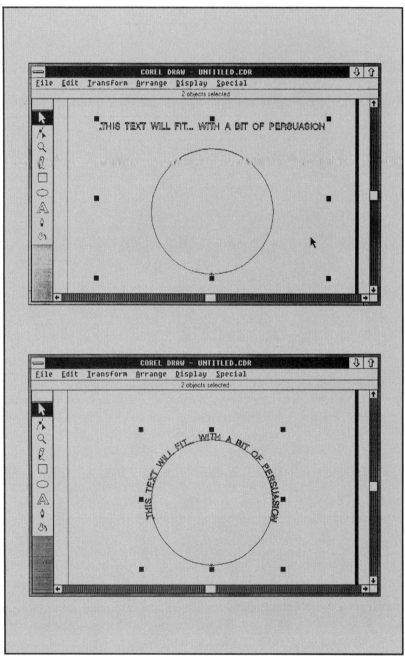

*Figure 3.25:* Fitting a text string to a path.

string, the baseline of the text will be straightened out. It's a handy feature for backing up and trying again.

It's worth noting that the Straighten Text function also aligns text vertically with the baseline and sets the characters to their original positions relative to each other. What this means is that kerning—something we'll discuss later in this chapter—is also undone by selecting this item.

## HOW TO DETERMINE WHERE TEXT WILL BE POSITIONED

One obvious question you might ask about wrapping text around an ellipse is how the starting point of the text is determined. In fact, a number of things help decide where on a path your text will be placed.

In part, the Alignment radio buttons in the Text dialog determine the placement of the text. If you select Center alignment, the text will be centered on the path. Left alignment will start it at the left end of the path, and Right alignment, as you might imagine, ends it on the right end of the path. The None alignment option is fairly obscure, and exists to deal with a particular problem, that of kerning, which will be discussed later in this chapter.

Figure 3.26 illustrates the effects of different alignment on text fitted to an ellipse.

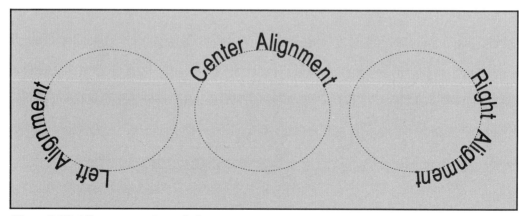

*Figure 3.26:* Alignment and text fitting.

This still does not completely explain where the text will appear on an ellipse. The following should help to define the factors involved.

The start and the end of an ellipse are at the same point on the object, this being the square node mark which is visible when you select an object with the shape tool. If the node mark is at the top of a regular ellipse, the center point on the ellipse path is at the bottom of the ellipse. Center-aligned text will thus be centered on the bottom of the ellipse in question. For left and right alignment, think of the node as a margin on a page. Left-aligned text will start at the node and spread to the right; right-aligned text will end at the node.

If you created the ellipse by starting in the upper left corner of the rectangle which bounds it and dragging your mouse to the lower right corner, any text fitted to the ellipse will appear *outside* the ellipse. If you started in the lower right corner and dragged your mouse cursor toward the upper left corner when you created the ellipse—the opposite of how one normally draws objects—any text fitted to the ellipse will appear *inside* the ellipse.

This approach also applies to open paths, such as curves. If you draw a curve from left to right, any text fitted to the curve will appear above it. If you draw the curve from right to left, text fitted to the curve will appear below it.

You can reverse the text direction along an existing path using the mirror function of the Stretch & Mirror item of the Transform menu. This should not make any visible changes to the path itself, but it will cause text to be fitted inside if it previously was fitted outside and vice versa.

Once you have fitted text to a path you can delete the path if you like. However, it's a better idea to retain the path and just prevent it from appearing in your finished drawing. To do this, select the path and give it no fill and no stroke. It will still appear in the work space, but the preview window and your final hard copy will not show it.

## *FITTING TEXT TO COMPLEX PATHS*

The idea of fitting text to paths often works better than the reality of it. There are a few important points to keep in mind when you go to fit text around complex paths.

Figure 3.27 is the letter A we first encountered in Chapter 1. You should now know roughly how this drawing was created. The path for the A was formed by setting an immense capital A and converting it to curves. The text which wraps around the A was entered as a straight text string—its length being determined largely by the 250-character maximum for a text string. Finally, the text and the capital A path were selected and the text was fitted to the path.

In fact, there's a lot more to it than this. To begin with, the choice of the typeface for the big A is very important. Text wrapped around sharp corners doesn't look very good. It was important to select a typeface in which the capital A was composed only of gently rounded paths. American Typewriter—what Corel Draw refers to as Memorandum—is a good choice for this.

Having been drawn on the page and converted to curves, the A was modified slightly by removing the paths that formed the inside of

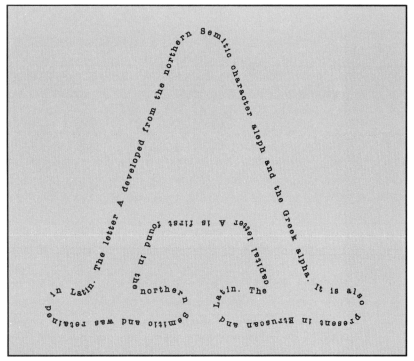

*Figure 3.27:* The return of the giant A.

the character. The stroke color of the path was then set to NONE so the path itself would not appear in the final hard copy.

The next tricky bit was to get the text to encompass the path which comprised the periphery of the big A with neither a gap nor an overlap. Actually, you'll never see any overlap using this technique: if you make the text too long Corel Draw will leave off the offending part of the string. Fitting the text without losing any of it was done through trial and error. The length of the text string can be adjusted by putting more or less space between characters and words using the Spacing adjustment of the Text dialog box. Having changed these parameters, Corel Draw will attempt to redraw the new text to the old path, which doesn't work. Therefore, after every change you have to straighten the text, again select the text string and the path, and again select Fit Text to Path from the Arrange menu to clean things up.

Figure 3.28 illustrates the steps in creating the A graphic.

## *MANIPULATING TYPE WITHIN TEXT STRINGS*

Corel Draw allows you to compress or stretch a text string such that the point size and aspect ratio of the text does not change. Only the space between the characters is affected, and this is adjusted proportionally. Thus, text which is fitted to an area larger than it would otherwise occupy still looks to be set properly—it's just a bit loose.

You can achieve this result by using the Spacing features in the Text dialog box, as we discussed in connection with the big A graphic earlier in this chapter. However, repeatedly having to pop back into this box in a trial-and-error attempt to fine-tune the spacing is inconvenient. Corel Draw lets you do the same thing by eye when this is more appropriate.

To adjust the spacing of a text string by eye, select the string with the shape tool. Along with individual node marks for each character, two special text-spacing marks will appear, one at each end of the last line of the string. The left text-spacing mark adjusts interline spacing. The rightmost mark adjusts the space between words and letters.

If you grab the right text-spacing mark and drag it to the right, the spacing between the letters of your text will increase proportionally. If you hold the Ctrl key down while you drag it, the space between the letters will not be affected but the space between the words will.

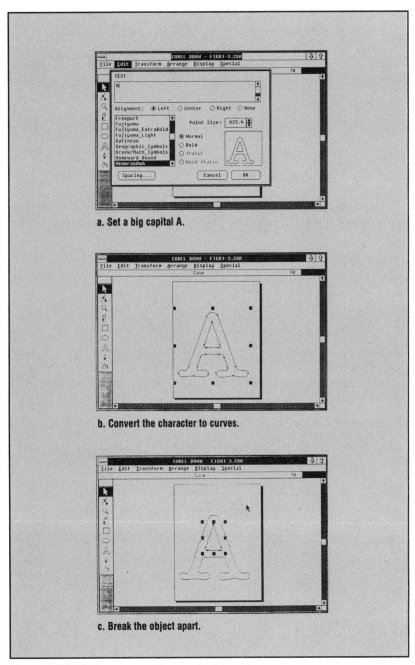

**a. Set a big capital A.**

**b. Convert the character to curves.**

**c. Break the object apart.**

*Figure 3.28:* Fitting a text string to the letter A.

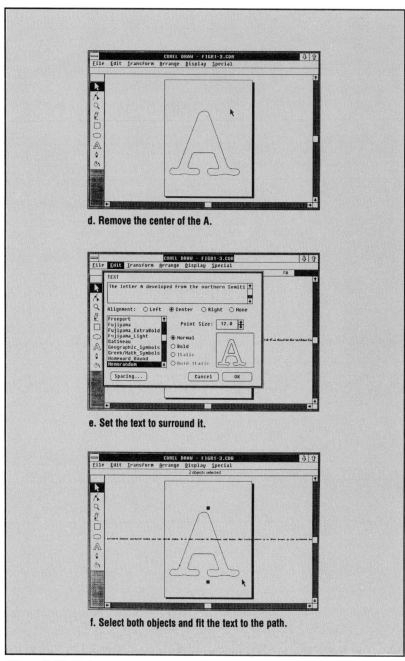

Figure 3.29 is the cover of the popular *Timewarp Quarterly,* a magazine which is rarely seen these days but will be very popular in the Late Middle Ages. As with most magazine covers, this design embodies several examples of text fitting and kerning.

The T and the Q of the main title have been made larger—by a process as yet undiscussed—and the T was shifted vertically. The text below the main title—"The Magazine for Temporal Tourists"—was

*Figure 3.29:* The cover of the July 1643 edition of *Timewarp Quarterly.*

set in Helvetica Narrow and fitted to the appropriate width with the right text-spacing mark. The issue date was handled in the same way.

The current fashion in using fitted text in this way is to have lots of space between the characters. If you like to keep up with such fashions, it's also not a bad idea to use a laterally condensed font (like Helvetica Narrow).

The cover contents, ''In This Issue,'' are all handled as a single block of text which has been expanded vertically using the left text-spacing mark. The text was set in University Roman; then the block as a whole was expanded by increasing the line spacing until the contents filled the cover.

The first line of this text block was then set larger than the rest of the type by the same as-yet undiscussed process.

Fitted text is rarely all that readable in quantity, and it is usually used more for decoration than to convey any serious amount of information. However, it's a powerful tool in creating contemporary looking type.

### *Setting Individual Character Attributes*

The as-yet undiscussed process in the previous section is that of setting individual character attributes. Corel Draw allows you to select individual characters in any text string and change their size, font, and several other characteristics.

You can manipulate the text attributes of every character in a text string. Figure 3.30 is an example of a text string in which each character has been given a different typeface. This serves to illustrate both the flexibility of Corel Draw and a good reason why you shouldn't overuse this powerful feature.

Let's create a text string in which the first and last characters are bigger than the rest of the text. The graphic is shown in Figure 3.31.

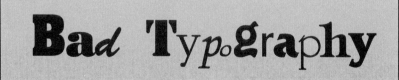

*Figure 3.30:* A text string with lots of different typefaces.

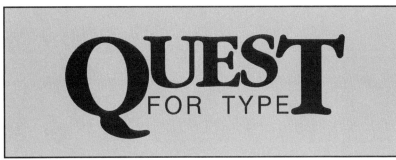

*Figure 3.31:* Changing the size of individual characters.

Here's how this graphic is created:

1. Set the word QUEST in 96-point Garamond, the face that Corel Draw calls Gatineau.

2. Select this text with the shape tool.

3. Double-click on the node for the letter Q (the one to the left of the letter). The Character Attributes dialog will appear.

4. Change the Point Size value in the dialog to 144 and the Vertical Shift to −35 percent. (This latter number was arrived at through trial and error.) The dialog box should look like Figure 3.32.

5. Click on OK, then repeat this process for the letter T.

6. Set "FOR TYPE" in Helvetica Light and fit it to the space between the Q and the T.

Any combination of attributes can be set for any number of characters. If you want to change the attributes of more than one character at a time—for example, to boldface one word in a sentence—use the shape tool to select the characters to be changed and click on one of the selected nodes. The dialog box in Figure 3.32 will appear, but this time any changes you make will pertain to all the selected characters.

This can be tricky if you've already changed some attributes in a text string. For example, the string in Figure 3.30 had a different typeface attribute for each character, although all of them were the same size. If you were to select the first two characters and

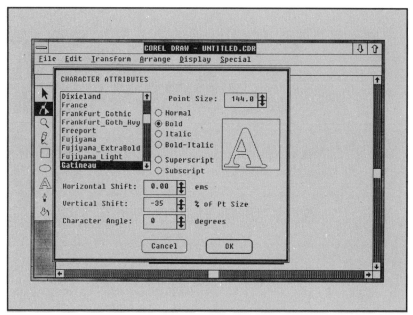

*Figure 3.32:* The Character Attributes dialog box.

double-click on the first node, the typeface displayed in the Character Attribute dialog box would reflect the typeface of the first character, the one you double-clicked on.

If you don't touch the typeface selection window each character's typeface attributes will still remain as they were. However, if you were to change the point size in this box, both characters would change in size. *In a situation where you have selected several characters with different attributes, only those attributes you explicitly change will be applied to all the selected characters.*

The Horizontal and Vertical Shift values in the Character Attribute dialog box correspond to the horizontal and vertical positioning which you can adjust with the shape tool in kerning text. These controls allow you to adjust these attributes numerically rather than by eye. This is handy for fine-tuning character positions which you've set by eye with the shape tool.

The units of the Horizontal and Vertical Shift values may seem a bit funny. The horizontal value is expressed in ems and the vertical value as a percentage of the point size of the text. There's a very good reason for doing it this way. An em is the width of the letter M in the current font at the current size. As such, this value will change along with the percentage of the point size if you change the size of the text object it's associated with. If you make the object bigger—either by stretching it with the pick tool or by using the Stretch & Mirror item of the Transform menu—both these values will change proportionally.

The Character Angle attribute allows you to cause selected characters to be rotated about their individual midpoints. This is not the same as skewing them so they look italicized, nor is it the same as rotating a whole block of text. These three effects are different, and they are illustrated in Figure 3.33.

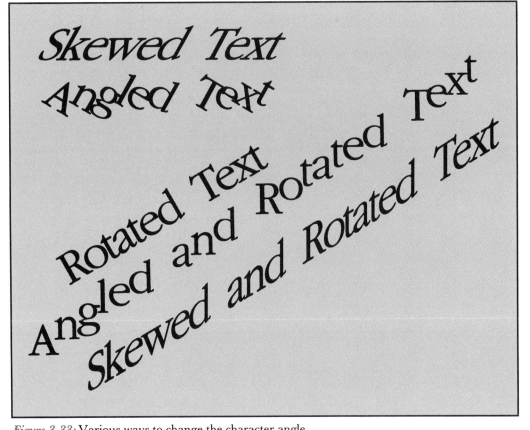

*Figure 3.33:* Various ways to change the character angle.

## *KERNING AND TEXT FITTING*

When you fit text to a path it's very often the case that the characters tend to bunch up in sharply concave areas and get spread out in convex ones. You can fix this by manually adjusting the spacing—or *kerning*—of the characters.

Figure 3.34 illustrates the effects of kerning text.

Kerning is a fairly contentious issue in the circles frequented by typesetters and type designers. If you read the graphics trade magazines you'll encounter all sorts of articles about why kerning is or isn't

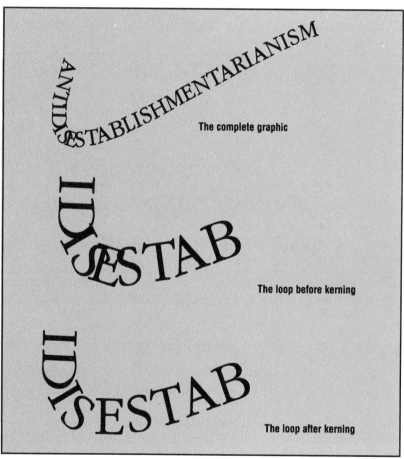

*Figure 3.34:* Kerning text.

desirable—impressive sounding arguments are to be had by both sides of the issues. A related subject, that of ligatures, gets still more violent. One suspects that many of the participants in these discussions wish they were back in the days of metal type so they'd have something substantial to throw at their opponents.

In setting body text—something which Corel Draw obviously does not do—reasonably sophisticated software usually manages to implement some sort of automatic kerning if it's required. Automatic kerning works by keeping a table of "kerning pairs," pairs of characters which should be kerned if they happen to appear side by side. This is not done in Corel Draw. If you want to kern text under Corel Draw, you must do so by hand. There are several good reasons for not implementing automatic kerning in a drawing package, not the least of which is that good kerning is a very subjective thing. The aesthetics of kerning become more debatable in larger text, where the result of kerning or the lack of it becomes more pronounced.

Text kerning is another of those operations which does not entail turning your text irretrievably into objects. Even though you will be dealing with the characters from a string individually, Corel Draw will still treat kerned text objects as text, allowing you to subsequently edit them and change their text attributes, as we've discussed.

### Simple Kerning

Figure 3.35 illustrates text which could do with some kerning. Note that this is a matter both of personal taste and of the typeface which was used to set this text. Some fonts, because of their design, are more likely to leave large or irregular gaps between certain pairs of characters. As a rule, fonts which are laterally condensed, such as Helvetica Narrow or University Roman, are less likely to encounter these problems.

Having placed this text in the work space, you can kern it by selecting it with the shape tool. This causes the individual character nodes to be displayed, one to the lower left of each character, as well as the two text-spacing marks, one at each end of the last line of the string.

If you click and hold on one of the character nodes, you'll find that you'll be able to drag the character around. This will let you adjust the kerning between any of the characters in the string. Figure 3.36 shows the letter W selected and kerned.

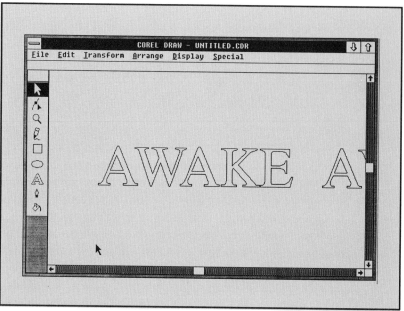

*Figure 3.35:* Some text to be kerned.

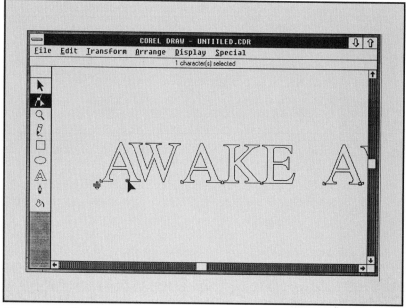

*Figure 3.36:* Kerning a letter.

In designing logos and other specialized bits of type, kerning text so that all the characters touch is a very effective technique. This does not make for particularly readable text—you would probably not want to do it to really fat text, for example—but it serves to make the text look solid and more like a single object than a group of characters. In the case of a logo, where you are really designing a symbol rather than a word, this frequently works well. We'll discuss logo design in detail in Chapter 10.

When you kern text like this, it's extremely difficult to keep from moving the text vertically while you're adjusting it horizontally. You might decide you *want* to put some vertical interest in your text string, but if you don't, there's a way around it. Once you're finished kerning a string of text, just use the Align to Baseline item of the Arrange menu. This automatically restores the text to the baseline without disturbing your kerning.

It's usually the case that you will want to kern only the occasional pair of letters in a text string, ones where the gap between adjoining characters is particularly noticeable. If you move the right character of the offending pair left, however, you will merely transfer the gap over by one character. You could, of course, kern all the other characters by hand, but this is tedious, and fortunately unnecessary. Instead, you can drag all the remaining characters in a text string by using the shape tool cursor to draw a rubber band box around the characters you want to drag. The node marks of the selected characters will turn black. Grab one of the selected node marks and drag the block of text into position. If you use the shape tool to move characters in a string which has already been set with one of the conventional alignment settings (Left, Center, and Right), and the moved characters end up beyond the previous beginning or end of the string, Corel Draw might reposition the other characters in the string when it goes to redraw the text. To avoid this problem, change the string alignment to None. This will prevent Corel Draw from imposing alignment on a string which you have taken pains to align by hand.

In selecting multiple characters with the shape tool it's not always immediately obvious whether you've selected all the text you think you have. Ingeniously, Corel Draw displays the number of characters which have actually been selected, in the status line above the work space.

*Creating Ligatures*

One of the more extreme uses of kerning under Corel Draw is in the creation of ligatures. Depending upon the graphic circles you frequent, using ligatures will have you regarded either as erudite and sophisticated or as a type snob.

A ligature is a single character formed by joining two or more characters, or, in the case of Corel Draw, by kerning two characters so close together they overlap in places. Ligatures usually involve lowercase characters. One common example is ''ff,'' as shown in Figure 3.37.

By using a ligature rather than two separate characters, the second example has allowed the word to occupy a bit less space on the line without looking unnecessarily crowded. In fact, used correctly, ligatures can be very attractive.

One ligature which is still frequently used is ''fi.'' In some fonts, the dot of the i will bump into the upper end of the f, which looks peculiar. In the days of metal type a special character was created in which the dot of the i was missing entirely—it was supplanted by the bulge at the top of the f.

The use of ligatures is not at all common anymore, for several reasons. One of these is that it's usually regarded as being too much work to bother with them. Secondly, the broad, flowing typefaces of the turn of the century—which supported ligatures nicely—have given way to type which is laterally condensed as designers have required typefaces which squeeze more words on a page. Fairly narrow faces neither lend themselves to ligatures nor really require them, and the minuscule reduction in line width offered by the odd ligature is rarely worth the effort.

In setting type with Corel Draw, you might want to experiment with making ligatures. None of the faces included with the package

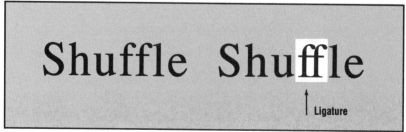

*Figure 3.37:* A ligature.

suffer from the problem cured by the fi ligature, but several of the more elongated ones—such as Cooper Black, what Corel Draw ships as Cupertino—look attractive when some adjoining lowercase letters are kerned together into ligatures. Particularly tall characters, such as f and l, lend themselves to forming ligatures.

## WRAPPING UP

To use the text facilities of Corel Draw effectively, you need to go beyond simply learning to work the software. The ostensibly un-involved task of slapping a few words on a piece of paper is really a rich, fascinating art form all by itself.

A lot more discussion of text will crop up throughout the course of this book. This will be especially true as we start looking at design techniques in Part II.

# chapter

# 4

## Using Fills

**T**HE TOPIC OF FILLING OBJECTS UNDER COREL DRAW
has been touched on in the previous chapters, but not really discussed. In principle, the subject is pretty simple. The realization of it,
however, can become complex, partly because Corel Draw offers a
lot of ways to handle fills, but especially because the capabilities of
your printer greatly affect the manner in which you specify fills.

There are a number of fills that Corel Draw will print on anything
that eats paper, but there are a lot more which are specific to certain
types of output devices, most notably laser printers.

There are also a lot of aesthetic and design considerations in using
fills, probably more so than in using the other facilities we have discussed previously. The aesthetically appropriate use of shading and
shadow, which can make your two-dimensional objects spring to life,
will be discussed in later chapters. This chapter will focus mainly on
the technical aspects of what goes on between Corel Draw (and, relat-
edly, other drawing programs) and printers.

## CLOSING PATHS TO ACCEPT FILLS

Any closed path can be given a fill characteristic. This includes text
and complex curves as well as simple objects such as rectangles and
ellipses. If you want to fill an open path you must close it first.

If you create an object out of multiple line segments, the path so
defined will probably not be closed initially even if the end nodes of
the segments line up. Similarly, if you create a single path which simply overlaps itself, it will still be an open path. You must therefore
check the status line above the work space to see if your currently
selected path is open or closed. If it is open, you need to "join" the
end nodes. The following steps show you how to do this.

1. Select the shape tool.

2. Select the two nodes you want to join, either by drawing a
   rubber band box around them or by clicking on one and then
   the other with the Shift key held down.

3. Double-click on one of the selected nodes. A pop-up menu will appear.

4. Select the Join item.

The two nodes will move together and Corel Draw will join them. (The Break Apart item in the Arrange menu can ''unjoin'' them later if need be.) Note that joining any two nodes will not necessarily form a closed path. The two nodes in question must be the ends of an otherwise closed path; if there are unjoined nodes within the course of the path, you'll have to join those too.

If you wish to join *two* paths into a single path, for the purpose of ultimately creating a closed path, you can do so by using Corel Draw's Combine feature. Select the two paths in question with the pick tool and then select the Combine item from the Arrange menu. (The paths can subsequently be uncombined using the Break Apart feature of the same menu.) For as long as they're combined, the two paths will behave as a single path.

## BASIC FILL QUALITIES

There are four basic types of fills under Corel Draw. The simplest, and most widely used, is a solid gray fill. Gray fills are the simplest sort of fill, and you'll probably find that they are the ones you use the most often. They are also the fill patterns which take the least amount of time to print, which is something worth considering. The second type is a solid color fill. The third is the fountain fill, and, finally, there are PostScript fills, or ''textures.'' As the name implies, PostScript fills are available only through PostScript printers. These will crop up later in this chapter.

It's easiest to think of a fill as being a color, even if the color in question is gray. If you imagine a closed path as being a container, filling it simply involves pouring colored ink into it. In fact, when Corel Draw draws a filled object on your screen or creates a bitmap of it for output to a printer, it performs a digital process analogous to this, algorithmically filling an enclosed area by starting with a single point and working outwards.

In addition to the fill patterns to be discussed in this chapter, Corel Draw also offers you a fill type called NONE, or no fill. NONE should not be confused with a pure white fill. The two are not the same, and in one case in particular the difference is significant. If you create two overlapping objects and fill the front one with pure white, the parts of the rear one which are overlapped will be obscured. However, if you give the front object no fill, it will appear transparent or hollow. Figure 4.1 illustrates the difference.

In cases where there is no overlap you won't notice this difference, and it would be easy to get these two apparently similar fills mixed up. If you mix them up when you're doing a complex drawing, parts of your drawing may vanish when they're not supposed to.

## UNDERSTANDING FILLS AND SCREENS

Laser printers, and the more affordable print houses as well, do not mix inks to arrive at specific shades of gray. To fill an area of a page with a particular shade of gray, printers utilize what is called a "screen" to place black spots of a certain size in a certain pattern such that up close the area looks like it was printed through a piece of screen or fabric. At a normal viewing distance the spots blend together over the white background to give an impression of gray.

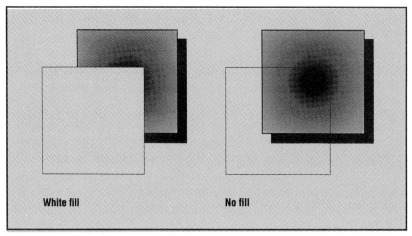

*Figure 4.1:* White fill versus no fill.

There are a lot of variables in handling screens. One way or another, they represent the most complex element of printing, whether you're doing it with a printing press or a laser. In order to work with fills effectively under Corel Draw, it's important to understand how they depend on the manner in which the screens are set up.

Note that in the following discussions, the word *dot* will be used to refer to one laser printer dot, that is, a black square 1/300th of an inch across for a typical laser. The word *spot* will be used to refer to an individual element of a screen. A spot may be larger than a single dot on your laser printer or a single pixel on your monitor. A spot may also be smaller than either of these.

### Screen Frequencies and Densities

Neither printing presses nor laser printers are perfect devices. Both have problems resolving fine details. This is true whether the details in question are fine lines or the tiny spots of a screened area.

When using an actual printing press, you will not be able to print details which are smaller than a certain size, because the ink will be too thick to flow into tiny areas of the plate. When using a laser printer, you will not be able to print details smaller than one dot. In practical terms, you won't be able to print even a one-dot detail unless the detail in question lies right where the printer prints its dots.

In dealing with computer images, there are two related factors that can be affected by the resolution of the output device. The first is the screen frequency, that is, the number of spots per inch in the screened area. The second is the screen density, that is, the percentage of black, determined by both the size and the shape of the spots. Depending on the type of printer you will be using, Corel Draw lets you control some or all of these variables.

Figure 4.2 illustrates a number of screened areas having different screen frequencies and densities. This figure may look a bit different than it did when it was first created due to the screen characteristics of the press which printed this book; however, you will notice that as the screens get finer they also begin to get more irregular.

Note also that the finer screens look darker than the coarser ones of the same density.

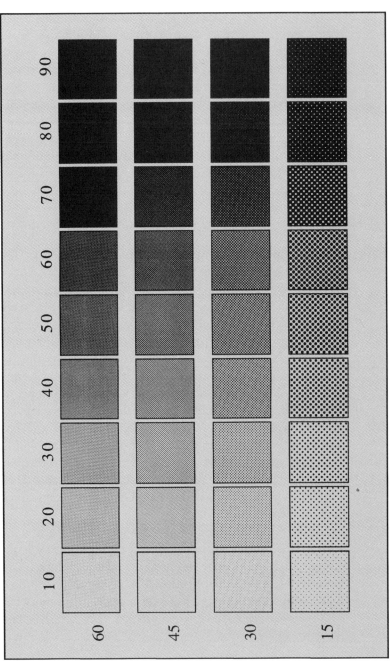

*Figure 4.2*: Different screen frequencies (up and down) and densities (across).

When the number of spots per inch of a screen approaches the number of dots per inch of the output device, aberrations can appear as a result of the algorithm which renders the screen spots as printer dots. The spots of the screen—which ideally are round—will begin to turn out ''pixellated''—in effect, chunky and irregular. If you attempt to print a 150-spot screen on a 300-dot-per-inch laser printer, for example, each spot of the screen will be drawn by no more than four dots of the laser. The results will certainly not be round, and they probably won't be arranged uniformly unless the screen of the image being printed just happens to ''register''—or align—perfectly with the dot pattern of the laser, not a likely occurrence.

If you're printing to a PostScript device, Corel Draw allows you to select the printer's frequency as the screen for your drawing. This usually results in the best fills, but it doesn't always. We'll discuss this in greater detail shortly.

For practical purposes, screens with more than about fifty or sixty spots per inch start to fall apart on a 300-dot-per-inch laser printer. You can improve on this if you will be using a higher resolution output device—for example, a Linotronic PostScript typesetter. However, this doesn't necessarily mean that you should. If you plan to reproduce your drawing, you need to take into account the screen capabilities of the device doing the reproducing.

Photocopiers—even good ones which have been tuned up recently—can't reproduce screens much above fifty or sixty spots per inch without starting to mangle them, so you'll probably find that you get more attractive results if you use a 45-spot-per-inch screen.

Printing presses have varying screen requirements, and you should consult the printing company you'll be using for the details of their presses. In general, though, web presses which will be printing on uncoated paper—newsprint—can't manage much better than 80-spot-per-inch screens (80-line screens in printer talk). Web presses running on coated paper can handle 120-spot-per-inch screens. Sheet-fed presses running on coated paper can typically deal with 144-spot-per-inch screens, and some of the really high-end ones can do even better than this.

If you can't afford to pay for a trial-and-error approach to getting your screens right, or if you aren't sure that you might not want to reproduce your images later, choose a screen frequency which is coarser than it has to be. For one thing, coarse screens don't necessarily look bad. Furthermore, as you saw in Figure 4.2, screens which are too fine can look muddy and unattractive.

## *SELECTING SCREENS*

Corel Draw is flexible in how it allows you to specify the frequencies of the screens used for fills. At least, it is if you're using a PostScript printer. LaserJet-compatible printers have only a single resolution as far as Corel Draw is concerned, and it outputs all screens to LaserJet compatibles at what its designers have considered to be an optimized resolution. In fact, Corel Draw handles LaserJet compatibles as well as any other drawing package available, and one would be hard pressed to find ways to improve on the arrangement.

PostScript printers offer dozens of screening options under Corel Draw. Like much of Corel Draw, these things default to sensible values if you ignore them, and you can use the fills under Corel Draw without touching any of these items. Once you've mastered the basic fill characteristics, however, you will want to use these controls to fine-tune the characteristics of your screen patterns.

Figure 4.3 illustrates the Corel Draw printing dialog box from the File menu. Normally, this will print to a PostScript printer with the default screen frequency for the printer in question. This means, for example, that you'll get a denser screen if your drawing is output to a Linotronic PostScript typesetter than you will if it's printed to a LaserWriter. However, for the most part it means that you'll never get wildly inappropriate screens no matter what you print your drawing on.

You can enter a different screen frequency by choosing Custom in the Default Screen Frequency box within the printing dialog box. The default screen frequency for your current output device will appear in the edit field first, allowing you to change it if you want to. This is usually 60 for a 300-dot-per-inch PostScript laser. If you do change the value, it's up to you to make sure you choose a frequency suitable for your output device. Corel Draw will not complain if you attempt to print your drawing with a 1500-spot-per-inch screen, for example—it'll just output a dreadful picture.

Note that the Default Screen Frequency control in the printing dialog box pertains only to objects which you have not explicitly filled with other sorts of screens in the course of creating your drawing.

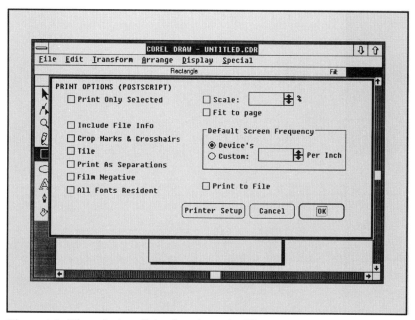

*Figure 4.3:* The printing dialog box from the File menu.

A PostScript printer allows you to control additional screen characteristics for individual objects in a drawing. In order to do this, however, you must find your way through a few dialog boxes and controls. First, you must select an object suitable for filling. Then select the fill tool, and click on the paintbucket icon to call up the precise-adjustment box for the fill tool. You should see the dialog box illustrated in Figure 4.4.

Ignoring the items concerning method, color, and tint—all of which will be discussed later in this book—click on the PostScript button. This will call up the PostScript Halftone Screen dialog box (shown in Figure 4.5), which allows you to choose a number of other interesting characteristics, including

- the frequency of the screen;
- the angle of the screen, that is, the angle at which the lines between the spots run; and
- the "type," or shape, of the spots.

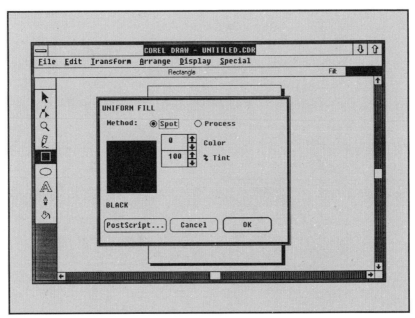

*Figure 4.4:* The precise-adjustment dialog box of the fill tool.

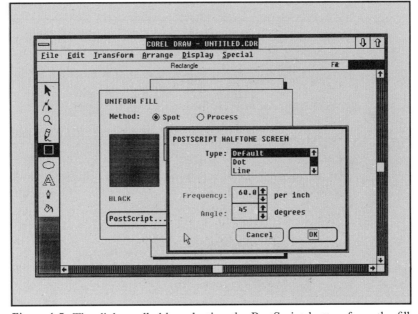

*Figure 4.5:* The dialog called by selecting the PostScript button from the fill tool's precise adjustment box.

The shape of the spots in a screen is a matter of considerable controversy in some circles. Round spots display aberrational characteristics at certain densities, something we'll touch on in a moment. Oblong spots are better; however, for special effects all sorts of shapes are possible. For example, you can create a fill out of lines or geometric figures. The selector window in the PostScript Halftone Screen dialog enables you to choose dot shapes other than the default shape for your printer.

Figure 4.6 illustrates some of the possible effects of varying the PostScript fill characteristics. You should plan to spend a while experimenting with these facilities to fully appreciate what they can do.

If you change any of the default values in the PostScript Halftone Screen dialog, the settings you choose will pertain only to the object you've selected at the moment. These will override whatever default screen frequency you select for the drawing as a whole when you're printing; so your drawing can contain some objects with the global

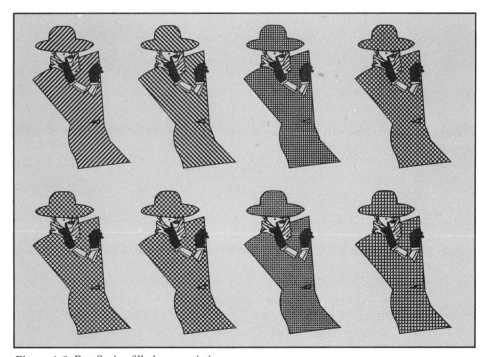

*Figure 4.6:* PostScript fill characteristics.

defaults you select when you go to print and some with the specific fill characteristics you specified earlier with the fill tool.

Note that the Corel Draw preview window will not show you the results of any changes you make in the PostScript Halftone Screen dialog. You'll have to print your drawing to see what effect they've had.

You should also know that Corel Draw allows for a second set of considerably more radical PostScript fill effects: its "textures." We'll be discussing these shortly.

## *UNDERSTANDING GRAY FAILURE AND SPOT PROBLEMS*

If you were to fill a rectangle with a varying gray level which went from 0 percent at one end to 100 percent at the other—which you can do with Corel Draw, though we haven't discussed it yet—you might expect that the result would show a uniformly varying gray field. However, this is one of those cases where the result would probably not live up to your expectation.

There are a number of factors which can cause the actual percentage of black in a fill emerging from your printer to differ from the specified percentage of black which was sent to the printer. The most commonly encountered one is called *spot failure*.

At the extreme ends of the scale—when the percentage of black approaches either zero or one hundred—your printer will find itself increasingly confronted with spots which are too small to print accurately. In the case of, say, a 2 percent gray screen, the spots of the screen may well be smaller than one dot of the laser. This will usually result in the printer simply filling the object in question with pure white.

Likewise, at almost 100 percent black, the white areas between the black areas can get smaller than one printer dot, with the result that the printer will probably fill the entire area with pure black.

Another type of spot failure occurs when the spot size is not significantly larger than the dot size. In this case, the printer will have difficulty in accurately forming some or all of the spots which make up a screened area. This can manifest itself in several sorts of visual effects, depending on how the errors work out. For example, in Figure 4.7, the configuration of dots (shown as squares) used to represent a regular pattern of spots (shown as circles) will exhibit two

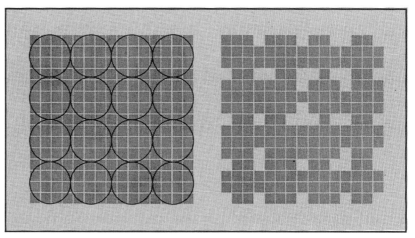

*Figure 4.7:* Screen spot errors.

problems: misrepresentation and interference. The right-hand part of the illustration shows which dots would show as black. None of the arrangements of the dots are very good representations of circular spots—for one thing, the representations are not symmetrical. Furthermore, because each spot aligns differently with the matrix of printer dots, each spot is represented by a different configuration. In a regular pattern, such as a gray fill, this variation in spots will lead to *interference patterns,* as the amount of black or white separating adjacent spots varies across the pattern. An interference pattern, also called a ''moiré effect,'' will look like light or dark patches or lines within a screened area.

On a 300-dot-per-inch printer, gray levels of more than 50 percent usually print darker than you might expect. This is because the printer usually errs toward using another printer dot rather than no dot to represent a partial dot along the edge of a screen spot. Higher resolution output devices, which can more accurately represent screen spots, suffer considerably less from this problem. This can create difficulties if you are using the output from one printer to give you an idea of how your final output will look on another printer. Screens printed on a 300-dot-per-inch laser printer will frequently look noticeably darker than the same screens printed on a Linotronic PostScript typesetter, for example.

The problem of comparability from printer to printer becomes more noticeable for screens which have more spots per inch. If you anticipate outputting your Corel Draw art to a higher resolution output device and your drawings call for accurate gray levels, you might want to reduce the screen frequency a bit.

A second facet of this problem involves what is called *dot gain*. A laser printer is effectively a photocopier; that is, it works by a process called xerography. As you may have noticed if you've used a photocopier a lot, black areas on photocopies tend to come out a bit bigger than those of the originals. This is due to the way xerography works and because the particles of toner on a photocopier's drum tend to spread slightly. The problem is shared by laser printers. The extent of the problem varies among different laser printer designs, and it's affected by things like the current humidity and the state of one's toner cartridge.

Dot gain doesn't affect type and lines noticeably, but it does affect the apparent density of screens. It is much less of a problem if your drawing uses relatively coarse screens. Many 300-dot-per-inch laser printers, however, can't print much more than 90 percent gray screens without having them fill in due to dot gain and come up as pure black. Purely photographic processes, such as the raster image processor of a high-end PostScript typesetter, do not suffer from this problem.

A final potential problem is that of *optical jump*. This isn't much of a concern on 300-dot laser printers, as it's caused by the interaction of very accurate screen spot shapes. It does crop up quite noticeably when you output certain sorts of Corel Draw drawings to a PostScript typesetter.

Optical jump is a change in the apparent gray level of a screened area due to the effect of screen spots which touch. For a screen which uses square spots in a checkerboard pattern, at densities of less than 50 percent the spots would all be isolated from one another. At more than 50 percent the spots would overlap, and the screen would effectively consist of a black area with white spots. At 50 percent, however, the corners of the spots would just touch, and the effect visually would be a screen which looked darker than 50 percent gray.

Corel Draw defaults to using round spots for its screens. This spot shape exhibits an optical jump at 25 percent gray. If you're sufficiently interested, you will discover that all spot shapes have optical jump problems at one density or other. Spot shapes which are oblong—elliptical spots, for example—exhibit two optical jumps.

None of the screen problems we've just discussed are crippling, especially if you're aware of them and keep them in mind when you're using Corel Draw. Many of them will only trouble you if you're planning to develop your artwork on a 300-dot-per-inch laser and then use a Post-Script typesetter for final output. Even then, a bit of experimentation and some common sense will help you work around them.

Here are a few useful rules of thumb which will help you avoid screen problems.

- Experiment with your laser printer to determine the minimum and maximum gray levels it can really reproduce.

- Avoid particularly high screen frequencies, especially for extreme gray levels.

- Avoid extreme gray levels when you're planning to send your output to a higher resolution PostScript printer, such as a Linotronic PostScript typesetter.

- Avoid filling adjacent objects with screens of similar density if you want them to be perceived as being distinct.

- If your applications call for predictable and repeatable gray screens, keep your laser well maintained and in an environmentally controlled area.

## USING COLOR FILLS

Color is treated in essentially the same way as gray fills under Corel Draw. However, Corel Draw provides some additional controls when you're using color fills to help you work with color in a convenient way.

If you have a color printer which is capable of handling fairly precise color specifications, such as a color PostScript printer or a Hewlett-Packard PaintJet, you will be able to output color Corel Draw artwork directly to it and see what your pictures look like. However, it's often more useful to be able to produce color artwork in a form that print houses like to use. Corel Draw will do this as well.

It's worth pointing out, before you get deeply into using color under Corel Draw, that Corel Draw's *monitor* graphics reflect the color facilities and limitations of Microsoft Windows. Windows really gives Corel Draw only 8 colors to work with, even if you have a 256-color VGA card installed in your system. Corel Draw shows color fills and objects by combining these 8 colors, using its best guess at the colors you have selected. However, the results are an approximation at best. This does not affect the final accuracy of the colors you print, of course, except insofar as you cannot see what you're dealing with before you print them.

A complete discussion of color can be found in Chapter 11. If you are unfamiliar with the details of process colors, spot (Pantone) colors, and so on, you might want to read that chapter before proceeding any further in this chapter.

## SPECIFYING COLOR FILLS

Having selected an object, you can give it a color fill under Corel Draw by popping up the precise-adjustment box of the fill tool. The color defaults to black (color #0), the density (% Tint) to 100 percent, and the color specification system (Method) to spot color. All of these things can be changed.

If you click on the arrows to change the value in the Color control, Pantone numbers will flash by and the swatch in the color sample window will change to approximate the colors. The Pantone colors change in such a way as to move smoothly through the ranges of colors. If you will be using Pantone colors, you should consider getting a Pantone color matching book. These are available from most graphics supply houses. They aren't cheap, but they're pretty much essential for accurate color matching.

You can type in a Pantone color number if you know what you're after. If you type in a number which does not represent a Pantone color, Corel Draw will tell you so.

If you select process colors rather than spot colors, the controls will change, allowing you to specify your fill color as percentages of cyan, magenta, yellow, and black ink.

Having specified a particular color, you can also specify a screen density for your fill. For example, if you mix up a medium blue ink—

whether as a Pantone color or from process colors—you can tell Corel Draw to fill your drawing with a 50 percent screen of it by adjusting the Tint control, just as you would for a gray fill.

You should think about what colors look like when they're screened. In effect, if you fill an object with a color screen, you will be mixing white with your specified color. For example, if you fill an area with a 30 percent screen of red ink (made up of 100 percent magenta and 100 percent yellow), the result will be pink, and not even a particularly attractive shade of it. Likewise, a lot of shades of blue that look forceful and interesting at 100 percent look like baby blue at lesser percentages.

A lot of fairly weird—and usually undesirable—effects can be achieved by printing process color fills at very coarse screen settings. If you use a 20-line screen, for example—an interesting technique in black-and-white—the result will probably be a lot of colored smudges with bits of process colors peeking out around them.

## USING COLORS AS LAYERS

There are other applications for the color facilities of Corel Draw. One of them is in handling complex drawings as layers. For example, plans often call for a lot of information to be overlaid onto a single drawing. If you draw each related group of information in a different color, Corel Draw will allow you to output each color as a separate layer simply by having it output a separation for each spot color. If you output the layers onto film rather than onto paper, you can stack them up to see the whole drawing or peel them apart to see one component of it.

In a mechanical drawing for a building, for example, you might want to represent the building's structural elements, electrical system, air-conditioning system, heating system, telephone system, computer data system, and so on. Drawn together, this would be an enormously complex—and largely unreadable—plan. Drawn in layers, however, it can be output one layer to a page, as needed.

To make this work, just select a different Pantone number for each layer. If you envision the whole works ultimately being output as separate color overlays you'll want to choose suitably contrasting colors. Otherwise, the colors won't matter. Corel Draw will output all Pantone colors as black for later use in the color process if you have it print separations for you.

If your applications for Corel Draw involve your doing a lot of this sort of work, you can have the program keep track of the names of the different layers for you. All the information about Pantone colors is kept in a text file called COLORS.SYS in the CORELDRW subdirectory of your hard drive. The following are a few lines from this file.

```
  9    8    13     2    MCOZ Black
547    9    49    81    OFYT
282   10    12    68    OSZN
668   10   113    96    NOZO 3285
  6   12     0   135    OSZA Reflex Blue
```

The first column is the Pantone number for the color in question. The rightmost column is for the color's name, if it has one. You can enter a name or modify an existing name using a text editor such as WordStar in its non-document mode to make it more useful. For example, you could change the second line in the preceding list to read

```
547    9    49    81    OFYT Electrical System
```

When you go to print your drawing as separations, the legends of these named colors will be displayed in the Color Separations dialog box from the Print dialog, allowing you to select the layers you want printed. Furthermore, if you are printing your separations with crop marks and file information—a procedure to be discussed momentarily—the legends will be printed in the margins, allowing you to identify them easily.

Adding names to previously unnamed colors in COLORS.SYS will in no way affect the normal use of spot colors under Corel Draw.

### Using Crop Marks

If you create color artwork to be sent to a printer—even if the color is only a single spot-color overlay—you can assist the printer and eliminate some potential errors by printing crop marks, alignment marks, and color information on your artwork. The printing dialog from the File menu enables you to implement these options. Figure 4.8 illustrates a drawing with its crop marks and other information included.

*Figure 4.8:* A drawing showing crop and alignment marks. This is the yellow plate of a four-color drawing.

The only drawback in doing this is that the crop marks for an 8½-by-11-inch page will print beyond the edges of the page. You must either use the Page Setup dialog box to choose a smaller paper size or arrange to output your drawing on a larger laser printer.

## USING FOUNTAIN FILLS

Any object which can be filled with a solid gray or colored fill can also be filled with a fountain. A fountain is a fill which changes its gray level or its color. Figure 4.9 illustrates the two types of fountains which Corel Draw allows for, these being linear and radial fountains.

*Figure 4.9:* Some fountains.

You can fill any object with either kind of fountain—an object need not be circular to be filled with a radial fountain. If you fill an irregular object with a fountain, the fill will be "clipped" to the object, just as with a solid gray or colored fill.

You can select a fountain fill from the fill tool's flyout menu by choosing the second-to-the-rightmost item. The Fountain Fill dialog box will then appear. This allows you to select the minimum and maximum gray level or the two extremes of the color range which the fountain will span. The color specifications can be handled using either spot or process colors, as with normal fills.

The Fill Angle pertains to linear fills. It determines the direction the fill will travel.

When you're selecting the extremes of a gray fill, bear in mind the foregoing discussion about extreme gray levels. Fountains do not look terribly attractive if their dark areas block up and their light areas vanish. In most cases, a fountain ranging from 10 to 90 percent black will look much nicer than one ranging from 0 to 100 percent black.

In creating a fountain which *changes* color, keep in mind how you plan to print your drawing. If you'll be creating four-color separations or printing directly to a color printer you can pretty well do as you like. On the other hand, if you plan to create spot-color separations, make sure that your fountain uses only one color, and change the *tint* level of it over the course of the fountain.

The Fountain Fill dialog box also allows you to specify the Post-Script fill parameters I discussed earlier in conjunction with normal fills. Fountains which use alternate spot shapes and such can be quite striking, and offer considerable opportunity for experimentation.

Fountains under Corel Draw are actually handled as a series of stripes or concentric rings. The number of stripes can be changed only globally, using the Preferences item of the Special menu. Thus, you cannot vary this value for separate objects—the value you set when you print your drawing will pertain to all the fountains in it.

The number of stripes you select will be a trade-off, and will require some experimentation to get the optimum results from your printer. If you choose a number which is too small, your fountains will print with discernible stripes rather than an apparently smooth transition between gray levels. However, the effect of having a small number of stripes is less noticeable if you print your fountains with fairly coarse screens. The trade-off is that if you err on the side of precision and choose a number which is too high, you'll find that your fountains take ages to print.

## *MOVING THE CENTER OF A RADIAL FOUNTAIN*

If you fill an object with a radial fountain, the center of the fountain will coincide with the center of the object. In order to produce the illusion of lifelike shading, you might want the center of the fountain to appear somewhere else in relation to the object. You can do this by combining the object with another object, in effect relocating the center. The preview window will be very useful here in helping you to see what you're doing with this procedure.

Let's start with a shaded circle. Figure 4.10 illustrates the procedure. (Note that you can do this with any object filled with a radial fountain.)

1. Draw a circle using the ellipse tool.

2. Fill the circle with a radial fountain using the fill tool.

3. Draw a short line somewhere below and to the right of the circle, using the line tool. By moving this line, you will be able to change the area taken up by the combined circle-and-line object, and the center of this combined object will change accordingly.

4. Give the line no color with the pen tool. This will hide the line while still allowing it to affect the location of the fill's center. You might want to set the line characteristics of the circle now as well.

5. Select both objects and combine them.

6. Use the preview window to view the results. You might want to break the two objects apart temporarily and move the line segment around to change the characteristics of the fountain in the circle.

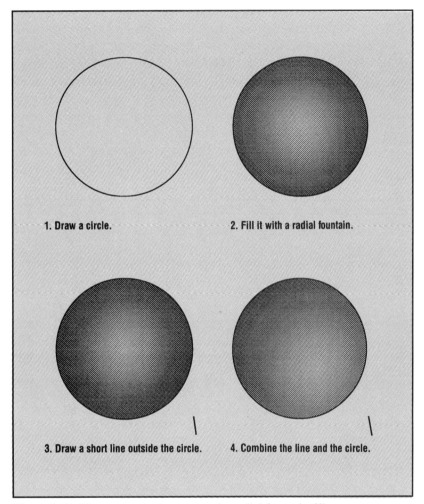

*Figure 4.10:* How to move the center of a radial fountain fill.

## WHAT TO DO WHEN YOU OVERDO IT WITH FOUNTAINS

As was discussed earlier in this book, fountain fills can make just about any object look more lifelike because they imitate the way in which our eyes see variations in light intensity. The only potential problem with fountains is in the way Corel Draw goes to print them on a PostScript printer: A fountain is actually drawn one spot at a time, with each spot handled as a PostScript path. As was mentioned earlier in this book, it's possible to create drawings which are too complex to print on a PostScript printer just by using a lot of fountain fills.

There is no easy way to tell when you've exceeded the bounds of good taste and available PostScript paths merely by looking at the Corel Draw work space. If nothing comes out of your printer when you have a lot of fountain fills, however, you should suspect them as the cause of it.

It's often possible to simplify your drawing a bit when this happens. If you use the PostScript Halftone Fills dialog from the Fountain Fill dialog box to select a coarser screen, the fountain will require fewer paths to print. Or, if you're filling text with a fountain, selecting a less ornate typeface might do it. Often, selecting normal weight type rather than bold type will reduce the path count sufficiently. Finally, since the problem is in the absolute number of paths, reducing the size of the filled area—such as by scaling your drawing down—will often let you print an otherwise reluctant picture.

Fountains take a long time to print to a PostScript printer because they make the printer do a lot of calculations. The time is proportional to the amount of area the fountain fills. All other things being equal, a 24-point character filled with a fountain will take four times as long as a 12-point character.

If you're working on a drawing with fountain fills, consider printing your intermediate versions scaled down to save time.

## USING POSTSCRIPT TEXTURES

Aside from the PostScript screen characteristics we've discussed thus far, there's a whole set of very elaborate PostScript fill patterns, or textures, available through the rightmost item—the PS—in the fill tool's flyout menu. While not without their limitations, these patterns can add some breathtaking effects to your drawings.

You will want to consult Appendix A of the Corel Draw manual for a complete list of the PostScript fills and some examples of the parameters used with them.

The PostScript fills are, as you might have expected, available only if you output your drawing to a PostScript printer. What you might not have expected is that they will not appear in the preview window. Any object filled with a PostScript pattern will show up in the preview with the letters ''PS'' pasted across it.

Each of the PostScript fills is actually a complex PostScript program. The text of these programs resides in a disk file called USERPROC.TXT in the CORELDRW subdirectory. The programs have a number of variables associated with them which you can set from within Corel Draw using the PS item of the fill tool's flyout menu.

There are a number of potential problems associated with the PostScript textures. For one thing, they are very complex programs, often creating large numbers of paths. As with the fountain fills—in fact, quite a bit more so—it's easy using the PostScript textures to create a graphic which is too complex for your printer to handle.

Even if you don't exceed this limit, you'll find that objects filled with PostScript textures take ages to print. Figure 4.11 illustrates a few of the many PostScript fills available. It took about seven minutes to print, on a fairly fast laser.

In using the PostScript textures there are a few things you should be aware of. First of all, the time and memory a pattern requires increases geometrically with the size of the area you fill with it. A two-inch-square object will contain four times as many paths as a one-inch-square object. Small objects are less likely to exceed the limits of your printer. Secondly, it's not uncommon when using PostScript textures to create a drawing that prints from Corel Draw but fails to do so when you export it and use it in, say, Ventura.

Most of the PostScript textures have variable levels of complexity. They get a lot more interesting as they get more complex. However, bear in mind that complex textures contain a lot more paths. Each of the examples of the textures in the Corel Draw manual has at least four possible sets of parameters to produce four variations on the effects. Because the textures dialog box allows you to enter any value you like, you can use parameters besides the ones listed in the book. Many of the patterns are based on random numbers, and even slight changes in the parameters or in the size of the object being filled will alter the resulting pattern.

You should also understand the use of the ''random seed'' parameter used by some of the textures. Computers can't actually produce random numbers—what they do is generate ''pseudo-random'' numbers.

*Figure 4.11:* Some PostScript textures.

These numbers do have a predictable pattern, but it's so complex as to be random for any useful purpose. The structure of the pattern is dictated by a seed number, which serves as the starting place in the random sequence. If you change the seed, you'll change the nature of the random numbers and hence the appearance of a texture based on some element of randomness. Choose any value you like for the seed. In keeping with its nature, it should be chosen randomly.

In all other respects, the PostScript textures behave just like the simpler fills we've discussed in this chapter. You can use them to fill any sort of object you like, provided you bear in mind that drawings created this way can take forever to print, and some might not print at all. Textures which create intrinsically complex patterns—the CrystalLattice texture is my favorite—are best used to fill fairly small, simple objects.

## *WRAPPING UP*

As with much of Corel Draw, fills can be as simple or as complex as you want them to be, once you've mastered the basic skills of using the package. If you've been following the examples in the book so far, you probably picked up enough basic information to use the fill tool under Corel Draw before you even reached this chapter.

If some of the details still seem a bit beyond you, don't worry. You'll come to understand them as you work with the package.

# chapter 5

*Importing and Exporting*

**A**LL BY ITSELF, COREL DRAW IS A POWERFUL TOOL for creating drawings. However, one of its additional attributes is that of being able to create and edit files for other applications. You can use it to modify Adobe Illustrator's encapsulated PostScript files, edit an AutoCAD drawing, create graphics for Ventura Publisher and PageMaker, generate pictures for PC Paintbrush, and quite a lot more. By virtue of its exceptional import and export facilities, Corel Draw is compatible with pretty much all of the major drawing and painting programs, and with other applications which use their files.

In discussing importing and exporting, you will encounter what Corel Draw calls "filters." A filter is simply a module of Corel Draw which relates two otherwise incompatible drawing formats. If you ask Corel Draw to import a file from Adobe Illustrator, for example, Corel Draw will load the appropriate filter and run the Illustrator file through it. Filters are used both for importing and exporting files under Corel Draw.

## BITMAPS AND OBJECT-ORIENTED FILES

There are really only two sorts of picture files found on a PC. These are bitmapped pictures and object-oriented pictures. To some extent, Corel Draw will allow you to work with pictures of either type.

As you know, Corel Draw files are object-oriented. Object-oriented files are generated by quite a few other PC applications, including AutoCAD, GEM Artline, Adobe Illustrator, and several Windows-based applications, such as Micrographix Designer, which can create Windows Metafiles and others.

Bitmapped images, or "paint" files, are pictures which are defined as a matrix of pixels. These are the sorts of images one associates with PC Paintbrush and with image scanners. Photographs which have been "digitized" are created in one of several bitmapped formats. Some things can be represented a lot better by bitmaps than by object-oriented art. Bitmaps can make photographic art look photographic even after your computer gets hold of it. Because it is a bitmap, however, it cannot be manipulated in the same ways as an object-oriented drawing. For example, if you attempt to rescale a bitmapped drawing you've imported, the result, while certainly scaled to fit the space you've requested, will not look very good. Bitmapped pictures simply don't scale well.

Corel Draw will allow you to import both object-oriented and bitmap files into a drawing, but it will deal with them differently. The object-oriented formats will be converted into Corel Draw's internal notation, and once such a file has been imported it will behave just like a normal Corel Draw drawing. You will be able to manipulate it as if you'd drawn it in Corel Draw yourself.

Bitmapped images can be imported as well, but only for two specific purposes. The first is to include a bitmap in a Corel Draw drawing. Bitmaps so imported can be resized (though not well), cropped, and placed on a page. However, Corel Draw does not allow you any facilities for editing them. If you'll be using PCX files, the native file format of PC Paintbrush from Z-Soft, you may well want to have the Windows version of PC Paintbrush running concurrently with Corel Draw in order to edit your bitmaps.

The other use of bitmapped art under Corel Draw is for tracing, the topic of the next chapter.

## *IMPORTING*

You will probably want to try the importing features of Corel Draw first. They give you access to much of the huge body of clip art which comes with Corel Draw, most of which has been saved in formats other than the native CDR files of Corel Draw. They also give you access to all sorts of other picture files from numerous other applications.

Recent upgrades in Corel Draw have enabled the package to import and export additional formats. If you discover that some of the formats discussed here don't appear in the import and export dialogs of your copy of Corel Draw, you might want to contact Corel Draw for an upgrade.

Many of the import and export filters which come with Corel Draw are somewhat memory hungry. If you happen to be printing something from Corel Draw such that the print spooler is active (see the discussion of this in Appendix A), many of the import and export facilities will not have enough memory to run, and will not appear in their respective dialogs. This isn't a permanent problem—they'll be available again as soon as the spooler completes its tasks.

The following are the most useful formats Corel Draw can import.

- *CDR.* Corel Draw will import its own files, something you might have reason to do from time to time.

- *DXF.* This is one of the object-oriented formats which Auto-CAD uses for its drawings. This filter was not available in early releases of Corel Draw.

- *EPS (Encapsulated PostScript).* This is an object-oriented format used by Adobe's applications, such as Illustrator. PostScript is also the language which drives PostScript laser printers.

- *GEM.* This is the object-oriented drawing format exported by several applications which run under GEM from Digital Research. More importantly, however, it's the native drawing import format for Ventura Publisher. Do not confuse this format with the GEM/IMG bitmap format, which Corel Draw does *not* import. This filter was not available in early releases of Corel Draw.

- *Lotus PIC.* This is the drawing format which the Lotus 1-2-3 spreadsheet package exports for its graphs. Corel Draw allows you to import Lotus graphs and smarten them up.

- *PCX.* This is the bitmapped-image file format of PC Paintbrush, from Z-Soft. It can also be created by the Delux Paint package from Electronic Arts, and by numerous specialized applications. Corel Draw does *not* read the 256-color PCX format generated by PC Paintbrush IV.

- *TIFF.* This is a bitmapped-image file format used by many scanners. The TIFF format is a bit complex, and it's not safe to assume that Corel Draw will read absolutely every TIFF file. It will read gray-scale TIFF files, however.

Figure 5.1 illustrates some files which Corel Draw has imported from other applications.

All importing is handled through the Import item of the File menu. When you select it, you will see the dialog box in Figure 5.2. Select the type of file you want to import and click on OK.

If you select one of the bitmapped formats, such as PCX or TIFF, the For Tracing option will become active. Leave this alone for the time being—it will be discussed in the next chapter.

*Figure 5.1:* Some imported files.

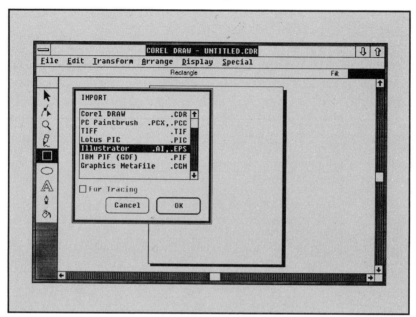

*Figure 5.2:* The Import dialog box from the File menu.

## IMPORTING BITMAPPED IMAGES

When you're importing bitmapped pictures, keep in mind how Corel Draw treats them. As we'll see in a moment, Corel Draw initially imports bitmaps with a whole-number relationship between the pixels and output dots, but you can change this by resizing the picture. It's not a good idea to do so casually. Bitmaps print best when they're sized such that each pixel of the bitmap corresponds to one dot of the printer. The next best output is available when each pixel of the bitmap corresponds to two pixels, or some other integral number.

Many PCX files are in color. The colors will not appear on your screen, however. As it imports a PCX file, Corel Draw converts it to black and white. Any pixel which was black in the original image stays that way. Any pixel which was any other color becomes white. This process can lose an enormous amount of detail in a bitmapped image. For this reason, you should try to work with monochrome PCX files whenever you can. Corel Draw will import PCX files with up to 16 colors.

Note that when you import a bitmapped image, Corel Draw shows you a vastly scaled down version of it on your screen. Your output will not look anywhere near this dreadful.

## IMPORTING OBJECT-ORIENTED IMAGES

Things are a lot less troublesome when one is importing object-oriented formats into Corel Draw. Some formats, such as GEM, have a pretty well one-to-one correspondence between what they can represent and what Corel Draw can handle. Importing them should result in no difficulties.

Importing EPS, or encapsulated PostScript, files can be frustrating under Corel Draw, depending on where the EPS files originally came from. PostScript is an extremely complex language—in order to import a PostScript file, Corel Draw must use the equivalent of a laser printer PostScript interpreter as part of its operational code. Having gone to these lengths, Corel Draw expects EPS files to be well behaved, in computer terms.

Corel Draw will import EPS files from Adobe Illustrator without complaint. Other applications which generate EPS files might not be quite so well received by Corel Draw. For example, Corel Draw can import EPS files, and export EPS files, but it can't reimport its own exported EPS files.

One important thing to note about importing a foreign file, as opposed to opening a Corel Draw drawing, is that whatever is currently in your work space when you do so will not be erased. You can add as many imported drawings to your work space as you like, subject to the bounds of available memory.

This is why Corel Draw allows you to import its own files, by the way. You can, for example, work separately on different sections of a large drawing and later import them into a new work space to assemble them into the complete picture.

## SOME IMPORTING CONSIDERATIONS

Despite the substantial range of foreign files Corel Draw deals with, it rarely complains or mangles a drawing unless you deliberately try to feed it something it doesn't like.

It's not difficult to overuse Corel Draw's import facilities, however. If you attempt to import several fairly complex files into your work space at one time, the resulting drawing may be so complex as to slow Corel Draw down when it goes to redraw its screen. A two-minute wait every time you want to change magnifications will probably put you off the idea of handling enormous pictures, even if Corel Draw is prepared to work with them. Large compressed TIFF files and complex GEM files are among the formats which tend to bog Corel Draw down noticeably.

You can import color bitmapped pictures into Corel Draw by first converting them to gray-scaled TIFF files. Programs such as The Graphics Link Plus by TerraVision will convert most color bitmapped images to TIFF files. The results, when printed to a PostScript printer, are photographic looking black-and-white halftones. Figure 5.3 illustrates a halftone of this sort incorporated into a Corel Draw drawing.

*Figure 5.3:* An imported gray-scale bitmap and some objects.

Imported bitmaps can be treated like any other objects as far as Corel Draw is concerned. You can resize them, rotate them, skew them, and so on. However, the results often turn out to be unattractive. Unlike drawn objects, bitmaps are not "cleaned up" by Corel Draw after a transformation. If you resize a bitmapped object, for example, the results may look crunchy and unattractive. Rotating one by something other than an even multiple of 90 degrees may also introduce some aberrations into the picture. This is one of those cases, then, in which Corel Draw allows you to perform an operation which you might do well to avoid.

If you transform a bitmap in some way other than simply resizing it, the rough screen representation of the bitmap which Corel Draw normally shows you will vanish, to be replaced by a gray rectangle with one corner missing. Transformed bitmaps can be printed on PostScript printers only.

Imported bitmapped images require a long time to print, and take up lots of memory as well. Both of these concerns grow with the size of your bitmapped objects. If you can keep them small, the performance of Corel Draw will be improved.

We've discussed the relationship of the pixels in a bitmap to the dots in your printed output. If you can arrange to keep your imported bitmapped images at the same size they'll be printed, you'll get the nicest looking output. Should you want to scale them up or down, use the Transform menu rather than freehand scaling, and expand them by an integral amount. Expanding by 200 percent will mangle your picture a lot less than expanding by, say, 187 percent.

## EXPORTING

You can export Corel Draw drawings in different formats as object-oriented drawing files or as bitmapped-image files. In the former case, the resulting drawing will be as scalable as the original Corel Draw drawing was. If you export an object-oriented file such as a Windows Metafile or a GEM file from Corel Draw and import it into Ventura Publisher, for example, the resulting picture will have all the attributes of line art under Ventura, including the ability to resize it without distortion.

If you output a bitmapped file, that is, a PCX or TIFF file, the resulting image will have a fixed resolution. However, you'll be able to use it in applications which require image rather than drawing files. For example, you could output a Corel Draw drawing as a bitmap and then use the resulting PCX file in PC Paintbrush. Exporting a PCX file from Corel Draw is also a quick way to generate graphics for inclusion in FAX documents if you have a FAX board in your computer.

You can export all or part of a drawing by means of the Export item from the File menu. Selecting this will pop up the dialog box shown in Figure 5.4.

The less-than-obvious controls in this box will be explained as we get to the various file formats they pertain to. The important one is the file-type window in the upper left corner.

Note the option called Selected Object(s) Only. If you choose this feature, only those objects of your drawing which were selected when you opened the Export dialog box will be exported. This allows you to export part of a drawing without having to delete the parts of it you don't want to include.

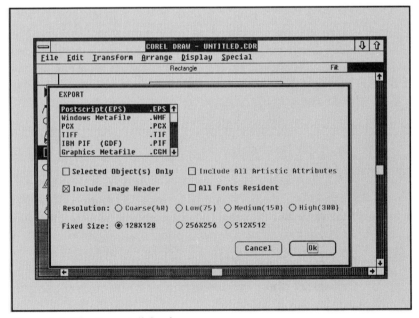

*Figure 5.4:* The Export dialog box.

Exporting is a bit more complicated than importing, because you have to take into account the applications you'll be using your exported files with, something Corel Draw can't really do by itself.

Let's look at some common applications of exporting Corel Draw drawings.

## *PCX AND TIFF FILES*

You can export a bitmapped version of your drawing as a PCX or TIFF file. In creating a bitmap, Corel Draw does essentially what your printer would do when it generates the huge bitmap which represents your final output. It chooses a fixed size for all the objects in your drawing and renders them in memory, doing whatever fills and so on as specified. It then writes the whole works to a file rather than to your printer.

The features in the Export dialog box which concern outputting a bitmapped version of a Corel Draw drawing are the Resolution options. These allow you to decide how many dots per inch your PCX or TIFF file will use. Neither of these formats has any inherent limitations on how big a picture you create, so you can select whichever resolution is appropriate so long as you have the disk space to accommodate the resulting file.

At the low end of the resolution scale, 40-dot resolution will leave you with a PCX or TIFF file containing something like the screen images Corel Draw shows you in its work space for imported bitmapped files. This is usually too ugly to contemplate. The 75-dot resolution is roughly equivalent to the resolution of a monitor. If you select 300-dot resolution, you'll get an image file with as much detail as you'd get from a typical laser printer. The results of these different resolutions are illustrated in Figure 5.5. Keep in mind that if you export a full Corel Draw page with 300-dot resolution, you could wind up with a PCX or TIFF file which occupies up to a megabyte of disk space.

Most of the programs which import PCX files, such as PC Paintbrush, have some limitations as to how big a file they'll work with. Consider this before you select the 300-dot option.

As with many other things under Corel Draw, doubling the resolution you select will quadruple the effect, in this case the size of the file you export in one of the bitmapped formats.

*Figure 5.5:* The results of using various Resolution options.

PCX files exported from Corel Draw will always be monochrome. Colored areas in the original drawing will be filled with gray screens.

Many desktop publishing packages, such as Ventura and Page-Maker, allow you to import either PCX or TIFF files or several object-oriented formats. Given the choice, you should always export an object-oriented file from Corel Draw rather than a bitmap if the destination of your export will accept both.

The size of your exported PCX or TIFF file will usually be determined by the amount of the Corel Draw work space your drawing takes up. However, you can use any of the Fixed Size options in the Export dialog box to force the picture to reside within defined dimensions. This will leave you with a pretty crude picture, but it's usually good enough if you want a small image which won't actually be used for reproduction.

## EPS OR ENCAPSULATED POSTSCRIPT FILES

If you know that your exported file will ultimately be printed to a PostScript printer, the encapsulated PostScript format isn't a bad choice. It offers the least opportunity for aspects of your drawing to be lost or mangled in the conversion between file formats.

If you wanted to export a Corel Draw drawing for use in a Ventura Publisher document, for example, you might consider doing it as a GEM file. However, Ventura would then have to convert it to an internal PostScript program for printing. On the other hand, if you were to output your drawing directly as an EPS file, Ventura would not have to do any conversion. In fact, it would not even really look at your EPS file beyond simply reading it in and shipping it directly to the printer.

Encapsulated PostScript files do have a few possible drawbacks, however. To begin with, they're big—much more so than any of the other object-oriented formats. They're also potentially troublesome. Unlike Corel Draw, most applications which use EPS files can't actually interpret them. Instead, they read a short header at the beginning of the file which tells them about the size and general nature of the drawing they're about to use. Everything else is dealt with using a great deal of faith. (Note that versions of Ventura Publisher prior to 2.0 are unable to display an EPS header even if one is present.)

Because an application like Ventura Publisher cannot interpret a PostScript file, it can't show you what an exported Corel Draw EPS file contains when you include one in a Ventura document—at least, not directly. In order to get around this, EPS files can include a ''preview,'' a small bitmapped image tacked onto the end of the file which applications such as Ventura can display. Ideally, the preview will contain enough detail of the original image to allow the EPS file to be positioned and cropped. In fact, because of the limited resolution of an EPS preview, the relationship between what you see and what you get isn't always terribly good. Accurate positioning of an EPS file is difficult in some cases.

If you are exporting EPS files to be used with a Macintosh system, you should export plain EPS files with no previews, because the preview structure differs between PC and Macintosh architectures, even though the file format itself does not.

Finally, PostScript is a bit temperamental and version-dependent. Corel Draw's exported files assume a fairly recent version. If you print your exported drawing on a really old LaserWriter, for example, odd things may happen: certain objects might not print, lines might not appear where you expect them, or fills might not do what you planned. The PostScript language, like most things having to do with computers, has grown and evolved somewhat since its inception.

As long as you appreciate the potential catches in using EPS files, they're a good way to export Corel Draw art for applications which will use them. They usually produce the best results with the least fuss.

### Relevant Controls for EPS Export

Several options in the Export dialog box pertain to EPS files.

*Include Image Header*   The Include Image Header option controls the generation of the preview image. You should choose this option if you plan to use your exported image in a program which does not interpret PostScript (but which will show you the preview), such as Ventura or PageMaker. You can disable it if you'll be using your exported file in Ventura 1.1, which can't read EPS previews, or if it will be going to Adobe Illustrator, which can interpret the PostScript code directly, making a preview image unnecessary.

Disabling this option when you don't need the preview will reduce the size of the EPS file somewhat.

*Fixed Size* The Fixed Size option allows you to select the resolution of the EPS preview in your exported file, assuming that you want a preview. A higher resolution Fixed Size image will make your EPS preview a bit easier to see and position. You should select one of the larger options if your drawing has details you anticipate needing to see when you import the file into its intended application.

A large, high-resolution preview image will take longer to update and work with as well as occupy more disk space. Corel Draw does not compress its preview images, so selecting a larger one will result in a substantial increase in the size of your exported EPS file.

*All Fonts Resident* The All Fonts Resident option tells Corel Draw to assume that all the fonts you've used in your drawing are available at the printer which will ultimately be printing your exported file. This means that if your drawing contains some straight, untouched text, Corel Draw would output the text as such with a request for the destination printer to supply the font, rather than drawing the text with paths as it normally does.

This option is useful if you know that the destination printer will have the fonts you want to use, particularly Adobe fonts. It allows you to take advantage of some of the more subtle aspects of Adobe fonts, such as "hinting," which we discussed in Chapter 3.

It also makes for a smaller EPS file.

If you select this option when all fonts are not in fact resident in the destination printer, the affected text will be printed in Courier type if it prints at all.

## WINDOWS METAFILE AND GEM

Windows Metafile and GEM can be interpreted by any applications which can import them. If you import a GEM file into Ventura, for example, it will draw each object on the screen just as Corel Draw will do with a CDR file. This being the case, these formats do not require a PostScript printer to output them. They're portable to any output device the application will drive.

These file formats generally give you better position control of your drawings for cropping if you're importing them into a desktop publishing program. However, there are certain drawbacks to using GEM or Windows Metafile drawings rather than encapsulated PostScript files when you know that the final output device will be a PostScript printer. A Corel Draw drawing exported as a GEM file, for example, will contain no PostScript font information. Thus, the more subtle features of Adobe fonts which might be resident on the destination printer, such as hinting, will not be accessible if you use a GEM file.

A small minority of drawings don't handle their fill characteristics as well when they're exported as GEM files, and you will occasionally find the fills bleeding out of the objects which contain them. There's no simple rule as to when this will happen or why.

There are some size limitations to both these file formats. You'll encounter them at odd times if you try to export large or complex drawings. In most cases Corel Draw will allow you to export a drawing which exceeds a file format limitation, but it will warn you that your exported picture will not contain all the objects in your original drawing.

Most Windows-based applications which can use object-oriented art will accept Windows Metafile drawings. However, the Windows Metafile format doesn't always import very well into Ventura Publisher. Since Ventura converts all its imported line art files into GEM files anyway, you can save yourself some time, disk space, and potentially unwanted extraneous lines in your drawings by exporting in the GEM format in the first place when you plan to use your drawings with Ventura Publisher.

## OTHER FORMATS

There are a number of export formats supported by the more recent versions of Corel Draw which are unique to certain applications. You may have cause to use them if your work involves exchanging applications with these programs. For instance, WordPerfect users may want to export drawings in the WPG—Word Perfect Graphics—format to allow them to be imported directly into Word Perfect without any conversion. (The WPG filter was not supplied with early releases of Corel Draw.)

If you work with AutoCAD, you might find it helpful to be able to create objects in Corel Draw for use in an AutoCAD drawing. It's unlikely that you'll want to do actual AutoCAD-type drawing in Corel Draw—Corel Draw is convenient, but it lacks many of the features that make AutoCAD, after all, a drafting and design package rather than a drawing program. However, Corel Draw can do a lot of things with progressive transformations and with text which Auto-CAD cannot. For these possibilities, Corel Draw now supports the DXF format.

You should note that when it's exporting DXF files, Corel Draw will not include any fill information that might have been present in the original drawing. The resulting AutoCAD drawing will consist solely of outlines—paths. There are several reasons for this. The most obvious one is the rather different natures of fills in Corel Draw and AutoCAD, the latter application using hatching rather than screen fills. There are also certain logistical problems in allowing Corel Draw to create fills for AutoCAD, in that Corel Draw has no way to define a situation where the pen of a plotter is lifted from the paper. Allowing it to create fills for AutoCAD would result in extraneous lines in many cases.

## *WRAPPING UP*

You'll probably find that it takes a lot longer to discuss the importing and exporting features of Corel Draw than it does to actually try them out. The best place to start importing files is in the subdirectory where you keep your Corel Draw clip art. Most of this is supplied as EPS files which are compatible with Corel Draw's EPS import filter.

Until you plan to use Corel Draw's files in other applications, you probably won't have any need to export. If you do want to export your drawings, chances are the program which will be importing them will already have defined most of the file types and other variables offered by Corel Draw.

*chapter*

**6**

*Tracing*

TRACING BITMAPPED IMAGES IS ONE OF THE RATHER magical facilities of Corel Draw. Although not without limitations, the tracing features let you import a scanned image as a PCX or TIFF file and more or less automatically draw an object-based version of it. The results are often far better than the original.

While you could trace images by hand with most drawing packages, Corel Draw will actually do the whole thing for you. All you need do is point to the things you want to trace and turn it loose. It will draw curves around the shapes in your original bitmapped picture.

Nothing this useful could really be as easy as it seems, and this is certainly true of tracing bitmaps. It takes very little time to explain how the process works, but you will need to practice to get a feel for how to make it work well.

## HOW TRACING WORKS

It's important to understand what Corel Draw does when it goes to trace a bitmapped object. First of all, it treats each pixel in question as either black or white—if you attempt to trace a gray-scale TIFF file, Corel Draw will treat it as a high-contrast black-and-white picture for the process.

When you click the tracing cursor—what the pencil cursor turns into when you've selected a bitmapped object—Corel Draw ascertains whether the cursor is resting on a black pixel or a white pixel. It then begins to work its way outward from this point until it encounters a pixel of the opposite color. When it finds one, it decides that it has located the edge of the object you want to trace, and it works its way around the periphery of it, constructing a path.

When it's looking for the edge of an area, Corel Draw always works to the right, that is, in the direction pointed to by the long arm of the tracing cursor. Figure 6.1 illustrates an area being traced.

It's generally the case in tracing complex drawings that you can start in either a white area or a black area. The resulting paths,

*Figure 6.1:* The tracing cursor at work, positioned to trace the model's left eye.

however, will be slightly different. (Note that if you start in a white area far away from any black areas, the program may fail to find the object to trace.)

Although it may look like Corel Draw traces by working its way around the actual image on your screen, the fact is that it works with the bitmapped image in memory. Thus, if the area you're tracing extends beyond the edges of the Corel Draw work space, the whole thing will still be traced. This also explains why the program is able to continue tracing even when you've hidden the bitmap.

In tracing an area, Corel Draw always creates closed paths *and fills them*. By default, it fills them with black. This can produce some unexpected results if you don't check the stroke and fill characteristics in the preview window.

## CHOOSING ORIGINALS

The most important step in successfully tracing a bitmapped image is in choosing the bitmap you want to trace. Good originals can produce excellent tracings. Poorly chosen ones—however interesting their subjects may be—will probably just frustrate you.

Figure 6.2 shows a bitmapped image and the result of a Corel Draw tracing of it. The picture on the left illustrates a type of drawing that makes for a good tracing original. It has few details, and lots of clean, sharp lines. There is no cross-hatching, and there are no occurrences of single pixels. There are a lot of round surfaces, none of which will suffer if they lose a bit of accuracy in the tracing process.

## TRACING THE ORIGINAL

The picture on the right in Figure 6.2 illustrates a tracing of the bitmap. You might want to try tracing the picture for yourself. It's a file called ARTDECO.PCX, drawn from the clip art provided with Corel Draw. The basic process is easy to use.

1.  Start with a clean work space. Import ARTDECO.PCX from wherever you keep your clip art. Make sure you select the For Tracing option in the Import dialog box.

2.  Select the resulting bitmap by clicking with the pick tool on the bitmap's perimeter.

*Figure 6.2:* A good bitmap for tracing (left), and the traced results (right).

3. Zoom in on a section of the picture—the man's head is a good place to start.

4. Select the pencil tool. If you have selected the bitmap properly, the cursor turns into an oblong cross. (If it turns into the regular pencil icon, you need to start again from Step 2.)

5. Place the cursor on one of the black areas and click. You might have a bit of a wait, depending on how complex the detail you've selected is, as Corel Draw constructs a path around the detail.

6. Repeat Step 5 for the rest of the black areas you want traced.

The Show Bitmaps option of the Display menu can be used as a toggle to hide the bitmapped image temporarily, leaving the trace by itself so you can see what you've actually drawn. Because paths created through tracing usually have a lot of nodes, they seem unusually messy in the work space. The preview window will improve the view by not showing the nodes. As usual, you should also use the preview window to check your results in terms of stroke width and fills.

If you use the preview window to check what you've done, chances are you'll find that the paths you've created by tracing have been stroked with a fairly fat rule, obscuring many of the details of the drawing. You might want to use the Select All item of the Edit menu and assign everything no stroke width.

You may also find that some objects in the picture will appear to have vanished in the preview. The hat-check girl's face, for example, will probably be missing. This is because Corel Draw fills each traced object with black, and her face is an object. After tracing a drawing, it's usually necessary to go through it and pick out the objects where this has happened, bringing them forward if necessary and filling them with white.

Note that bitmaps imported for tracing will not print, so if you elect to leave the bitmap in place it will not affect your final output. However, when you're completely finished using a bitmap, you can reduce the size of your CDR file considerably by selecting the original bitmap object and deleting it.

## FINE-TUNING TRACED OBJECTS

There are two adjustments in the Preferences dialog box of the Special menu which affect the way Corel Draw handles tracing. By setting these appropriately, you can make Corel Draw do a lot of the work in creating a well-traced bitmap.

When Corel Draw attempts to trace an area of your bitmapped image, it has to decide how accurately to follow the contours of the surfaces it encounters. On the one hand, if it tracks everything perfectly, the result could be a very complex outline with countless individual paths. On the other hand, if it ignores all small details, it might well ignore some important ones. Obviously, the amount of detail Corel Draw should preserve will vary with the nature of each image you trace.

The Autotrace Tracking item of the Preferences menu allows you to set the number of pixels below which Corel Draw will ignore details. If you set this value low—below four—Corel Draw will create fairly intricate traced lines which will represent every detail and hiccup in the surfaces of your original, possibly including some you didn't really want. If you set it high, Corel Draw will trace your bitmaps with smooth, flowing lines.

It's often helpful to change this value repeatedly throughout a tracing session.

The Straight Line Threshold value in the Preferences dialog is the other important control in handling tracing. It tells Corel Draw how close a curve can come to being straight before Corel Draw can just go ahead and use a straight line to trace it. Using straight line segments will keep the straight lines of the original from taking on slight curves due to tracing errors. It will also speed up the final printing of your drawing. If you're tracing a bitmap which is all straight lines to begin with—an architectural drawing, for example—set this value high. High would be eight to ten. In this case, only surfaces which are obviously curved will be traced as curves. Everything else will be handled with straight line segments.

Having traced a bitmap, you will very likely have to do a bit of path manipulation by hand. The tracing algorithm in Corel Draw is not flawless, and its work usually needs some polishing up. The shape tool is very useful for moving paths around, removing unwanted nodes, and so on.

Figure 6.3 illustrates one quarter of the rose of a lute—in fact, the rose that was missing from the lute we drew back in Chapter 2. This is a good example of the sort of drawing which needs some fine-tuning. The original in this figure was scanned from the designer's blueprint for the lute. The individual elements of the center of the rose traced well enough, but the rings surrounding it did not. The tracing algorithm couldn't get them to come out round. As such, I replaced them with actual circles.

In tracing the rose, what Corel Draw really did was to draw objects which described the spaces between the wooden parts of the rose—the cutouts rather than the lines. It was occasionally necessary to clean these up by dragging their nodes around.

*Figure 6.3:* The lute rose: original (left) and trace (right).

## USING TRACED OBJECTS

The objects you create by tracing can be treated just like anything else you draw in Corel Draw. Having traced an image and set the line stroke and object fills to your liking, group the objects together. You can now duplicate them, transform them and position them easily.

You can fill traced objects with any of Corel Draw's fills—you aren't restricted to black or even to solid fills, although you should keep in mind the potential complexity problems if you elect to use fountains. Figure 6.4 illustrates a traced image with some interesting fill patterns.

The chief problem with tracing *per se* is in tracing bitmaps which will result in a picture with an excessive number of paths. The cutout cat in Figure 6.5—shown here in both its bitmapped and object-oriented forms—is a classic example of this.

*Figure 6.4:* Using fills with a traced picture.

*Figure 6.5:* Killer cat.

This picture looks like it would be an ideal subject for bitmap tracing. It is, too, except that all the little white areas resulted in a picture with so many objects that Corel Draw bogged down enormously toward the end of the tracing session. In addition, the resulting picture took an extremely long time to trace and was too complex to print to a PostScript printer. This output was done with a LaserJet.

This might give you an idea of what the practical upper limit of detail is for tracing bitmaps.

## WRAPPING UP

Despite the enormous amount of work which goes on inside Corel Draw when you trace something, the work you'll have to do to get good results from the tracing features of the package will be pretty trivial. Corel Draw handles tracing very well, with the result that there's little to concern yourself with in using it.

If your applications involve tracing, plan on working with the tracing features a bit to get used to what they'll do for you. This is one of the areas of Corel Draw which is very much an art, requiring patience to get the most out of it.

# part

# II

## A Guide to Design

# chapter 7

WINDSURFING
MONTH

*Designing
for Good Effect*

Y OU'VE PROBABLY REALIZED BY NOW THAT COREL Draw is not as difficult to use as it first appears when you peel the shrink wrap off its box. At this point you have largely mastered the mechanics of making the package go, thanks in large part to its combination of a well-thought-out user interface and simple tools.

The next section of this book will deal with the real function of Corel Draw—that of design. Most likely, the reason you bought Corel Draw was not to create complex Bezier curves, to set optimum screen densities, or to be able to create type in 36 fonts. It was to create finished art.

It may well be argued that any book which purports to make you into an artist is lying to you. Design—whether it's done with pencils or done with paths and nodes—is very much an art, and one which cannot be learned over the space of a couple of chapters. The real task in mastering Corel Draw is in learning to use your mechanical skills in an artistic way.

In this chapter we'll look at some of the fundamental elements of design, and some approaches to using Corel Draw in ways that will make your graphics visually interesting and eye-catching—which is, to an extent, the whole objective of commercial art. With an eye for design and Corel Draw, you will be able to produce quick and effective commercial art without going to the expense of using a graphics house.

Some of the examples in this chapter are actually complete pages, incorporating both Corel Draw's output and some text, in this case from Ventura Publisher. We'll discuss the finer points of importing Corel Draw into desktop publishing documents later in this book.

## CREATING INTEREST

It's difficult to look at a visually exciting image and define precisely why that particular picture appeals to you or attracted your attention when other, similar ones did not. However, it's in developing an intuitive sense of these intangible characteristics that you'll make the transition from a Corel Draw operator to a Corel Draw artist.

You probably have seen photographs of the most mundane things—computer circuit boards, jet engine turbines, sunglasses—which have been rendered striking and exciting because of the way in which they were photographed. People get paid a lot for making computer circuit boards look interesting and, considering how many of them there are and how much they all look alike, perhaps rightly so.

A computer circuit board is a thin green slab of epoxy resin with some black chips soldered to it, and there's nothing in the least bit sensuous or exciting about one as you hold it in front of your face. However, the interesting images of these things which turn up in magazine ads are never photographed as they would appear in front of your face. The camera is often positioned at an impossibly oblique angle, such that you see the board as if you were very small and standing amongst its circuitry. Sometimes the board will be lighted in an unusual way, or placed in unlikely surroundings.

The reason that high-priced photographers can make you look at a photograph of a computer circuit board when you thought you had no real interest in doing so is that they can show you the beast in a way that you'd not normally see it. While they cannot make the board itself any less dull, they can apply a unique *treatment* to the subject, and it is this treatment that makes you look at the photograph.

Human beings are sensual junkies. If you create visual art which looks like other visual art they have already seen, you will not provide them with any new experiences, and you will not attract their attention as a result. If there were a set of numbered rules for designers—fortunately, there is not—this would be the first: Make your graphics innovative and different from the backdrop of everything around them. This is one of the keys to making graphics effective.

## DEFINING YOUR AUDIENCE

Before you can create effective graphics, you have to define your audience (or your "vidience," as it were). More specifically, you have to ask yourself two important questions concerning your potential viewers, to wit,

- What are you trying to say to them with the graphic you're attempting to create?
- What are they predisposed to be told?

A good graphic—that, is, an effective graphic—is by no means a universal thing. Visual messages are only meaningful if they are created with the framework of their intended audience in mind. Unfortunately, it's often very difficult for an artist to separate his or her own framework from that of a prospective audience.

Before you can create effective graphics, it's often necessary to do a bit of long-distance psychoanalysis of the attitudes and predispositions of the people you expect to see it. There are a number of other things you might want to think about in defining your audience. For example, if you perceive your audience as being characteristically busy, then complex graphics which take a lot of time to appreciate would be inappropriate. If your audience can be expected to be cultured and refined, you can use classical allusions and sophisticated images effectively. If your audience has some special characteristic—they're all jet engine turbine designers, for example, or all teachers—you can create images which involve their "inside knowledge." Such images can be both visually interesting and effective, because they involve your audience directly.

None of this sort of analysis is particularly easy, and it's usually complicated by the problem of trying not to color your observations about your audience with your own predispositions.

## *RULES AND THE BREAKING THEREOF*

One of the best general approaches to design is to create images which obviously have a set of rules associated with them and then to break those rules strategically. Figure 7.1 illustrates two magazine pages. They both have essentially the same contents, but the rightmost one is arguably more eye-catching because it deliberately violates an obvious rule, that of keeping its graphics in boxes.

Most graphics are ultimately constrained to some sort of fixed boundaries, and these frequently represent the most appealing targets for breaking rules. Consider, to begin with, that every piece of art which emerges from your laser printer does so with a frame around it, this being the periphery of the paper it's printed on.

Figure 7.2 illustrates two illustrations of the same graphic. They're both the same size, but the right one has violated the boundary of the box it resides in, and thus seems to imply greater size. By failing to be successfully constrained by the box it's printed in, it suggests that it's big.

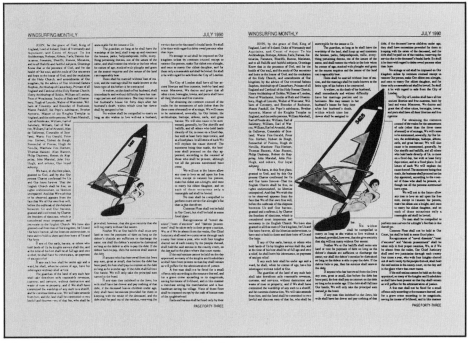

*Figure 7.1:* Breaking an obvious visual rule.

One of the most effective boxes to do this with is the periphery of a sheet of paper. Having a picture which is printed partially off the paper implies that its subject is big or strong—or some superlative characteristic—without having to say so.

One of the longstanding rules of typography is that the characters in text shouldn't touch. However, consider the two headlines in Figure 7.3. The second one might be said to be bad typography, but it's visually striking. It seems to imply that the message in the text is so potent and full of meaning that the width of the text is barely able to contain it.

As with all design elements, this sort of headline has its place. If you use this effect constantly it will soon cease to be an effect at all. Secondly, if you use it in the wrong place it will be counter-effective. Fat, bulging titles might be very badly out of place on a menu, for example.

One of the more effective design effects is that of juxtaposition, of combining images which would not normally be seen together. Corel

Two ships passing in the night.

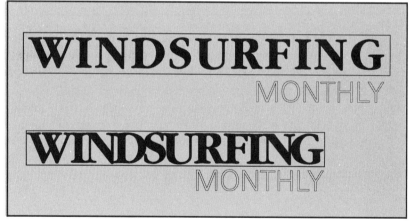

*Figure 7.3:* Two approaches for doing titles.

Draw is, of course, a superb tool for this, as it will allow you not only to combine disparate graphics but to manipulate them so that they fuse together seamlessly.

The picture in Figure 7.4 is an example of using two unrelated images. The zipper graphic, one of the clip art images supplied with Corel Draw, has countless possibilities.

If a flock of pigs flew over your town you'd probably notice them. Just about everyone would notice them. There's a perfectly obvious reason for this: it violates another rule. Pigs don't fly. Showing a squadron of them in a V formation would be an example of creating a graphic to show something that has never been seen.

A few years ago, most designers would have felt that you could use any color you like in a design—with three notable exceptions, these being cyan, magenta, and yellow. These primary colors were only for the eyes of printers and pressmen. However, in attempting to create eye-catching designs, someone must have observed that there

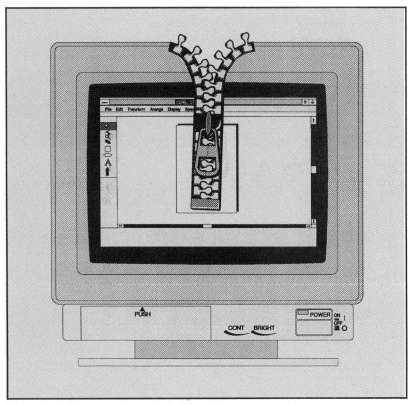

*Figure 7.4:* The popular prefaded Levi Strauss personal computer.

were three colors which, as if by mutual conspiracy, had never been seen. They've become quite common by now.

Another important rule of typography is that type should be easily readable. There are more reasons for violating this rule than can readily be counted with small numbers. One which has been cropping up a lot in magazine design of late is the apparent thyroid problem which drop caps seem to be having. Consider Figure 7.5.

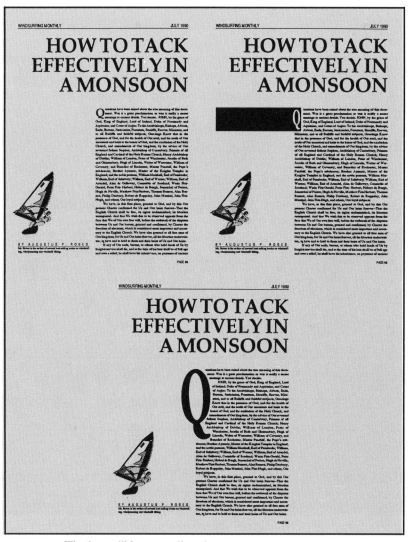

*Figure 7.5:* The incredible expanding drop cap.

This is another example of violating a rule to express something through the impression of size. The statement which the immense drop cap in the last example makes is that the page it is part of is extremely important. It would be nice if it could be printed on a billboard so that *all* of its important words could be set in enormous type, but, the constraints of publishing being what they are, the first thing you read will have to set the tone.

## *CREATING EFFECTIVE GRAPHICS FOR INTANGIBLE THINGS*

Perhaps more often than designers would prefer to admit, the visual message in a graphic is to convey the characteristic of something being superlative—or, at least, of having more of something than it used to have, or more than its competitors have. We have become a somewhat graph-oriented culture, and designers are often asked to represent non-visual things as visual. Consider the graphics in Figure 7.6, which represent some non-visual phenomena in perfectly understandable visual forms.

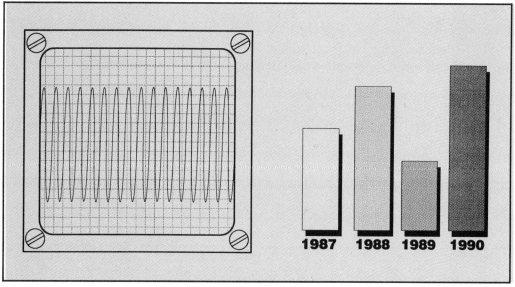

*Figure 7.6:* Expressing non-visual phenomena as visual graphs.

Expressing that a non-visual quality is *greater* has generally involved presenting it occupying more *area*, or an area which is further removed from the bottom of the page. Even people who are not by nature analytical have a certain predisposition to graphs and analogous structures.

Consider the problem of depicting an amplifier with the intent of creating an effective amplifier advertisement. Most people buy amplifiers because they want to hear music. Allowing that even mediocre amplifiers have pretty good specifications these days, the deciding factor will probably be how loud the amplifier in question can make your music sound. Unfortunately, loudness is a characteristic which is difficult to convey in visual terms. However, consider that most people will regard an amplifier which is capable of rocking the foundation of the building and setting off seismographs as being strong. Although it might turn into an ambitious project, these are occurrences which can be illustrated with drawings. On a simpler level, big amplifiers will be regarded as being stronger than little amplifiers. Thus, while you probably can't depict a loud amplifier all that well visually, you can certainly depict a big one.

Another of the obvious rules of design is that graphics should depict their subjects accurately. You can often break this rule very effectively. In Figure 7.7, the picture on the left is a more accurate drawing of a Porsche than the picture on the right. However, the picture on the right implies that it's a drawing of a much faster Porsche: the visual implication is that the car was so fast that it was half off the page before the picture could be printed.

*Figure 7.7:* Two views of a fast car.

If your graphic is intended to sell Porsches, you might consider that anyone who's likely to buy a Porsche will probably already know what one looks like, and will not require the advertisement merely to be able to recognize one. One of the things which really recommend Porsches is their ability to go fast. Depicting a fast Porsche is therefore a lot more important than depicting a whole Porsche.

There are, to be sure, all sorts of qualities which cannot be expressed with graphics that imply bigger, stronger, or otherwise more potent. Creating effective graphics in these situations requires a bit more of the aforementioned long-distance psychoanalysis.

Let's start with a fairly obvious example. Consider how you would create an effective graphic which depicts a really appetizing hamburger. You could draw a picture of a burger, but this has a lot of potential pitfalls. If you draw a burger with pickles on it, it will not be appetizing to people who don't like pickles. Of course, you could leave off all the things which *might* be unappetizing, but then you'll be left with a pretty bare burger. If your graphic is viewed by someone who's just eaten, it won't be effective no matter how you draw it. Finally, it would be hard to create a really sensuous-looking rendition of a hamburger in a drawing program like Corel Draw.

This particular example is useful because it has been solved countless times. In effect, this allows you countless opportunities to cheat, to turn to the back of the book and look up the answer. Just look at the advertisements for McDonalds. McDonalds is very effective at selling hamburgers. They do so without ever implying that their burgers are good to eat, and they run their advertisements during the evening, when they might well assume that most of the people watching them have already eaten.

McDonalds doesn't actually sell hamburgers in their advertisements. They sell characteristics of McDonalds which are more readily depicted in a universal way through the essentially visual medium of television—things like fast, friendly service, clean restaurants, and still more subtle things, like happy families or an exciting lifestyle, depending on which ad you happen to catch.

There's an important rule to be learned by studying McDonalds' advertising: In attempting to create effective graphics, you must often consider which qualities of the thing you want to depict can be conveyed to your audience visually.

Here's a slightly less commercial problem. Draw a picture of perfume. In this problem, let's assume that budgetary constraints preclude the use of a scratch 'n' sniff sample of the perfume in your drawing.

It's wholly impossible to convey the aroma of perfume visually. However, smells are evocative, perfumes especially so. Since you can't draw a picture of the smell, you should probably give some thought to drawing a picture of what the smell evokes. This is another, fairly major violation of the rule that a drawing must accurately depict its subject.

## DESIGNING PAGES

If you leaf through the clip art catalog which accompanies Corel Draw, you'll find a lot of great *images*. You won't find any good *pages*, though. It is, after all, a catalog.

As we discussed earlier in this chapter, just about every application of graphics involves some sort of a boundary. Most often it is the edge of your page, but if you're designing graphics for packaging, for example, it might be the edges of the box. Whatever your boundaries consist of, you should regard them as being part of your complete design. A graphic stuck on a page is a picture; a graphic which becomes part of the page is a design.

With the exception of the sorts of conceptional art which are no longer considered fashionable—paintings of polar bears in snow storms or black cats in tar pits, for example—every page will have a *focus,* either intentionally or not. A focus is that which first draws your eye to the page and leads you into whatever else is there.

You might consider that absolutely everything you look at contains a focus of this sort, this being the thing which draws your eye out of the background of visual images. At the moment, you can probably see not only this book but also the room around you. However, the book is the focus of your attention.

An important distinction between this book and most of the graphics and subsequent pages you'll create is that you bought this book, and you are presumably motivated to read it because you *want* to know what it has to say. In many cases the audience of your graphics will not be so motivated, and the first task of your work will be to keep them from simply turning the page or focusing on something else.

If you merely create images without regard to the final design of the pages they'll rest on, the ultimate focus will be left to chance. However, if you take into account the way people look at things, you can focus their attention to great advantage. You can attract them into your page and direct their attention where you want it when they first start considering the contents of the page in general. This is true with both wholly visual pages and with pages which combine graphics and text.

In creating an effective page design with an unequivocal focus, you must once again think about both your audience and what you're trying to convey. This second point bears some discussion, because it's often unclear to designers what they're really supposed to focus the attention of their audiences on.

For an example of this, try to read a coffee-table book. It's very nearly impossible. Coffee-table books consist of pages which are mostly pictures, drawn together with a thread of text that runs from page to page and fills up the left-over spaces. The text is hardly the focus of the pages. Each time you turn a page, your eye will be drawn to the photographs, which typically occupy a lot more real estate than the text does. When you do try to read, you will find that your reading is constantly distracted.

Coffee-table books aren't meant to be read. The text is usually little more than an ornament, or a condescension to people who feel that there's something less than refined in looking at books which have nothing but pictures in them. The focus of the pages is the pictures.

Coffee-table books also have the advantage of a captive audience, something which few applications for graphics can assume.

Consider the things which catch your eye, that is, things which focus your attention to a particular part of a page. These things fall into two broad classes. The first is simply that which is visually different from its surroundings—a picture in a page otherwise filled with text, a dark area in an otherwise light image, a brightly colored object against a background of otherwise muted colors. The second is an image which you find interesting or remarkable for its content.

The first class of focus elements is universal. These things will work for everyone who sees them. The second tends to be more audience-specific.

A page which lacks a clear focus is much less appealing than one which implicitly directs the attention of someone looking at it. People are lazy in this respect, especially if they're in a hurry. They want their eye to be told where to go and how best to appreciate the page with the least amount of effort on their parts. This may be kind of slothful and un-zenlike, but it's the way things are.

The elements of a well-designed page are often said to "lock together." There is a clear path for the eye, from the initial focus through the material on the rest of the page. The arrangement of objects on the page is visually pleasing. The page conveys an amount of information which is in keeping with the ability of the person regarding it to absorb.

Figure 7.8 illustrates two examples of the same page. They both have the same information, but the one on the left doesn't really lock together. The picture is obviously the focus of the page, but it doesn't lead one's eye anywhere in particular. There's type all over creation, and if you want to read the type you have to wander around trying to find it. There's no obvious order to it, either—your eye will have

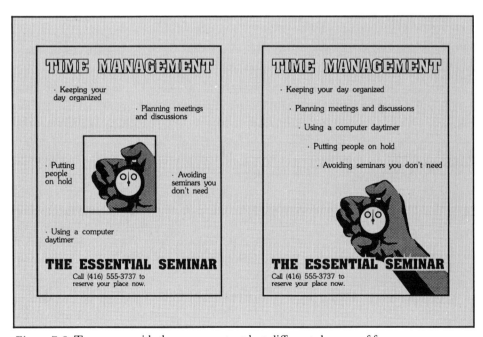

*Figure 7.8:* Two pages with the same content but different degrees of focus.

to pause frequently to decide where to look next. By contrast, the page on the right pulls you into its center to look at the picture and then up to the copy fairly effectively.

## USING WHITE SPACE

One of the principal pitfalls of Corel Draw is actually its ability to create complex pages. Someone once remarked that music consists of both the notes and the pauses between them; the same can be said of page design. In creating a page, you should try to find the balance between a page which is too sparse to have any sort of direction to it at all and one which is too cluttered and busy to have an obvious direction amidst the tangled underbrush. Pages which consist primarily of white space—unless it's done deliberately for effect—suggest that there's nothing to look at on the page, or at least not enough to make it worth pausing to consider what might be there. Pages which consist of a wall of type or a barrage of images, on the other hand, are intimidating. They convince someone considering the page that it will take a lot of mental effort to figure out what's happening.

There is very little point in conveying a lot of information which no one reads. It's arguably better to create pages which say less, but which do so in a way that makes them hard to skip over.

You can open out a dense page—"let it breathe," in designers' terms—by introducing some white space into it. If you're working with color, of course, this may translate into colored space. The important thing is that the space in question not have anything distracting in it.

There are all sorts of ways to introduce some white space into a page. If you have a large graphic on the page, consider reducing it or positioning it so that only part of it is visible. Inasmuch as Corel Draw lets you change the density of the fills in your drawings, you might want to try lightening the graphics you've used. A fainter picture can often be a lot less dominating. If the page contains text, set some of the text in a large spindly font with lots of leading. We'll discuss the uses of text in this regard in greater detail later in this book.

Most publications—books, magazines, quarterly reports, and so on—have a lot of text and graphics in them. Designing one of the pages with a larger amount of white space can be an effective way to call attention to it.

Multiple-page publications, furthermore, offer superb design opportunities for setting up rules and then breaking them deliberately.

## DESIGNING WITH TWO PAGES

The possibility of having more than one page is something many designers overlook. If you're creating pages for a magazine, pamphlet, or anything which is bound—like a book—consider that although you may work on one page at a time, your audience will regard your work as two facing pages. When someone opens a magazine, the initial focus of what's before them will be a pair of pages.

By ignoring the fact that there are two pages in front of someone looking at your graphics, you could easily create a *page spread* that doesn't work very well. On the other hand, if you bear in mind that most of your pages must work with at least one other page, you can often do some clever things with the spread.

Most double-page spreads are intended to focus initial attention somewhere in the upper left corner of the left page. If this area is occupied by an interesting graphic, it will lead the eye of a reader naturally into the page. If it starts with some unremarkable-looking type, the reader will tend to wander around the two pages, looking for an obvious focus.

Spanning the *gutter* between two pages is a singularly effective way of tying the two pages together. However, you can't actually print a picture which prints right to the edge of a page on a conventional laser printer. If you want to be able to do this, you'll probably have to have your final pages handled by an output service or a typesetting house with a PostScript typesetter.

## WRAPPING UP

The best drawing package in the world is useless without someone who can use it, and using it involves a lot more than knowing which menu items to click. Creating graphics with Corel Draw is a mechanical process, but creating good, effective graphics takes a sense of design.

One of the best ways to develop a sense of design is to analyze designs which are effective for you. Try to make a point of noticing advertisements, magazine page designs, and other examples of commercial art which catch your eye. Having done so, figure out why they caught your eye. It's neither ethical nor particularly productive to lift ideas from existing graphics, but the exercise of figuring out why particular graphics have worked can teach you a lot about design.

# chapter

# 8

## Integrating with Desktop Publishing

WHILE IT'S A GREAT TOOL ALL BY ITSELF, COREL DRAW really shows its versatility when it's used in conjunction with desktop publishing packages. The strengths of something like Aldus Page-Maker or Ventura Publisher—primarily in text formatting—ideally complement the graphic strengths of Corel Draw. In addition, Corel Draw's rather generous contingent of typefaces makes it a first-class source of headlines and other small bits of display type.

If your applications involve creating complete documents, as opposed to just discrete pictures, you'll probably find that Corel Draw and Ventura or PageMaker will form an ideal working environment.

There are two fairly disparate areas to concern yourself with when you load up Corel Draw with the intention of creating art for exporting to another application. The first concerns the actual mechanics of handling the exporting of your picture. Much of this was dealt with in Chapter 5, but we will discuss a few more considerations here. The second and perhaps even more intangible aspect of this task is creating graphics which work in the design of the pages they'll ultimately become part of.

In the first part of this chapter we'll deal with exporting Corel Draw's graphic files—to Ventura Publisher documents for the most part. Ventura is a good example of desktop publishing software, as it embodies most of the facilities—as well as most of the gremlins—found in other packages of this type. If you use a different desktop publishing package, you'll find that most of the exporting issues are about the same from the point of view of Corel Draw.

The second main part of the chapter, the design discussion, will be essentially independent of the software you use to implement your pages.

## BASIC EXPORTING CONSIDERATIONS

The CDR files which are native to Corel Draw are, at the moment, unique to it as well. No other application will read them. However, by now you know that there are all sorts of ways to represent a drawing in a disk file.

Each of the drawing file formats which Corel Draw will import and export has its own ways of representing the basic paths and other elements which make up a drawing. Each format also has certain limitations.

As a simple example of this, the GEM drawing file format—which Ventura Publisher likes to use for most of its drawings—doesn't handle text in anything like the same way that Corel Draw's CDR files do, with the result that a Corel Draw drawing exported to a GEM file invariably has all its text reduced to paths. If you import a GEM file with text in it back into Corel Draw, the text will not be editable as text for this reason.

This sort of basic problem often makes exporting Corel Draw files for use with other applications something other than painless.

## *VERY SIMPLE EXPORTING USING THE CLIPBOARD*

Let's start with a very simple example of exporting, one in which most of the catches have been ironed out beforehand. All Microsoft Windows-based applications which can exchange graphics through the Windows clipboard do so using a common file format. This is called a "Windows Metafile." In fact, the data exchanged between Windows applications in this way never actually winds up as a disk file. As far as the programs which use the clipboard are concerned, the data is simply handed transparently between applications.

The clipboard has cropped up occasionally before in using Corel Draw. Let's use it once again to investigate the operation of a Windows Metafile.

For this exercise, boot up Windows and then load Corel Draw. Load or create a small drawing. The operative word here is "small": the amount of object data you can store in the Windows clipboard is extremely limited, and if you attempt to export too big a picture from Corel Draw using the clipboard, Windows will refuse to handle the operation. If this happens, you'll see a dialog box which tells you that you're attempting to deal with too much Metafile information.

Having created your drawing, select it and copy it to the clipboard using the Copy item of the Edit menu. Although nothing will appear to have changed, your drawing will now be living in the Windows clipboard.

Load up Write, the word processor which comes with Windows. You can leave Corel Draw running while you do so. (Running concurrent applications under Windows is discussed in Appendix A.) Write will open with a blank document. Select the Paste item from Write's Edit menu. Your original Corel Draw drawing will appear at the top of the page which Write is creating.

Figure 8.1 illustrates a Write document with some imported Corel Draw art.

Because both Write and Corel Draw can use this common export format—the clipboard—there is little possibility for something to go wrong in the transition between applications. Admittedly, this was a fairly trivial example: the clipboard does not allow for very large or complex drawings to be exported in this way, and, further, Windows Write is hardly a desktop publishing program. Bear in mind, though, that you can use this process quickly and easily with any suitable Windows-based application, and this includes PageMaker and the Windows version of Word.

## EXPORTING BITMAPPED IMAGES

As we discussed earlier in this book, Corel Draw allows you to export drawings in a host of formats in order to make your Corel Draw artwork suitable for use with as many import applications as possible. In the case of desktop publishing software—which typically import a large number of file formats for much the same reason—you will usually find yourself confronted with several format possibilities.

The simplest and most foolproof way of exporting drawing files is to export your file as a bitmap. Although on the one hand this method has serious drawbacks, on the other hand it overcomes a large number of potential file format inconsistencies—by simply ignoring them.

As you know, Corel Draw exports bitmaps in two formats, these being PCX and TIFF. Of these, TIFF is most often the least desirable, as it's ill-defined and likely to cause trouble. Therefore, for simple monochrome graphics, you should consider always using

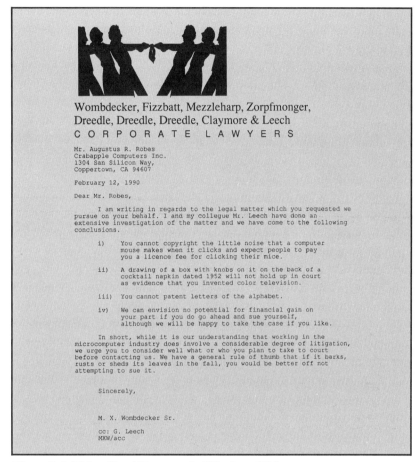

*Figure 8.1:* Using Corel Draw art in Windows Write.

PCX files for bitmap files (as far as Corel Draw is concerned). The following discussions, in fact, will assume that you are using the PCX format for bitmaps.

If you export a Corel Draw drawing to a PCX file, the resulting bitmapped image will be unscalable and quite inflexible as graphics go. If you want it to appear at its best upon importing it into a desktop publishing document, you will be forced to use it at the size you exported it. Furthermore, if your final output is bound for a Linotronic typesetter, you will find that bitmapped images don't improve in appearance with higher resolution printers.

The advantage to exporting a bitmapped image, on the other hand, is that there will be virtually no possibility that anything nasty will happen to your drawing in the trackless wastes between Corel Draw and a desktop publishing program. A bitmap file—especially a monochrome one—is a pretty immutable object, and what you see on your monitor is really what you'll get in printed output. Very few things in desktop publishing can get away with making this claim.

Exporting a Corel Draw drawing as a bitmap file requires lots of forethought. Because a bitmap file cannot be scaled once it has been exported without losing some quality, you must make sure that your image is properly sized before you export it. Furthermore, you must export it at the 300 dots per inch it was created with if you want it to look as good as it could have simply as Corel Draw output. This also requires some forethought, in that you'll have to allow for a lot of disk space to hold really big 300-dpi bitmap files. Finally, bitmapped files take a long time to print. The larger they are the longer they take.

In summary, exporting Corel Draw art to bitmapped files is fool-proof, but, because of the work and planning necessitated by this format, it's best left as a last resort, for use if every other option has failed.

### Using PCX Files with Ventura

In Ventura, imported graphics are always poured into frames on your document pages. In order to load a graphic into a document, you would select the Load Text/Picture item of the Ventura Files menu, choose the appropriate file format, and select your file.

Having poured a PCX file into a frame in Ventura, you will have to use the Sizing and Scaling box from Ventura's Frame menu to ensure that it gets treated properly. Ventura defaults to scaling imported bitmap files to fit the frames they're poured into—much to the dismay of the graphics themselves, which often look dreadful as a result.

In order to force Ventura to let your imported PCX file find its natural scale, select the By Scale Factors option in the Sizing and Scaling box, as shown in Figure 8.2. The Scale Width field on the lower left will be enabled, and will be filled in with the natural scale of the image at the resolution you selected with Corel Draw. If you don't alter this value, you'll get essentially the same picture that

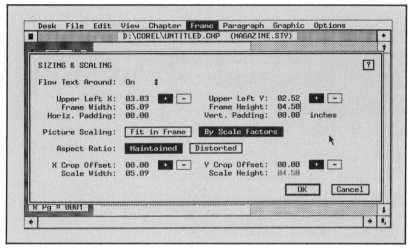

*Figure 8.2:* The Sizing and Scaling box in Ventura Publisher, showing the By Scale Factors option selected.

you would have gotten had your exported graphic been printed directly from Corel Draw to a 300-dpi laser printer.

You can crop PCX images with Ventura with no loss of quality.

There are a few potential bugs in even this simple example of exporting. First of all, you should know that when you import a PCX file into Ventura, it creates a second file called an IMG file. This is just another image-file format—it happens to be the one which Ventura likes to use. It's a bit better at compressing bitmapped data than a PCX file, but not much. If you start out with a 120-kilobyte PCX file exported from Corel Draw, plan on there being at least that much more space occupied by the resulting IMG file when Ventura gets through with it.

It would be convenient if Corel Draw could export directly to IMG files, but it doesn't do this at the moment. You can, however, use an external file-conversion utility such as The Graphics Link or Graphic Workshop to convert PCX files to IMG files before Ventura gets to them, allowing you to delete the PCX files and have only one copy of your exported image on hand, rather than two.

The use of IMG files by Ventura can create a second, rather weirder problem, but this will be discussed a bit later in the chapter, in the ''Exporting EPS Files'' section.

The other difficulty you might encounter is a genuine bug in Ventura. It's visible in Figure 8.3. This is a PCX file which was exported from Corel Draw and subsequently imported into Ventura Publisher.

If the horizontal dimension of a PCX file is not evenly divisible by eight—which can happen quite easily under Corel Draw—the exported file may have up to seven unused pixels at the end of each line. The PCX file instructs Ventura to ignore them, but Ventura chooses to ignore the instruction instead, and rounds the image width up to the next highest eight-pixel boundary. Corel Draw, for its part, should clear the unused pixels at the ends of the lines, but it doesn't. They usually contain random black or white dots. The result is frequently the accretion of fur at the right edges of Corel Draw files exported as PCX bitmaps.

*Figure 8.3:* The attack of the hairy right margin.

Fortunately, this is an easy thing to get around in Ventura. Simply reduce the horizontal dimension of the frame which contains the image, cropping the fur in the process.

## EXPORTING LINE ART FILES

The best way to export line art—such as a Corel Draw drawing—is as line art. Corel Draw can produce readable line art files in all sorts of specialized formats and in three fairly general ones, these being Windows Metafile, CGM, and GEM. Virtually all applications which can import line art files will read at least one of these. Page-Maker, for example, uses Metafile. Ventura will read all three.

Note that early releases of Corel Draw lacked the export filter for GEM, which would be a considerable drawback for Ventura users. If you don't find GEM listed in the list of exportable file formats, you should probably contact Corel for a software update.

In theory, when Corel Draw exports a drawing into a GEM file, it simply translates its own notation for each object in the drawing into GEM notation. In practice, things don't always work out that well. There are some things which a CDR file can do which a GEM file cannot, as was discussed in Chapter 5. In addition, the GEM format has a size restriction. It can only hold drawings of a finite level of complexity. This level is none too great, and you will find that it's pretty easy to create a Corel Draw drawing which cannot be exported to a GEM file because it exceeds the format's limits.

The principal catch in this for Ventura users is that while Ventura will import many types of line art files, it actually converts them all to GEM files before it goes to use them (with one exception, which we'll discuss in a moment). Therefore, even though it's frequently possible to export Corel Draw art to a Windows Metafile when it cannot be successfully exported to a GEM file, you will not really have snuck around the problem if your ultimate destination is a Ventura document. Ventura will be unable to translate all of your Windows Metafile into its GEM work file, and you won't be any further ahead.

PageMaker is a bit less troublesome in this respect, in that the Windows Metafile format is far less restrictive than GEM files in terms of what you can put into it. It also avoids many of the bugs which GEM files are heir to.

The original CDR file from which the drawing in Figure 8.3 was created was too complex to export to a GEM file. If you encounter such a drawing, Corel Draw will warn you that some of the objects in your original drawing will not be present in your exported file.

You should also note that there is not a one-to-one correspondence between the drawing objects in a GEM file and those in a Windows Metafile. This occasionally results in extraneous lines cropping up in Metafiles imported into Ventura chapters. For this reason, it's preferable to export your Corel Draw art to GEM files if it's to be imported into Ventura chapters rather than having an extra stage in the translation process.

Exported GEM files are typically pretty compact as line art goes. GEM can support most of the basic attributes that you're likely to use in drawings under Corel Draw. This includes color, and if you have installed Ventura with one of its color screen drivers—the last two in the standard screen driver list for EGA cards—you will see your imported GEM files in the same colors that Corel Draw shows them to you in if you use the preview window.

This is more than just a light show. Ventura allows you to output separate black and spot-color plates, just like Corel Draw does. With a bit of coordination, you can export Corel Draw art with spot-color into a GEM file and have Ventura produce two-color pages for you, handling both its own spot-color text and Corel Draw's spot-color art.

GEM files have problems with some of Corel Draw's more sophisticated effects. Fountains, for example, frequently bewilder them. Figure 8.4 is a fountain which was created under Corel Draw, exported as a GEM file and imported into Ventura Publisher. Likewise, PostScript effects and PostScript-related parameters, such as screen frequency and dot shape, are ignored by GEM files. The Corel Draw PostScript textures cannot be exported to GEM files. Fountain effects survive exporting into PageMaker a lot more readily.

The major advantage to using GEM files in Ventura or Metafiles in PageMaker is that what you see on your screen is really what you'll get when you print your output. Your desktop publishing software will actually interpret the GEM file or Metafile you import and draw what it finds right on your screen. The position of a line art graphic on your screen will match up perfectly with its final position on your

*Figure 8.4:* A Corel Draw fountain exported to a GEM file, with unsatisfactory
results.

printed pages, making it possible to wrap text around a GEM
graphic without having to worry about the picture overlapping it.

GEM and Metafile graphics are true line art. If you output a Ventura or PageMaker chapter containing some GEM or Metafile art
exported from Corel Draw to a high-resolution PostScript typesetter,
you'll get to see the advantages of having a high-resolution printer
in your art as well as in your text.

Because they are line art, you can stretch both Metafiles and GEM
files with no loss of quality once they're imported into PageMaker or
Ventura.

Finally, Ventura chapters which include GEM files can be printed
to any of the output devices which Ventura will drive. This is also
true of bitmap files, but it's not true of the next sort of file we'll look
at, EPS files.

If you want to export simple black-and-white line drawings of mid-
dling complexity from Corel Draw, the best way to handle it is as line
art. This means GEM files for Ventura, but it would be Metafiles for
most Windows-based applications.

The algorithm which translates the paths of a GEM file into laser printer data in Ventura is not quite as clever as the one in Corel Draw. The lines it forms are often not as neat as you might like them. For example, when it is confronted with a path which is formed with half dots (a problem we discussed earlier in this book), Ventura usually manages to guess wrong. Therefore, Corel Draw graphics which have lots of small, delicate paths often don't look as good as you might like them to when you handle them as GEM files and output them to a 300-dot-per-inch laser printer. This affects text, among other things, and small text a lot more noticeably than large text. The text problem often manifests itself as type in which the lines forming the characters are noticeably thicker or thinner than they should be in some places.

In instances where you want to export small or precise graphics and you want to ensure that they make the trip with as little distortion as possible, the final solution is usually to use EPS files. However, this approach is not without its drawbacks.

## EXPORTING EPS FILES

We have discussed EPS (encapsulated PostScript) files to some extent in Chapter 5. In order to understand how best to export graphics from Corel Draw using EPS, however, you'll have to immerse yourself in its lore for a few more pages.

To begin with, encapsulated PostScript files can only be used with a PostScript printer. If you plan to use a LaserJet Plus to print the documents you'll ultimately be importing your files into, PostScript files will be of little use, except perhaps in the area of printing ''preview'' images, which we'll discuss shortly.

PostScript is actually a programming language, rather than a line art graphic format. It has been specifically fine-tuned to write programs which deal with printed pages. In its simplest sense, when an application wants to print a page to a PostScript printer, it writes a program which defines the page and sends the program to the printer. Ideally, the printer interprets the program and does what it says, generating the page the program had in mind.

In order to import a PostScript file and show it to you on your screen, as Corel Draw does, the software which does the importing must have the equivalent of the PostScript language which is resident in a PostScript printer. Corel Draw is one of the few PC applications which has this facility. Ventura Publisher is one of the many PC applications which does not, even though it is capable of importing PostScript files.

Adobe, the creator of PostScript, recognized that not every program which would be importing PostScript files could be expected to contain the considerable complexity of a PostScript interpreter. To alleviate this situation, Adobe dreamt up something called PostScript "encapsulation." The principle of encapsulated PostScript is simple. Allowing that the body of a PostScript program is a great black mystery for most applications, files which are intended for use by programs like Ventura are fitted with headers that tell Ventura in capsule form everything it needs to know about the drawing the rest of the file will produce when it finally hits a PostScript printer. This includes things like the size of the drawing, called the "bounding box." The bounding box is a rectangle which just encloses the final drawing. Knowing this, Ventura can fit the drawing into a frame even though it doesn't really know what the drawing is.

Not being able to interpret a PostScript file directly, Ventura would be unable to show you what one looked like before sending it on its way to a PostScript printer. To address this deficiency, Adobe added another element to the PostScript encapsulation process, involving the creation of a "preview" image. This is simply a bit-mapped picture which looks roughly like the drawing which should ultimately emerge from a PostScript printer. The encapsulation header tells programs like Ventura how to find the preview image, and the preview is tacked onto the end of the PostScript program.

In Ventura, if you import an encapsulated PostScript file which has a preview, the image will appear in the frame you've put the graphic in. If there is no preview, Ventura will draw an X through the frame. The graphic will still print, but you will not be able to see it on your screen. Note that versions of Ventura prior to 2.0 did not deal with previews, and always drew an X through a frame containing an encapsulated PostScript file whether it had a preview or not.

You should note that if you print a Ventura document containing an encapsulated PostScript file to a LaserJet Plus printer, the preview image itself will appear in place of the graphic. This is invariably not as good as real PostScript output would be, but it's better than nothing.

Corel Draw allows you to specify the resolution of the preview image when you are creating an encapsulated PostScript file. If you anticipate outputting Ventura documents with Corel Draw EPS files to a LaserJet, select the highest-resolution previews.

## *POSTSCRIPT LIMITATIONS*

In theory, exporting Corel Draw art to an encapsulated PostScript file is the best way to import it into another application—assuming that the ultimate destination of the art in question will be a PostScript printer, of course. PostScript files never get translated; thus they never lose anything in the process. They take full advantage of the superb graphics-rendering facilities resident in PostScript printers. They allow you to have PostScript-dependent things like font hinting preserved in your exported files. Exported PostScript files can employ the whole range of Corel Draw's substantial talents, including PostScript textures, fountains, and the like.

There are a few catches to all of this in practice.

The system of preview images in PostScript files has one obvious weakness: You don't see your actual exported drawing when it has been poured into a Ventura document. Instead, you see the preview. While Corel Draw's EPS previews invariably look more or less like its EPS files, the position of the preview in a Ventura frame is frequently quite different from that of the actual art.

Figure 8.5 illustrates an example of this problem. The frame on the left is the PCX file from Figure 8.3, above. The frame on the right is the printed output of the same graphic imported as an EPS file. The two frames appeared to have the same pictures in the same positions in Ventura, but the right picture has actually been output slightly lower in the frame.

Unfortunately, this phenomenon is not at all consistent. The disparity between what you see in Ventura when you import an EPS file from Corel Draw and what actually gets printed can be quite pronounced. If you require that your EPS graphics be very accurately positioned, plan on having to undertake some trial and error.

This is an irritating problem, but it's often worth putting up with in order to get the best possible results from graphics exported by Corel Draw.

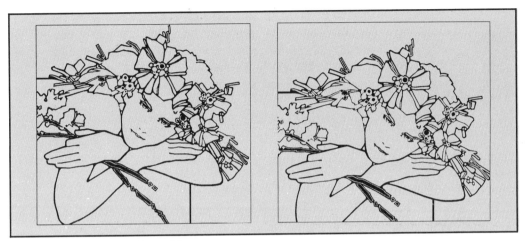

*Figure 8.5:* Lies my preview told me.

Part of the aesthetic of drawing for export, to be discussed in the next section of this chapter, involves creating simple graphics which do not detract from the page they're to be imported into. More fundamental than this, however, is the practical requirement that imported graphics not be so busy that they overwhelm your printer.

A document output by Ventura to a PostScript printer faces the same limitations that a graphic printed by Corel Draw does. Every PostScript printer has a finite number of paths which it can deal with on a single page, and if you attempt to exceed this value, the results will not be as expected. Usually the page won't print at all, as we've seen previously.

If you import an EPS file from Corel Draw into a Ventura document, the number of paths in the Corel Draw drawing will be added to the number of paths in the Ventura page it has become part of. A Ventura page with lots of type, rules, and other elements may have a pretty good helping of paths on its own.

Complex documents with complex graphics imported into them often attempt to print things which are beyond the scope of your printer, even though the page and the graphics were printable before they were combined. It's very difficult to tell when you've exceeded the available number of paths for your printer just by looking at a page.

As a rule, if you're using Corel Draw to create graphics for export, make sparing use of fountain fills and PostScript textures. When you do use them, try to do so in small, fairly simple objects. Along the same lines, avoid using lots of complex line graphics on the same page. For example, the girl in Figure 8.5 will print if she finds herself on a Ventura page. You can usually get away with two of her if the page doesn't have an inordinate amount of type on it. When I tried having one of her at each of the four corners of a page, I found that it was certainly more than the printer was interested in dealing with.

## VENTURA AND IMG FILES

Ventura has an unusual quirk which might sneak up on you if you aren't aware of it, should you attempt to create pages having certain combinations of imported graphics. It can cause things you weren't anticipating to print or appear on your screen.

When you first import an EPS file from Corel Draw into a Ventura document, Ventura looks for a preview image. The preview image actually lives at the very end of the PostScript file, which can be quite a way in for a complex graphic. To avoid having to find its way to the end of the PostScript file every time it wants to update its screen with the preview image, Ventura makes a copy of the preview and stores it in an IMG file. If your EPS file is called PICTURE.EPS, Ventura will create PICTURE.IMG to store the preview in.

As you may recall from earlier in the chapter, Ventura will also translate your file into an IMG file if you attempt to import a PCX or TIFF file into a Ventura document. As it happens, this sort of IMG file and the sort in which Ventura stores previews aren't structured quite the same inside, but this doesn't actually matter. The important thing is that both sorts of files are named the same. If you import a file called PICTURE.PCX, Ventura will create a new file called PICTURE.IMG.

This is where the quirk comes in. If you create a Ventura document and attempt to import two files called PICTURE.PCX and PICTURE.EPS, they will each be translated to PICTURE.IMG, and one of them will overwrite the other. Depending on which file gets loaded first, you may find that the preview of your EPS file suddenly looks an awful lot like the contents of your PCX file, or that your PCX file prints like a very crunchy looking version of your PostScript graphic.

It's important to bear in mind that Ventura doesn't treat its imported files in the way that Corel Draw does. If you import a file into a Corel Draw document, the contents of the file become part of the document. Importing a file into a Ventura document, on the other hand, simply tells Ventura about the existence of the file. Each time you open a Ventura document containing imported graphics, Ventura must retrieve each graphic from its original file. Because every graphic is a separate file residing on your disk, its contents can be modified without Ventura knowing it—even if it is Ventura which is inadvertently responsible. Thus, if a graphic gets modified or trashed after it has been imported into a Ventura chapter, it will stay trashed, and it will print trashed.

This is true whether you trash it yourself or Ventura does it for you.

You can avoid this problem very easily. Make sure you never have two graphics in the same directory having the same file names and different extensions if you plan to import them into Ventura Publisher.

*Ventura's Cropping Problem*

If you import a large graphic into a Ventura document and subsequently attempt to alter its position in its frame interactively—that is, by holding down the Alt key and dragging the graphic with the mouse—you will quite likely find that all or part of the contents of the frame will suddenly become littered with scraps of the Ventura side bar. The results can sometimes look like a bitmapped Dali painting, and they are the sort of thing which usually precedes a major system crash. In fact, this is a harmless bug, and as soon as you release your mouse it will vanish. It has to do with the way Ventura allocates memory for large graphic files while it's working with them.

Figure 8.6 illustrates a lesser degree of this problem. The side bar in the middle of the frame, the one with the hand pointer, is not supposed to be there.

## *DESIGN ELEMENTS AND EXPORTING*

Creating graphics which export successfully from Corel Draw is largely a mechanical problem. Having read the first part of this chapter

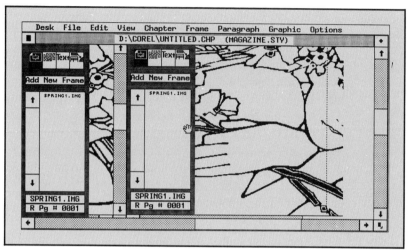

*Figure 8.6:* Ventura's cropping bug.

you should be fairly versant with the options you have available for getting your Corel Draw art into the documents of other programs.

Creating graphics which really work when they're imported into complete pages is quite a different problem, one of design rather than of software. Unfortunately, the features which make Corel Draw really powerful also make it capable of producing wildly inappropriate art if you don't think about the final destination of your pictures.

It might well be argued that some of the PostScript limitations we discussed a while ago aren't limitations so much as they are features. If you create an imported graphic which is so complex as to keep your page from printing, consider that what PostScript might be doing is telling you that you may be creating a page which is far too busy to be attractive.

This would probably be argued most stridently by the customer-support people at the company that made your printer should you call to complain about this limitation in their hardware.

Graphics which look good all by themselves don't necessarily look good when you import them into a desktop publishing page. The addition of a few columns of type and some potentially distracting headlines can often destroy the effect of an otherwise attractive piece of art.

## FINDING A FOCUS

As we discussed in the last chapter, a page which really works is a page with a focus. The design must lead one's eye into the page and then to wherever the contents of the page actually start. In a publication having a lot of similar pages, a well-designed page will be eye-catching enough to be noticed amidst all the others. Page design can often do more to make a page readable than the content itself, especially when you're dragging yourself along to the last page of a long, dry article.

You should also consider that pages of type suffer from an inherent flatness—they're two-dimensional by nature. Graphics which stand out from the pages they've been poured into will give the entire page a sense of depth, and make it more interesting.

There are lots of ways to do this. One of the effects which magazine publishers use a lot at the moment is to pour fountains into otherwise flat graphics, such as bar charts. Depending on the complexity of the overall page, you might be able to use them too. Consider the two pages in Figure 8.7.

It's also advisable to plan your graphics with a bit of rule-breaking in mind. If you deliberately create art which doesn't fit easily in regular rectangular frames, you'll have a good opportunity to do something interesting with it when it has been imported into pages. Figure 8.8 illustrates a couple of somewhat uncommon shapes for graphics.

## CLIP ART AND ORNAMENTS

In some cases, the graphics you export from Corel Draw will have been created for specific reasons. For instance, charts, graphs, and technical illustrations are specifically created to augment the information in the text they'll ultimately be surrounded by. It's probably not a good idea to get too creative with these sorts of graphics. A design which diminishes the informational value of graphics that have been created primarily to be informative is a design that has allowed art to get in the way of the publication's purpose.

To a large extent, however, graphics are meant to serve as ornaments. A page which has nothing but type on it is intimidating, and perhaps uninteresting and difficult to read. The inclusion of a few pictures, even if they're only tangential to the nature of the text, will

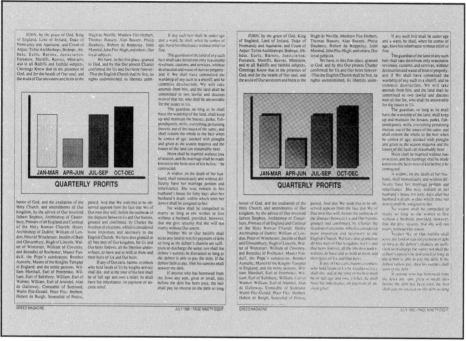

*Figure 8.7:* Giving a chart some depth.

make your desktop publishing chapters more approachable. Further, if you are creating a document with multiple pages, graphic ornaments can serve to tie the pages together. Publications with multiple pages frequently tie their pages together by using a large graphic on the first page and then smaller versions of it or fragments of it on subsequent pages. Figure 8.9 illustrates an example of this technique used over a multi-page spread.

In Ventura, you can pour graphics into frames and then make the frames appear on every page using the Repeating Frames item of Ventura's Frames menu. This is a handy way to use graphics of the ornamental sort, as new graphics will automatically appear as you add more pages to your document.

## ICONS

One of the more functional applications of ornamental graphics in desktop publishing is icons. Probably something of a by-product of

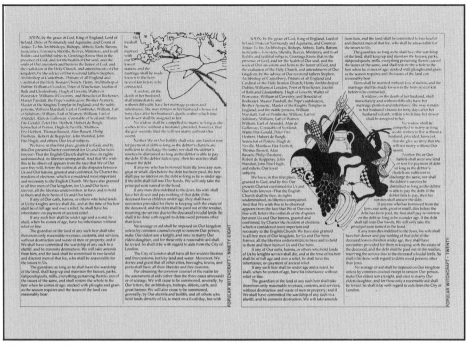

*Figure 8.8:* Using nonrectangular graphics.

the growing use of graphic user interfaces like Windows, icons are nonetheless an elegant way to highlight important areas of text or to allow your readers to locate pertinent parts of a document quickly.

Figure 8.10 illustrates the use of icons.

You can use just about any graphics you like as icons, but they work best when the icon images are fairly simple and easy to spot. This is handy, as the sorts of images which make good icons are also the easiest ones to cook up in Corel Draw.

In Ventura, the frames containing your icons can be tied to the text they're associated with, so that if you do something to cause the text to move, even to change pages, the icons will reposition themselves. Having created an icon and poured it into a frame, give it a name using the Anchors and Captions box of Ventura's Frames menu. Then you can place an anchor for the named frame in the text you want it to be next to by hitting Ctrl-C and then F5. If you later

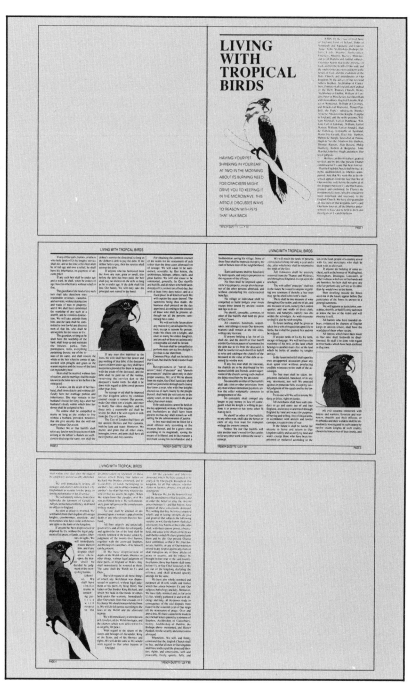

*Figure 8.9:* Using graphic fragments to tie pages together.

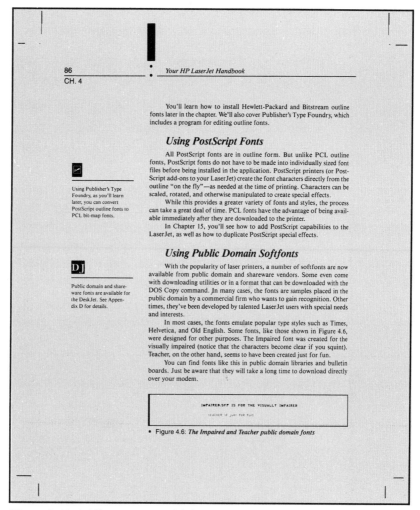

*Figure 8.10:* Adding some graphic icons to a document.

change anything in the text or layout such that the icons are no longer positioned where you'd like them, you can reposition them by selecting Anchor Frames from the Chapter menu.

If you plan to create large documents with lots of pages and lots of icons—a book, for example—you'll probably find that setting up all the individual instances of the icons is a bit tedious. There's a short cut of sorts which you can use with Ventura if you plan ahead.

1. Use Corel Draw to create all your icons and export them to GEM files.

2. Create a dummy chapter for your book in Ventura.

3. On the first page of the dummy chapter, create the frames for your icons and pour in the GEM files from Corel Draw.

4. Duplicate the frames enough times to allow for the greatest possible number of icons in your longest chapter. Give each new frame a unique and easily predictable name, such as "Warning 1," "Warning 2," "Warning 3," and so on.

5. Place the frames such that they're all at a constant distance from the left side of the page. Their vertical position doesn't matter, and they can overlap if need be.

6. Go through the text files for your chapters and install the anchors. The syntax for an anchor under Ventura is as follows:

<$&Warning 2[^]>

The text after the ampersand is the name you gave the icon in question with the Anchors and Captions box. You can use a named icon only once in each chapter, which is why you had to make lots of duplicates. The caret in the square brackets tells Ventura that this frame is to be relative to and above the anchor.

7. Pour your text into the dummy chapter and save the chapter under a new name.

8. Select Anchor Frames from the Chapter menu. Ventura will position all your icons for you.

9. Delete the unused icons from the first page.

As a final note, a few icons on a page are effective. Having an icon for every other paragraph is distracting, and the effectiveness of your icons will quickly diminish. Icons can be a superb use of exported graphics, but, as usual, only if you apply them sparingly.

## *HEADLINES*

The type facilities of Corel Draw have been expounded upon at length earlier in this book, and if you've played with them a bit you could probably expound on them yourself as well. The range of typefaces and type effects which Corel Draw offers far exceeds anything you could manage with desktop publishing software all by itself.

While it requires a bit of forethought to achieve, you can easily create your headlines in Corel Draw and export them to Ventura. Because the PostScript typefaces available under Ventura are also available under Corel Draw, you can easily match the fonts in your headlines to work with the type for your body copy. Helvetica under Corel Draw looks like Helvetica under Ventura, for example.

There is a multitude of effects you can add to headlines with Corel Draw. Figure 8.11 illustrates a variety of them, but these are only a small fraction of what you can get together.

When you go to export your headlines, you will probably have to give a bit of thought to the format you should use. The positioning problems inherent in EPS files make them less than ideal for headlines which will have to be placed accurately relative to the other elements on your page. Moreover, the path constraints of GEM files make some complex heads impossible in this format. If your headlines include fountains, intricate drawings or PostScript textures, you'll be stuck with EPS files and a bit of fine tuning once you get to Ventura.

From a design perspective, you should consider that a large headline will invariably serve as the focus of your page. As such, the nature of your headlines should set the tone of whatever your publication actually deals with. Headlines set in antique Germanic type, however interesting or eye-catching they may be, would probably not be appropriate for the stockholders' report of a computer manufacturer.

Consider using smaller versions of an interesting looking headline instead of graphics as ornaments or as a way to tie the pages of an article together. Some documents don't lend themselves to text used in this way, but varieties of headlines can often work where graphics can't.

It's a good rule to insist that all the type effects on a page look as if they have a reason for being there. It's another good rule to limit yourself in the variety of typefaces and effects you use. A corollary to

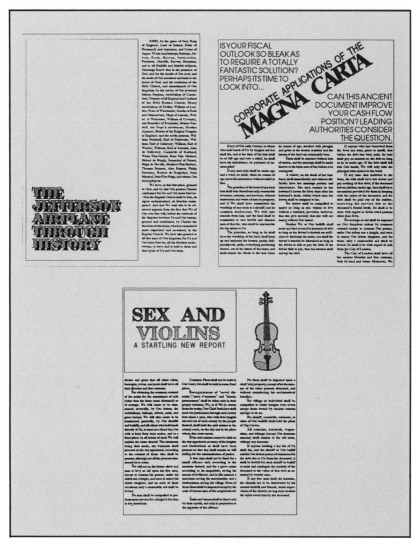

*Figure 8.11:* Some headlines created in Corel Draw and exported to Ventura.

this rule suggests that most pages should have no more than one serif face and one sans serif face on them.

If you use a particular font for your headlines, consider using it as well for subheadings, captions, and other non-body text to make the headline face relate to the rest of the document. Try to avoid creating a dominant, bold headline graphic if the rest of your page design uses fairly light type and thin rules. It's important to observe the difference between a headline which serves as a focus for your page and one which dominates it, distracting one's eye long after a focus is no longer needed.

It's said of type that nobody reads it if it's bigger than 14 points. In fact, people do not, as a rule, read headlines. They look at them, but they don't analyze them for meaning in the way that they do body text. There are a number of things you should bear in mind about your headlines in this light.

To begin with, avoid creating ornate heads which are hard to read, or people will be even less likely to bother trying. Secondly, avoid headlines with lots of words in them.

The really important thing to consider about large type is that, as most people are conditioned to ignore it, it's notoriously hard to proofread effectively unless you really think about what you're doing. There's a legendary example of this which took place quite a few years ago. Time magazine ran on its back cover an advertisement which contained the word "America" in enormous type across the page. Only as it was being printed did one of the pressmen notice that the word had been spelled incorrectly. He stopped the press and the error was fixed, fortunately before any copies hit the streets. However, in the aftermath of this it was discovered that over sixty people had proofed the ad without ever noticing the mistake.

## *DROP CAPITALS*

Ventura allows you to create drop capitals as a special effect in the formation of a paragraph tag, but its facilities are limited to the fonts it has and the effects it can manage with them. You can create far more interesting drop caps in Corel Draw and import them into Ventura chapters as graphics.

There isn't a lot you *can't* do in creating a drop cap. Some of them get pretty strange. If the opening headline of a document is fairly plain, you can focus the attention of someone looking at the page on the start of the text most effectively by using a noticeable drop cap. Some page designs extend the idea of a drop cap to the entire first word of the text.

Figure 8.12 illustrates some drop capitals and other similar effects created in Corel Draw and exported to Ventura. Note that we can get away with using fountains and PostScript textures in these examples because they are elements of pages which aren't very complex.

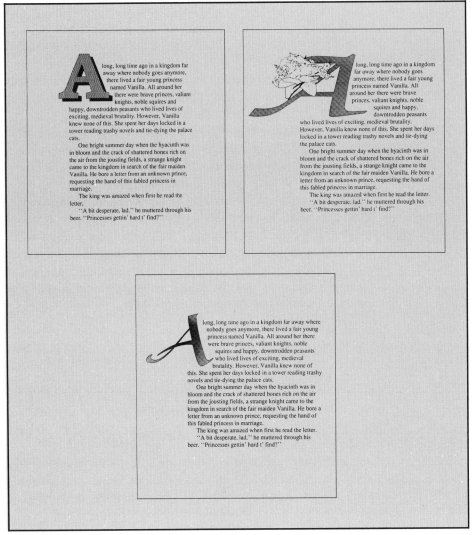

*Figure 8.12:* Some examples of drop capitals exported from Corel Draw.

Some magazine and book page designs use drop capitals rather than subheads. Occasionally you'll find one which manages to combine both, as shown in Figure 8.13.

## EXPORTING TEXT BOXES

One of the reasons why page designers like graphics so much isn't really artistic at all—it's wholly pragmatic. If you pour a text file into a Ventura chapter, you'll probably find that it doesn't fill the chapter perfectly. Depending on the luck of the draw, you'll either wind up a few paragraphs shy of a full final page or a few paragraphs over.

A good page design allows you to compensate for text files of inconsiderate lengths by having some flexibility built into the nontext elements. For instance, if you have lots of graphics on a page you can resize some of them a bit to force the text to fit. However, if this isn't practical, the next best thing is to use text boxes.

A text box, or "quote box," is nothing more than a box surrounding a bit of pertinent-sounding text set large and stuck in the body of your document. Figure 8.14 illustrates some examples of text boxes. Ventura can create these, but Corel Draw can do a lot more with

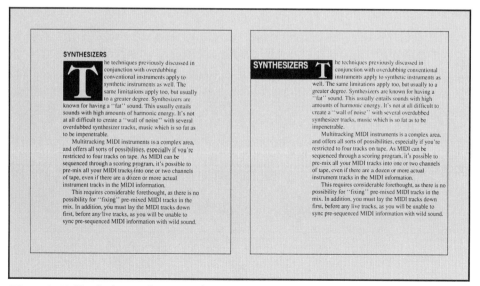

*Figure 8.13:* Replacing and augmenting subheads with drop capitals.

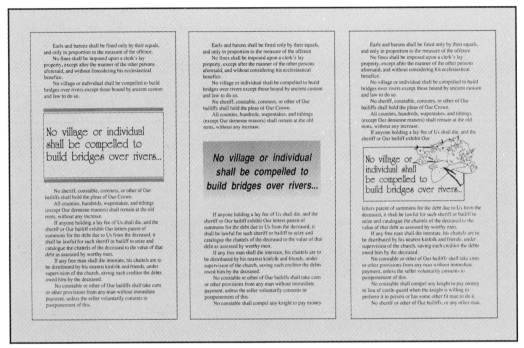

*Figure 8.14:* Text boxes exported from Corel Draw.

them in terms of using text effects. Also, if you export text boxes from Corel Draw as graphics, you can easily resize them in Ventura if you have to adjust the length of your document a bit.

One particularly elegant way to create text boxes is to use Corel Draw in conjunction with Windows Write, the word processor which comes with Windows. As was discussed earlier in this book, you can copy small chunks of text from Write to Corel Draw through the clipboard. While these chunks are limited to 250 characters, this is usually more than enough for a text box.

To create some text boxes, do the following:

1. Run Windows, then run Write and Corel Draw at the same time.

2. Load the text of your document into Write. Chances are your document will not have been written in Write format, in which case you can just load it as an ASCII file. You will not

be modifying the document itself, nor will you be saving it back to disk when you're done.

3. Find a suitable line or two of text in Write. Highlight it and copy it to the clipboard using the Copy item of the Edit menu in Write.

4. Bring Corel Draw forward. Use the text tool to open the Text dialog box.

5. Paste the text in the clipboard into the Text dialog box by holding down the Shift key and hitting Ins.

6. Set the text into a suitable text box. If the text you've used is a fragment of a sentence, it's appropriate to indicate this with an ellipsis. You can use three periods if you like, or you can use the special ellipsis character, character 0145. Hold down the Alt key and type 0145 on the numeric keypad to enter this character. What you get in the Text dialog box will probably be an apostrophe, but what will be printed will still come out as an ellipse. (See Chapter 3 for enlightenment on this apparent glitch.)

Having created a text box, it's usually practical to export it as a line art file, that is, as a GEM file for Ventura. If your application for Corel Draw and Ventura involves laying out a lot of chapters which might use text boxes in this way, you might want to create four or five of them for each chapter before you start, pulling interesting quotes from various parts of the chapter, and using them as needed when you start working through your pages.

Text boxes do help to break up pages which are otherwise nothing but type, and as such their use isn't wholly a layout convenience. However, you'll probably find that their major attraction is for getting you out of awkward situations when there's just not enough text to fill in the spaces.

Page designers are often accused of regarding body copy as ''fill'' or ''gravel,'' that stuff that occupies the white space around their design elements. Editors are often accused of regarding graphics in the same light. You might want to consider where your sympathies lie, and attempt to strike a balance, keeping an open mind concerning possible conflicts.

# *WRAPPING UP*

Using Corel Draw in conjunction with a desktop publishing package allows you to marry two powerful applications and get the best out of both. However, more than this, it allows you to be editor, page designer, and artist all at the same time. While this might leave you busier than you would have been otherwise, it will also allow you to bring a more unified perspective to the chapters you create. Having control over all the elements of a page gives you the potential for creating designs in which the graphics really suit the text, and the overall page design accurately reflects the mindset of its intended audience.

Italic
Bold
a Bold Italic
ica Black
tica Black Italic
ica Light
etica Light Italic
etica Narrow
etica Narrow Italic
vetica Narrow Bold
elvetica Narrow Bold Italic

*Designing with Type*

**T**YPE CAN BE AMONG THE MOST POWERFUL OF design elements. It can communicate far more than just the meanings of the words you set: used correctly, it can evoke deeper levels of meaning, suggesting culture, setting, and style. If your applications for Corel Draw include using it to set type, you should give some thought to the basics of type as an art form.

The richness of type as an art form is evidenced by its diversity. You already have a feel for this to some extent if you've played with the wide variety of typefaces which accompany Corel Draw. However, this is actually a very tiny fraction of the typefaces which have been created in the long and rather twisted history of type. If you find the diversity of type available in Corel Draw inadequate as it stands, you might want to consult Appendix B of this book: it deals with using the WFNBOSS program, included with Corel Draw, to add still more faces to the package.

## *UNDERSTANDING TYPEFACES*

One of the distinctions which will turn up in this chapter is that between "body copy" and headlines, which is reflected in the fact that typefaces are designed specifically for use as either body faces or display faces. (This was touched on in Chapter 3, but it's worth clarifying it here. You're reading body copy now, in a Baskerville typeface. In a moment you'll probably notice a line which reads "The History of Helvetica," which is headline copy, in bold italic Baskerville.)

Many type "families"—we'll discuss these shortly—have both body- and display-face variations. However, it's important to distinguish between these two applications of type and not to interchange them. Body faces are designed to be set small and used in words that are to be read, as in the body copy of an advertisement or the paragraphs of text on a book page. They tend to be light and simple. Display faces are designed to be set large and have visual impact, as in headlines, titles, banners, and posters.

Body faces don't make for interesting headlines. They lack the intensity to stand out from a page. Display faces, on the other hand, don't produce body copy which is easy to read—the type has too much detail, and is too busy to allow one's eye to get on with reading the words.

Most of the faces which come with Corel Draw are display faces. Some, such as Times or Helvetica, are really intended for use as body faces, but are included with Corel Draw because they frequently find themselves pressed into service as display faces too. You might want to use them as such to match the type in an existing design, for example. In general, though, Corel Draw's typeface assortment is heavily weighted in favor of display faces because just about everything it does with type is a display-face application. At any rate, it cannot set more than 255 characters at a time, because it is not intended to be a replacement for a word processing program.

## THE HISTORY OF HELVETICA

You certainly do not need to understand anything about the history of typography in order to use the type facilities of Corel Draw. However, much of the rationale behind applying type to design problems may be seen in the way type has evolved into its present form. The forces which drove it were at least partially a result of the demands of designers for specific typographic features. (The other part was the demand of type foundries, the companies which design and manufacture type, to dominate their respective markets and sell lots of faces.)

The Helvetica typeface has a long, fairly convoluted history which will probably help you to understand a lot about why type is as it is.

Helvetica is a sans serif typeface, and though it has a long history, it is a comparatively recent development as movable type goes. The first typefaces were considerably more ornate. Helvetica is called a "lineal" typeface, that is, one in which all the stalks and elements of the typeface design are essentially lines of the same width.

The earliest precursor to Helvetica is thought to be a face called Egyptian, released by William Caslon IV in 1816. Caslon was a noted type designer, among other things—you may have noticed that the Casablanca typeface which comes with Corel Draw is in fact Caslon, named after him.

Egyptian was not particularly Egyptian in appearance; nor was it much like the faces which Caslon and other type founders of the period were used to. It lacked all vestiges of the then common ornamentation of type, and was exceedingly plain. Its most notable absence was serifs, which made it look rather sparse and did not endear it to the typesetters of the period. In those days, type was set entirely by hand and the serifs on the characters helped to keep the edges of the type from wearing down prematurely.

The Egyptian face created only a mild stir in typographic circles. Several similar faces appeared for a short while, but it was a long time before sans serif type gained any significant acceptance.

Mechanical typesetting was born in the latter part of the nineteenth century with the invention of hot lead type. While one may regard this as being simply a convenience, a quicker and perhaps more economical way to arrive at the results previously managed by hand, it was really as much of a revolution in its day as laser printers and desktop publishing are now. The advent of typesetting machines made books and newspapers of the sort we're used to a practical reality, and it also made the use of sans serif type less problematic.

Much of the early design of type and typesetting originated in Germany—Gutenberg seems to have founded a tradition of typesetting there which long survived him. When mechanical typesetting had grown to be widely accepted, Berthold AG, one of the great German type foundries, released a face called Akzidenz-Grotesk. It looked a lot like Helvetica does now. It was also one of the earliest instances of the appellation Grotesk, or grotesque, applied to sans serif type.

Despite what you might think, this does not imply that its designers thought the face was particularly ugly. The etymology of "grotesk" is a bit complex; the term has been applied in typography mainly as an alternative to "gothic." Gothic is a somewhat vague term in typography, and it would be very hard to define concisely—you'll probably get a feel for it as you become more familiar with various typefaces. It is usually used to imply that the face in question is somehow evocative of traditional or conservative type design.

Akzidenz-Grotesk was originally intended for use as a display face. In a world rich with ornate faces, the simple, decisive lines of a sans serif face stood out, and made for a good display face. It was released in medium condensed and bold condensed faces.

Early in the history of commercial printing, typeface designers realized that type naturally lent itself to being designed in "families," that is, in a number of weights which were visually distinct from one another but which had similar enough characteristics to appear to have sprung from the same root.

The initial weights of Akzidenz-Grotesk were eventually added to until there was a moderately full family around it. This included a medium-weight face, which no one particularly liked. It also included several more varieties of display faces. There was a light face, an expanded face, and an extremely light version called Akzidenz-Grotesk Skelett, that is, skeletal.

There are quite a few important things to note in the evolution of Akzidenz-Grotesk. First of all, it was well received because it was distinct from the faces which were in common use at the time. Secondly, it was well received as a display face, that is, as a face intended for use in headlines, titles, and so on. The normal weight, added to the family fairly late in its development, was intended for use in body copy, but it was something of a failure. This may be attributed to the general apprehension of designers, both then and now, that one body face looks pretty much like another, and that there was little cause for embracing a new one. It also might be attributed to the rather "unfriendly" appearance of sans serif faces used to set body copy.

Akzidenz-Grotesk became quite popular, but its name, among other things (it didn't sound any less weird back then), precluded its successful marketing in the English-speaking world. The name eventually faded away in German typesetting circles, too, although it returned briefly in the late 1950s as Akzidenz-Grotesk 57. Very recently it has again been reborn as AG Old Face, a phototypesetting face faithfully copied from the original metal type of 1896.

It's worth noting that Akzidenz-Grotesk found its greatest popularity in Switzerland. Helvetica, in fact, was commissioned by a Swiss type foundry. It was designed in the 1950s by Max Meidinger, and it is clearly based on Akzidenz-Grotesk. At about the same time, a French type designer, Adrian Frutiger, was creating Univers. Helvetica and Univers look exceedingly similar, although you will notice a few design differences. If you become very conscious of type, you may come to feel that Univers, with its slightly more flowing style and more sensuous feel, expresses something subtly different from Helvetica. Both Helvetica and Univers are included with Corel Draw—you can see them both in Figure 9.1.

One of the important distinctions between Akzidenz-Grotesk and both Helvetica and Univers is that the latter two faces were designed

*Figure 9.1:* Helvetica and Univers.

as complete, unified families of type. We will discuss the significance of this in greater detail later in this chapter. However, Helvetica suffered from a lot of name troubles early in its life, as its various weights got called different things in different circumstances. Hence, at various times Helvetica Light and Helvetica Extralight were in fact the same face, and it became difficult to specify something in a particular weight of Helvetica and know what one was going to get. The Helvetica family as it appears today in Corel Draw (under the name Switzerland) is shown in Figure 9.2.

Univers, by comparison, was always named consistently—with numerical values for its various weights—Univers 45 for the light weight, for example. While perhaps not as descriptive as the names

Helvetica
*Helvetica Italic*
**Helvetica Bold**
***Helvetica Bold Italic***
**Helvetica Black**
***Helvetica Black Italic***
Helvetica Light
*Helvetica Light Italic*
Helvetica Narrow
*Helvetica Narrow Italic*
**Helvetica Narrow Bold**
***Helvetica Narrow Bold Italic***

*Figure 9.2:* The Helvetica family.

applied to Helvetica, the numbering system was consistent. There are designers who favor Univers over Helvetica for this reason.

There are countless variations on the original Akzidenz-Grotesk face extant today. This includes buckets of authorized Helvetica derivations designed by the descendants of the type foundry which created Helvetica itself. You'll encounter extended Helvetica, rounded Helvetica, Helvetica designed expressly for body copy—book weight Helvetica—and so on. There are also countless knock-offs of these fonts under other names.

The evolution of Helvetica was unquestionably commercially driven to some extent, but in it you can also see the demands of designers for particular sorts of type, or for type to perform certain functions. These functions will probably crop up in your applications of type under Corel Draw. You might consider the problems in type evolution when you're thinking about the problems of suiting type to your graphics.

## TYPES OF TYPE

Type design is a rather esoteric art. The plethora of software packages which ostensibly allow one to design custom typefaces will attest to this. They make designing bad type exceedingly easy. Actually, if you have a background in typeface design (or if you're presently employed by one of the type foundries), you *can* design good type with some of them.

Figure 9.3 shows a character under construction. This is the sort of thing which goes on for each character of a typeface being designed.

In considering type, it's important to realize that every typeface was designed with a lot of reasoning behind it, and that all that reasoning was expended to design it for a specific function. Before anyone reads your type, they'll see it as a graphic element. Its visual appearance, and whatever it evokes or fails to evoke as a graphic, will color their perception of your words.

Consider the type samples in Figure 9.4. All four of these paragraphs have the same words in them, but they read differently. If you came upon each of them in isolation, your approach to what they had

*Figure 9.3:* How a character is designed.

to say would probably be modified by their appearances. Before you read it, the visual style of the type speaks.

The type samples in Figure 9.4 are a bit extreme. The ornate details of the second sample, for instance, are extremely evocative but hardly ever used, except as an effect. The message in the typeface is too broad, too evidently a message to appeal to our sense that type itself should be evocative. Rather than a subtle suggestion, it's something of a pie in one's face.

*As soon as peace is restored, We will banish from Our kingdom all foreign knights, crossbowmen, attendants, and mercenaries who have come with horses and arms to the harm of the kingdom.*

𝔄𝔰 𝔰𝔬𝔬𝔫 𝔞𝔰 𝔭𝔢𝔞𝔠𝔢 𝔦𝔰 𝔯𝔢𝔰𝔱𝔬𝔯𝔢𝔡, 𝔚𝔢 𝔴𝔦𝔩𝔩 𝔟𝔞𝔫𝔦𝔰𝔥 𝔣𝔯𝔬𝔪 𝔒𝔲𝔯 𝔨𝔦𝔫𝔤𝔡𝔬𝔪 𝔞𝔩𝔩 𝔣𝔬𝔯𝔢𝔦𝔤𝔫 𝔨𝔫𝔦𝔤𝔥𝔱𝔰, 𝔠𝔯𝔬𝔰𝔰𝔟𝔬𝔴𝔪𝔢𝔫, 𝔞𝔱𝔱𝔢𝔫𝔡𝔞𝔫𝔱𝔰, 𝔞𝔫𝔡 𝔪𝔢𝔯𝔠𝔢𝔫𝔞𝔯𝔦𝔢𝔰 𝔴𝔥𝔬 𝔥𝔞𝔳𝔢 𝔠𝔬𝔪𝔢 𝔴𝔦𝔱𝔥 𝔥𝔬𝔯𝔰𝔢𝔰 𝔞𝔫𝔡 𝔞𝔯𝔪𝔰 𝔱𝔬 𝔱𝔥𝔢 𝔥𝔞𝔯𝔪 𝔬𝔣 𝔱𝔥𝔢 𝔨𝔦𝔫𝔤𝔡𝔬𝔪.

*As soon as peace is restored. We will banish from Our kingdom all foreign knights. crossbowmen. attendants. and mercenaries who have come with horses and arms to the harm of the kingdom.*

As soon as peace is restored, We will banish from Our kingdom all foreign knights, crossbowmen, attendants, and mercenaries who have come with horses and arms to the harm of the kingdom.

*Figure 9.4:* Different body faces.

Let's consider four more type samples, as seen in Figure 9.5.

These four faces are a bit less extreme, but each has a particular style and a particular message. The paragraph set in Helvetica looks crisp and sterile, and suggests something of a technical or business-like nature. The passage in Caslon looks gothic—in the typographic use of that word—and suggests age and stability. The sample of Optima seems sparse and ascetic, suggesting that its words will be to the point, with no ornamentation. The text in Times Roman has a sense of neutrality about it, perhaps because Times is such a commonly used font.

As soon as peace is restored, We will banish from
Our kingdom all foreign knights, crossbowmen,
attendants, and mercenaries who have come with
horses and arms to the harm of the kingdom.
Helvetica

As soon as peace is restored, We will banish from
Our kingdom all foreign knights, crossbowmen,
attendants, and mercenaries who have come with
horses and arms to the harm of the kingdom.

Caslon

As soon as peace is restored, We will banish from
Our kingdom all foreign knights, crossbowmen,
attendants, and mercenaries who have come with
horses and arms to the harm of the kingdom.

Optima

As soon as peace is restored, We will banish from
Our kingdom all foreign knights, crossbowmen,
attendants, and mercenaries who have come with
horses and arms to the harm of the kingdom.

Times Roman

*Figure 9.5:* Four more conventional typefaces.

It may well be argued that only type gurus and perhaps owners of
Corel Draw will analyze type to quite this extent. However, the subtleties of type affect people who see it, whether they think about it or
not, and you can make this visual aspect of type work for you by
choosing type which suits the direction of whatever you're designing.
There are a lot of useful guidelines for choosing type, but the first one
is always to make sure that the message of your typeface agrees with
the message of the rest of your drawing (or poster or page).

Consider the two graphics in Figure 9.6. The images are the same,
as are the words which have been appended to them. However, the

*Figure 9.6:* Type and a drawing, two examples.

two typefaces involved alter the overall effect of the two graphics considerably. The upper version, set in Helvetica, lacks any cohesiveness between the text and the graphic. The elegant, flowing lines of the picture jar with the hard, sharp edges of the type. One has a feeling of the type and the picture existing as separate entities, with little in common save that they've been placed on the same page.

The second image works a great deal better. The lines of the type—in the Benguiat face this time—work well with the drawing, and the picture complements the words. The whole graphic locks together, and one is not confronted with two contradictory visual messages upon considering it.

There are certainly reasons to break the rules, although, as we discussed in Chapter 7, you should do so consciously and creatively. One fairly obvious example is in setting small type. Text which is smaller than about nine points begins to get difficult or impossible to read if it's handled in an ornate font. A simple, sans serif font like Helvetica will survive at small point sizes far better than a serif one.

One is often confronted with similar mechanical constraints. The chart in Color Plate 7 in this book, for example, was originally all set in Caslon. It looked better in Caslon, but it spread out far too much. The solution was to set all the type in a horizontally condensed face. Corel Draw comes with few such faces, one of which is Helvetica Narrow. I could also have used Futura Light—a font which is almost as condensed—without a significantly different visual effect.

It might be argued that the chart could have been done using a serif face by simply transforming it into a compressed one, squeezing the type horizontally until it fit. This approach seems elegant in theory but isn't all that workable in practice. Condensing an ornate font this way usually leaves you with rather ugly type. Genuine condensed versions of typefaces are designed as such, from scratch.

You also might decide simply for effect that you want to break the rule of having your typefaces match your graphics. The results of doing so can be eye-catching and effective simply because they *don't* work as unified graphics; rather, they contrast. Consider Figure 9.7.

As with all elements of design, try to do this sort of thing with a reasonable measure of subtlety and with some thought as to whose eye you're trying to catch. A graphic which is eye-catching because it's simply bad or loud and obnoxious isn't necessarily effective.

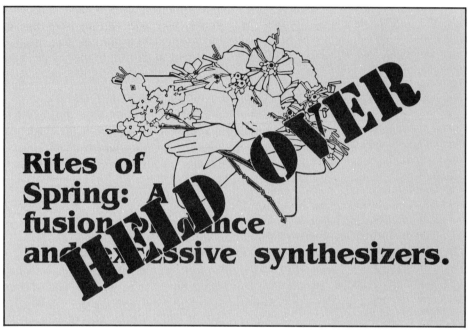

*Figure 9.7:* Deliberately mismatching type to a graphic.

## TYPE FAMILIES

The typefaces which come with Corel Draw are, for the most part, supplied in families. If you use a font like Garamond, for example, you can introduce variations in your text using the italic, bold, and bold italic versions of the face.

If you've used a Macintosh, you might have noticed that the Mac algorithmically produces italics from medium type by simply skewing the font slightly, and bold by laterally expanding each character a bit. This works for crude dot-matrix printing, but it isn't nearly good enough for true typesetting. For instance, each of the faces of Garamond is a separate font—someone originally designed Garamond four ways.

One important rule in creating graphics of any sort—and especially when using type—is that human beings subconsciously attach meaning to everything they see, or, perhaps more precisely, look for meaning in everything they see. For this reason, everything you do in creating a design should appear to have been done for a deliberate reason.

The subtle differences between fairly similar typefaces can be used to make an excellent illustration of this rule. Consider the type in Figure 9.8.

In reading the paragraph in Figure 9.8, you may have been struck with the sense of something being wrong with it. It seems peculiar without there being an obvious reason for it. If you look closely, however, you might be able to pick out the reason: some of the words have been set in Times Roman and some in Garamond. These two faces are very similar, but they're different enough that they look distinct side-by-side.

Figure 9.9 illustrates the same text with very different fonts. This may be a good example of bad typography, but it isn't as disturbing as the first one. In this case it's obvious that something has been done, and it might be the case that the designer did it for some conscious reason.

As soon as peace is restored, We will banish from Our kingdom all foreign knights, crossbowmen, attendants, and mercenaries who have come with horses and arms to the harm of the kingdom.

*Figure 9.8:* Some type.

As soon as peace is restored, We will banish from Our kingdom all foreign knights, crossbowmen, attendants, and mercenaries who have come with horses and arms to the harm of the kingdom.

*Figure 9.9:* More type, in this case with a more obvious reason for being this way.

Typefaces should be selected and used with some conscious reasoning in mind. If you have a good reason for choosing Garamond, say, over Times Roman at some place in your graphic, chances are that you will not have an equally good reason for using Times Roman rather than Garamond somewhere else in the same graphic.

As a rule, you should not have type from more than two families in a single graphic or on a single page. Furthermore, the two families should be visually distinct. The best application of this rule is to make one of the families a serif font, and the other a sans serif font. The functions the different families are put to should also be distinct—the serif face for body copy and the sans serif face for heads, for example, if you're designing complete pages.

Once again, you can break this rule if you have a good reason to, but think about it carefully before you do. A design which incorporates a welter of different typefaces can be eye-catching if it's done for the right reasons, but it's far more likely simply to be confusing.

The faces which have condensed, extrabold, and other variations offer a powerful facility for introducing variations on your type without violating the two-family rule. For example, Helvetica and Helvetica Narrow look pretty good together—they're different faces, but they still appear to be from the same family.

## USING BOLD AND ITALIC

Corel Draw allows you to employ the usual additional type fonts of italic and boldface. In some cases, you can use the condensed or extrabold versions of standard faces for additional effect. These facilities offer a world of opportunity for bad design if you don't apply them with restraint.

The expressive potential of typography has probably been expounded upon at sufficient length. Aside from being able to evoke, through your choice of typefaces, a particular state of mind in someone looking at your design, you can also add emphasis and direction to the words you set through the use of related faces. However, just as you can visually misdirect or confuse someone by choosing the wrong typeface, so too can you render your words ineffective by misapplying the family members of a good typeface.

If you look through a few pages of this book, you'll probably notice all the section heads. They're very obvious and eye-catching, in that they're in boldface. Because this book is intended to serve at least partially as a reference work, the effect of having heads snagging your attention is appropriate. It allows you to skim through the book and easily identify the subjects of the various sections.

Boldface text within a paragraph will also snag your eye. In most cases, though, you should probably not try this technique. Reading body text with boldface words scattered through it is uncomfortable. Your eye will be constantly distracted by the nearest bold word or passage. Boldface should never be used in body text for emphasis unless you particularly want your readers to pick out key words at the expense of the meaning of the copy in general.

If you want emphasis in body text, use italics. Because they are the same weight as the rest of the type, italics will not immediately stand out from the page (unless, of course, they are overused). They *will* be noticeable as the text is read, which is when you want them to be noticeable.

As with other attention-getting devices, changes in type fonts are at their best if you use them sparingly. Text which is largely italicized with bold heads between every paragraph quickly negates the effectiveness of all the emphasis these differences usually convey.

When you apply text to a Corel Draw graphic, you can do a lot toward integrating the text and your picture by considering how best to apply certain types of text. For example, consider that boldface type might integrate nicely into a drawing which has a lot of dominant black areas. Likewise, a simple but elegant application is to use italicized text if your drawing has any slanted elements. If the slant of your drawing doesn't happen to match the slant of your italics you might have to skew the text mechanically.

Type purists will probably lurch about the room in horror at this idea—italics are not merely slanted type, they say. However, it's often necessary to take a few liberties with the typefaces to make them do what you want. This is what makes Corel Draw so useful.

## GUIDELINES FOR USING COREL DRAW'S FACES

As you know, there are all sorts of reasons to recommend one typeface over another. For example, a graphic with many curved objects lends itself to a serif typeface, preferably one with lots of curves of its own, such as Garamond or Caslon. A graphic which looks sparse and mechanical might work well with a similarly designed face. Friz Quadrata is a particularly useful typeface in this regard, in that although it is a serif face, it still maintains the appearance of being rather chiseled and lean, without flowery ornamentation.

The rest of this chapter consists of some discussion about the specific typefaces included with Corel Draw and how you might want to apply them. These ideas are by no means rigid—you can ignore them whenever you feel it's appropriate—but they might help you to find the most applicable faces for your applications.

Bear in mind that this discussion incorporates a lot of personal bias as well. You'll quickly develop your own attitudes about type as you work with it, quite probably disagreeing passionately with mine. Art will do that to you.

The following discussion is arranged alphabetically by the proper commercial names of the fonts. The corresponding Corel Draw pseudonym is shown alongside in parentheses.

## AACHEN BOLD (AARDVARK BOLD)

Aachen is a massive and rather eye-catching display face. It doesn't actually look all that attractive, but it's hard to miss. It's also hard to read if you set it small. Aachen doesn't purport to be subtle.

This would be a good face for applications in which you want a headline or title to be noticed but you don't really care what people think of it. Ugly type may not be very pleasing, but it's difficult to ignore. If you're printing in color, set the Aachen type in purple against a black background and it will have its maximum effect.

If you can get more than a dozen words on a page in Aachen, you've set them too small.

## AMERICAN TYPEWRITER (MEMORANDUM)

American Typewriter is obviously a gadget face, a special effect. It doesn't really look like it has come from a typewriter—for one thing, it's proportionately spaced. It is evocative of typewriters, however, and is useful for this reason. It's also useful in all sorts of type-based graphics, as it's a serif face with a lineal design—there are no points, picks or other sharp edges. It worked well as the basis for the giant A graphic at the beginning of this book for just this reason.

Despite appearances to the contrary, American Typewriter does not make a good body face. It's great for heads in which you want to suggest a connection with an office, with writing, with archaic machinery, or with individuals as opposed to machines or corporations. Type-writers are evocative of individual typists or authors; type is evocative of companies and organizations big enough to afford typesetters. This distinction may vanish as laser printers become common household appliances.

## *AVANTE GARDE (AVALON)*

Avante Garde is certainly one of my favorite sans serif faces. It has the clean, distinct lines of Helvetica but, as its name implies, it's a bit more daring and adventurous. It's a good choice when your application calls for a sans serif face and you consider Helvetica or Univers too overused or too conservative. Some of the capital letters of Avante Garde, such as the Q, are particularly attractive, and it's tempting to work in text with Q's in it just be able to see them.

Much of the appeal of Avante Garde is its clean, breezy appearance. This tends to vanish when you use the bold weight of this font. Bold Avante Garde isn't ugly—it's just not quite as appealing as the medium face is.

Avante Garde makes a good face for doing headlines and other bits of display type, especially if the other font in your design is something fairly pedestrian, like Times Roman.

## *BENGUIAT (BANGKOK)*

Benguiat is a particularly ornate serif face, evocative of turn-of-the-century poster art, among other things. It looks a bit bohemian, and suggests that the design it's part of is sensual and perhaps some-what debauched. Benguiat is a rather specialized typeface, and one which you probably won't have call to use all that often. However, it's very effective in the right context, because it's so rich in images.

Obviously, the aforementioned richness is somewhat audience-dependent. It may conjure up allusions to the heyday of turn-of-the-century Europe, but only for people who are familiar with these ideas. It will just look flowery and overdone if you apply it as the headlines for a book on chartered accountancy, for example.

Perhaps the biggest drawback to Benguiat is that it's attractive enough to lead one to use it in places where it doesn't belong. I've yet to find anything practical to do with it, although I'd like to.

## *BODONI POSTER (BODNOFF)*

Bodoni is another special-purpose typeface. It's not quite art deco, but it's reminiscent of the period. As such, it doesn't have the too-obvious, campy appearance of simply using art deco type, but it still manages to evoke the period and culture.

Ignoring this aspect of its design, Bodoni is also a rather attractive display font in its own right. It's as bold and noticeable as Aachen, but it's nowhere near as unpleasant to look at. It looks sophisticated and dignified even though it's kind of enormous. Like Aachen, however, you should not use Bodoni to set small type—it gets very nearly unreadable.

Bodoni, as with so many other specialized faces, makes a good effect when it happens to match the direction of the rest of your design. It's not suited for general use, however. You wouldn't want to use it as the display face in book design, for example. Its distinctiveness would work against you in this case—one's eye would become so interested in the visual appeal of this interesting font as to be distracted from the principal intent of your design.

## *BOOKMAN (BROOKLYN)*

Bookman, as its name suggests, is a very well crafted body face for setting books. It's included with most PostScript printers, and it is used quite frequently for body copy in desktop publishing applications. Having it available in Corel Draw therefore allows you to create graphics which perfectly match or complement the type in a desktop-published document.

As a body face, Bookman is a bit less horizontally condensed than Times Roman. It takes up more space, which is both handy if you want to fill a lot of paper with relatively few words and functional if you want those words to be more easily read.

If you apply Bookman to a stand-alone graphic in Corel Draw, you'll probably notice that it's unusually easy to read. While visually unremarkable, it's useful for this purpose.

## *BRUSH SCRIPT (BANFF)*

Brush Script is one of the more severely abused special-effect typefaces. This is at least partially because it makes good press-on lettering, having fat stalks that are less likely to break off, and it has worked its way into letterhead, business cards, and other sorts of quick printing for this reason.

While not unattractive in isolation, Brush Script suffers from over-exposure. It has become something of a cliché, and it's probably worth avoiding for this reason. It seems to cry out "Look here—special effect in progress—film at eleven!"

Besides all that, there's a certain perversity in using a four-thousand-dollar laser printer to simulate handwriting, the very thing it was created to do away with.

## *CASLON (CASABLANCA)*

I'm never sure if I like Caslon better for its appearance or for the typographic traditions it evokes. If it's the latter case, it'll be effective only for other people interested in type. Visually, though, Caslon manages to be eye-catching yet restrained and distinguished at the same time. Its disproportionately large caps and ascenders make type set in it look large without seeming massive.

Caslon doesn't make a bad body face, although its real strength is in doing heads and titles. It's well suited to designs in which you want to suggest age, stability, conservative values, and so on.

## *CENTURY OLD STYLE (CENTURION OLD)*

Century is a somewhat gothic—"grotesk"—serif face. It's a bit more ornate than Times Roman, but also more horizontally condensed than Bookman. It doesn't work badly for heads, although it appears to be a body face. It's enough like Times to get away with using Times for a body face and Century for large, bold heads.

Gothic faces are another of those subtle applications of type that only other type gurus will consciously recognize. Century suggests stability and permanence without being really obvious about it.

## *COOPER BLACK (CUPERTINO)*

It's said that Cooper was designed by a "farsighted printer with nearsighted clients." It's a nice-looking typeface for titles, although it might be alleged to suffer a bit in that it looks like the sort of face a press-on lettering company would embrace. Cooper has the advantage of standing out from an otherwise busy page by virtue of its boldness, while at the same time not detracting from its surroundings by looking ugly or weird. It seems to evoke hand-set type and an age of simpler things.

Because Cooper covers a lot of real estate, it's a great face to use for extreme type-based Corel Draw graphics. Like American Typewriter, it's a good base for fitting text to.

## *FRANKLIN GOTHIC (FRANKFURT GOTHIC)*

The subtleties of sans serif faces are often hard to appreciate. In isolation, one Helvetica clone looks pretty much like another.

Franklin Gothic is different from Helvetica in that its caps and ascenders are quite a bit smaller in relation to its normal lowercase letters. Type set in Franklin has a rather dominant look to it. It suggests that whatever it says is so important as to entail filling up every square inch of the paper it covers.

If your design calls for a sans serif font and you've done Helvetica to death, Franklin is a particularly attractive alternative. It's provided in an extrabold face, too, which adds to its usefulness.

## *FREESTYLE SCRIPT (FREEPORT)*

Given the choice between Freestyle Script and Brush Script— assuming that you must use a script face at all—the former is probably a better choice. For one thing, it looks more like handwriting. It's also a great deal less common. If you use it very sparingly, such that its precision as a font doesn't become apparent, it might even be mistaken for handwriting.

A script face such as this one can be effective if you apply it cleverly. The juxtaposition of a precise graphic and an apparently analog bit of handwriting can be very eye-catching. Consider using it to add your signature to a graphic in the way that a painter might sign a painting.

If you have more than a couple of dozen characters set in Freestyle Script on the same page you're probably overdoing it.

## *FRIZ QUADRATA (FRANCE)*

Friz Quadrata manages to combine the hard, crisp lines of a sans serif font with the attractiveness of a serif face. It looks businesslike and technical, and, as its name suggests, somewhat contemporarily German. Friz is a font which is rarely used, and as such is a good face to use for doing something different with type.

Friz Quadrata works well in heads for things like corporate reports and technical publications, and in graphics where the subject is mechanical, technical, scientific, or perhaps financial. It suggests that its demeanor is serious, but that there is an element of humanity in this otherwise serious subject.

## *FUTURA (FUJIYAMA)*

Futura is a sans serif font which is both more condensed and bolder than Helvetica. It's better suited to heads in which you want to get a lot of type into a small space, and the generally punchier appearance of Futura is more likely to get noticed.

Futura is arguably a bit less interesting and appealing than Helvetica—what it gains in visibility it lacks in appearance. It's good for applications wherein its contribution to your design is secondary to its usefulness in other areas, specifically that of being a good, unmistakable headline face. It's extrabold version is extremely hard to ignore.

## *GARAMOND (GATINEAU)*

Garamond is one of the most attractive serif faces, and its appeal grows the bigger you make it. It's particularly ornate, but its ornamental elements, predominantly its serifs and large, flowing capitals, seem to have been designed with precisely the right amount of subtlety to go unnoticed most of the time. Garamond is one of the few serif faces which looks just as good in bold as it does in medium.

Garamond is a good face for use in headlines and titles if you want to convey a sense of culture and style without adding elements of other, specific design criteria; that is, it doesn't look too gothic or too antique or too modern and so forth.

One unique quality of Garamond is that it looks good tightly kerned. If you use the Corel Draw shape tool to squeeze all the space out from between its characters, Garamond flows naturally into a sort of quasi-graphic font. Headlines created this way don't lose too much readability, and they do make really attractive design elements.

## *HELVETICA (SWITZERLAND)*

Helvetica is often accused by designers of being unadventurous, dull, overused, lacking in dynamics, devoid of distinction, and the opiate of typesetters everywhere. All of this may well be true. If for no other reason than its almost daily appearance in everything from newspapers to spaghetti labels, Helvetica is so common as to be a non-effect. It evokes nothing. It is the safest sans serif font you can use.

There are certainly instances in which you will want to set type that says nothing other than the actual words you set. Helvetica has its place for this reason. It doesn't presuppose anything on the part of its ultimate readers, either. Someone who dislikes anything old may take unkindly to type set in Caslon; the Luddites among us will be bothered by Friz Quadrata. While your readers will never get excited about Helvetica, they'll never object to it, either.

In addition, Helvetica as it appears in Corel Draw is available in an enviable family of faces ranging from condensed and light versions up to an extrabold weight. This makes it extremely versatile.

In summary, you should consider using Helvetica when you want your graphics to speak and your words merely to convey information. It's also applicable if you anticipate the words you'll be setting to be read by a large and varied group of people. Finally, if you can't decide on what you want your typeface to evoke, it may be better to have it say nothing than to have it say something inappropriate.

### HOBO (HOMEWARD BOUND)

Hobo is another special-effect face. It's not unattractive in small doses, but its rather obvious apprehension of being laid back and funky starts to pall after a while. It's good for effects, but you wouldn't want to see it every day.

Once again, Hobo looks suspiciously like it started life as press-on lettering.

There are some designs, especially for publications, in which the use of one-of-a-kind typefaces like Hobo works. Some magazines, for example, will have markedly different designs for the lead of each feature. In these cases, you can justify one head in Hobo, one in Chancery, and another in ExtraGalactica Condensed Gothic if you like without any one of them getting stale.

You might think of typefaces such as Hobo as being a joke. A lot of designers do. However, in this case, consider it in the following context, taken from Robert Heinlein: The first time you tell the joke you're a wit. The next time you tell it, you're a halfwit, and so on, in a geometrical progression.

### MACHINE (MOTOR)

Machine is clearly a special-effect typeface which has been created with the sole object of looking massive. It's very successful at this. However, lacking lowercase letters and being pretty ponderous to look at, it has relatively few applications.

### NEW BASKERVILLE (NEBRASKA)

New Baskerville is a nice, somewhat gothic serif face which is usually found in body copy. As a matter fact, you're looking at a version of Baskerville right now. It's not bad for heads, either, if you're trying to create a design in which the heads fit comfortably into the rest of a page—assuming that the rest of the page is a bit gothic too.

One way of regarding New Baskerville is that it's the ideal choice when you would have used Times Roman if it wasn't so badly over-used already. Baskerville is just a bit more interesting visually, but it stops short of really coloring your text with any real visual character to overshadow the intent of your words. An article concerning the great courtesans of seventeenth-century Moldavia and a pamphlet on the nutritional characteristics of baby food can both be set in New Baskerville with equal effect, although I'd much rather read the article about great courtesans.

## NEW CENTURY SCHOOLBOOK (NEW BRUNSWICK)

New Century Schoolbook is, rather obviously, another book face. It's actually a bit heavy for use as a body face unless you'll be setting it moderately large—say twelve points or better. It's a bit austere as a headline face unless you're deliberately trying to create very dry look-ing designs. Like Bookman, it's a bit more elongated than body faces tend to be. It fills up more space as a result, but it's a bit easier to read than something set in Times, for example.

Much of the rationale for using Baskerville is applicable to School-book if you have the space. I think that Schoolbook crosses the boundary between gothic and dull—Baskerville has just enough of a gothic flavor to it to make it interesting, while Schoolbook is just bland enough to make it lifeless. This is a really subjective point, of course, and one which you should consider carefully for yourself if you have applications for this sort of type.

## OPTIMA (OTTAWA)

Optima is a rather unique typeface, and one which you will proba-bly grow to appreciate as you work with Corel Draw. It's not really a serif face, but it's not a sans serif face in the way that Helvetica is, either. It bulges and curves a lot, and keeps one's attention in situa-tions where Helvetica would long since have lost it. Optima has the advantage of looking clean and modern without looking sterile and mechanical.

You'll probably find that Optima doesn't make a really good headline face. Set large, its starts to show its delicate curves and fairly thin lines far too much. It looks underfed, and one's eye starts looking for a valve on it to pump a bit more air into it. However, in less demanding applications where its lack of muscle isn't a problem, Optima can convey the impression of being refined, sophisticated, and elegantly understated.

### PALATINO (PALM SPRINGS)

Palatino has applications in much the same areas as Baskerville. It makes a good body face, and as it turns up in the PostScript font list of Ventura Publisher as such, you might find that having it available in Corel Draw is extremely helpful when you're creating graphics for export. Compared to Baskerville, Palatino is a bit less artsy, but it still manages to be visually interesting. Once again, it's a good choice for when you're weary of Times.

### PARK AVENUE (PARADISE)

Park Avenue is another special-effect typeface. It's a particularly troublesome one at times, as it's a bit inconsistent. Some of its characters, such as the uppercase A, for example, are kind of attractive, if rather overdone. Others, such as the lowercase e, seem out of place. The lowercase n always looked to me as if it had been lifted from one of those old Irish typefaces.

Used sparingly and in the right context, Park Avenue can be effective. However, it's a typeface that's really easy to overuse.

### REVIEW (RENFREW)

Review is a special-effect typeface with much the same problems as Hobo or Cooper Black. It's not unattractive, and it's certainly bold enough to get noticed almost anywhere. However, it seems to call attention to itself not so much because it has a particular style about it, but rather because it's obviously strange looking.

## *SOUVENIR (SOUTHERN)*

Souvenir seems to dangle just this side of being a special effect. It's a very attractive face, and manages to be sort of bold, to have a sort of serif design about it, and to evoke a sort of gothic flavor—but not quite. Not a face which is frequently employed, Souvenir is useful for this fact alone.

Faces like Souvenir are a good choice when you just want something different and you aren't sure what it should be. It doesn't have any particular feel to it, and it's unlikely to be inappropriate. At its worst it's still noticeable, and even moderately dignified looking.

## *STENCIL (STAMP)*

There's little opportunity to mistake what Stencil evokes. If your graphic has something to do with packing crates, military vehicles, or civil servants, this font was made for you.

## *TIFFANY (TIMPANI)*

Tiffany is a particularly ornate serif face, but a fairly well designed one. You might even be able to get away with using it on a regular basis for heads and titles if your application allows for a bit of character. Even in its medium weight, Tiffany is eye-catching, and it gets very hard to miss in its extrabold version, Tiffany Heavy. This latter case is probably a bit too nouveau something-or-other to suit serious designs.

You might want to regard Tiffany as being New Baskerville taken several steps further. It's a serif face which might be used in place of Times when you're not only tired of Times but want people to know that you've denounced it and everything that looks like it.

## *TIMES ROMAN (TORONTO)*

Most of what could be said about Times has already been discussed indirectly in discussing the faces that can be compared to it. By virtue of its extensive use, it shares with Helvetica a neutrality and lack of extreme character. Type set in it will not really be colored by the typeface. It also won't be particularly interesting visually, but there are times when you want this quality in your type.

Times is the model of a well-designed typeface. It's moderately condensed, but it still reads well. The boldface version looks bold and substantial without looking heavy. While Times was designed as a body face, the bold version is an acceptable headline face.

## *UNIVERS (USA)*

As we discussed earlier in this chapter, Univers was created for much the same reason as Helvetica, and the two fonts can be applied in similar contexts. However, Univers looks a bit different from Helvetica. Its light face flows a bit more, and doesn't look as constrained. Its extrabold weight, Univers Black in Corel Draw, is a bit more condensed than Helvetica Black.

## *UNIVERSITY ROMAN (UNICORN)*

University Roman is unquestionably a special effect, although it's a particularly pleasing one. It looks like Times Roman the morning after. While it would not do to apply it too frequently, the odd use of University Roman can be very eye-catching. In the right context, it might be regarded as an eccentric relation—entertaining for its peculiarities, but harmless and inoffensive.

One of the positive features of University Roman is its fairly condensed design. One of its negative features is that it's pretty hard to read. Don't set anything that really should be read and understood in this face.

## *ZAPF CHANCERY (ZURICH)*

In recent years, Chancery has come to be the forerunner in grossly overused display faces, by virtue of its appearance as one of the staple fonts in PostScript printers. While not a particularly bad face as ornate fonts go, Chancery is very easy to overuse. It looks like someone has deliberately attempted to be artistic. Looking at type set in Chancery often makes one think that a simple day-glo sticker saying "The designer is in" would have sufficed.

The hard lines and calligraphic appearance of Chancery make it ideally suited for specific design applications. However, keep in mind that Chancery is unfortunately easy to apply, so it turns up everywhere. Even with the most well-thought-out design criteria in mind, you might wind up creating a rather hackneyed bit of type inadvertently.

## *WRAPPING UP*

Until very recently, graphics and page creation software were pretty crude stuff, and required little concern for art. In many areas of microcomputer applications this is still true, and most computer users seem to feel that whatever comes out of a computer is either right or wrong, with no room for interpretation or creative argument.

Corel Draw, which is just dripping with nuance and subtlety, seem to fly in the face of attitudes such as these—and doubly so when it's dealing with typography.

If you're new to the nuances of typography, you might want to deliberately try to notice type. See if you can judge the effect that different typefaces and their applications have on your appreciation of the words you read. This is something which slips by the conscious perception of most people, but if you are to make full use of the expressive potential of type, you'll need to have a conscious understanding of it.

# chapter 10

BUGEX

PEST CONTROL

ZEBRA

ZEBRA

BRA

EANS

*Designing Logos
and Symbols*

**N**O OTHER AREA OF DESIGN SPEAKS TO THE REALITY of contemporary Western civilization better than that of designing symbols. A well-thought-out symbol conveys at a glance a lot about whatever it symbolizes, and a glance is the most that some people can spare. In a world where you can seldom hope for more than a moment of someone's attention, an art form which only requires a moment to fully appreciate seems destined to ascend in importance.

The most obvious use of icons outside of user-friendly computer interfaces is in corporate logos. Logo design has been refined to a high art, and with good reason. Logos are commissioned by the most rushed members of society, upper-management executives. It's not surprising that they regard them as being important.

Designing functional logos requires the application of many of the design criteria which have come up in this book, and it entails ignoring a few others. A good logo will catch the eye, say what it has to say, and be gone. Logos which seek to provoke curiosity, appreciation, subtlety, contemplation, or the enjoyment of good commercial art creatively executed have failed before they even start. People don't stare at logos that long.

In this chapter we'll have a look at the rudiments of designing logos and symbols with Corel Draw. By definition, a good logo will be one which has not been seen before, so you won't be able to just modify the examples in this chapter. Hopefully, though, you'll be able to use the approaches explained herein and apply them to your own logos.

## *APPROACHING LOGOS*

The intensity of your design effort for a logo or symbol will probably vary. If the project in question is to design a set of symbols for an annual report or a dinner menu, for example, you will probably not want to spend a day brainstorming what they should look like. Logos which look like they'll be around for a while, however, usually call for somewhat more involved research. The final result of your work may well be a pretty simple graphic, but designing a logo that says everything it's supposed to is by no means a simple task. You'll find this to be exceedingly evident if there are several people involved in the process of ultimately accepting the logo you're designing. Everyone seems to think that a logo should say something different.

A logo is a unique sort of symbol. Consider its requirements.

- It must express what the company it represents *is*.

- It must express what the company it represents *aspires to be*, or thinks it is or will be.

- It must please the eye, and express positive visual associations for the company it represents.

- It must communicate across great distances of culture, background, and personal predisposition.

- It must work very, very fast.

There are secondary, mechanical considerations, too. For example, logos which incorporate color should usually be reproducible in black-and-white as well.

There are few perfect logos, and few occasions in which everyone involved in the design and acceptance of a logo will agree that one is perfect, even if it actually is.

Let's have a quick walk through the above criteria. The first one is representative of the sorts of problems you'll encounter in working out a good logo design. Expressing what a company is involves finding out a lot about it and the people behind it. This is tied in with the second point, that is, finding out what it thinks it is and what it aspires to. A logo for a metal-plating company might properly depict an organization which dumps traces of cadmium into the local water table and kills fish, but you would probably find that a logo with dead fish on it will not be very well received.

Consider further that corporations, like individual people, will rarely tell you what they really want. One doubts that IBM told the creator of its logo that it wanted a design to convey its character as being monolithic, omnipresent, and immense. One of the skills of whoever it was that designed the IBM logo was the ability to read between the lines of what was said to find the true character of IBM—as seen by IBM, of course.

The most difficult element of logo design exists not in your Corel Draw workspace, but in the heads of the people who will look at it after it becomes reality. A symbol is a sort of substitution code. Consider the one in Figure 10.1.

*Figure 10.1:* The logo for Cow, Inc.

Printed out, this symbol weighs almost nothing. It doesn't smell, doesn't make basso honking noises at five in the morning, never needs feeding, and isn't good to eat. However, I trust it still conveys all the attributes of a cow.

The reason I believe this logo works is that this conception of a cow and that of pretty well anyone else likely to see the logo should be about the same. I believe I can safely use the symbol without worrying about its being misinterpreted.

In marked contrast to the cow circumstances is the Sanskrit symbol for good fortune (Sanskrit being an old pictographic language which originated around what is now Tibet). Upon consideration I have decided not to illustrate the symbol. Although it would have been a positive symbol for any Tibetan a few centuries ago, its meaning has been changed perhaps irrevocably because of more recent events. It is a swastika. This would not be a good logo for any company, even if it were run by historically-minded Tibetans.

These sorts of cultural predispositions are rarely as obvious or as easily understood as most people's reactions in this particular case.

The final criterion on the list of logo requirements is that a logo must work fast, for reasons we discussed above. This doesn't really put any immediate strictures on your designs, but it might provide you with some guidelines. Pictures convey ideas a lot more readily than words. Pictures are also a lot more universal. The word ''America'' would probably be meaningless to a Bedouin who spoke no English. On the other hand, there probably aren't many people on earth who wouldn't recognize an American flag.

Some things, however, don't represent well as pictures. Returning to a previous example, it's hard to draw a picture of IBM. It's often difficult to convince the owners of a company that the name of their enterprise should be reduced to a few squiggles and a bit of abstract art. In these cases, a logo which uses type and applies some graphic elements to it might well be more appropriate.

## *USING TYPE LOGOS*

The easiest way to create a symbol is to stylize some type. This will usually *not* result in the most effective logo—if you *could* represent what you want with a picture, the result would be a more universal logo which communicated its ideas a lot more readily. However, this is not always practical, and, more to the point, there isn't always the time available to do it.

We'll get into the design of pictographic logos later in this chapter.

Anyone can typeset a name, and even if after weeks of head scratching you really ascertain that the company you're designing a logo for would work best with just its name set in Helvetica with a box around it, you're not likely to get away with it. A logo has to look like a graphic—a piece of commercial art—rather than words.

One of the most effective ways to turn type into a graphic is to run the characters together. Using the shape tool in Corel Draw, select each character in the name which is to become your logo and move them until they touch. Experiment with different typefaces and amount of overlap between characters to produce different degrees of "logo-ness." Some typefaces work better than others for this effect. Garamond is my favorite victim in this case. Very lineal faces, such as Helvetica, don't work as well.

Figure 10.2 illustrates various degrees of success using this approach.

If the name of the company in question has some nonalphabetic punctuation in it, consider doing something with it. For example, ampersands are fertile ground for manipulation, especially if you choose a typeface with an interesting one. Figure 10.3 has some examples of the creative use of punctuation.

It would be a fair complaint to suggest that none of the preceding examples says anything about the companies they represent. This is very often the case when one is confronted with creating a logo out of text. There is almost nothing a logo can express visually about a law firm, for example, beyond vague ideas of honesty, stability, and so on.

In many cases, a text-based logo can aspire only to being eye-catching. If the logo will exist in an environment where the qualities of the company it represents are well known, this may be enough. For example, the Kraft Foods logo is nothing more than the word Kraft set in a pretty pedestrian-looking sans serif type. However, as pretty well everyone knows that Kraft makes food, one could argue that little more needs to be said.

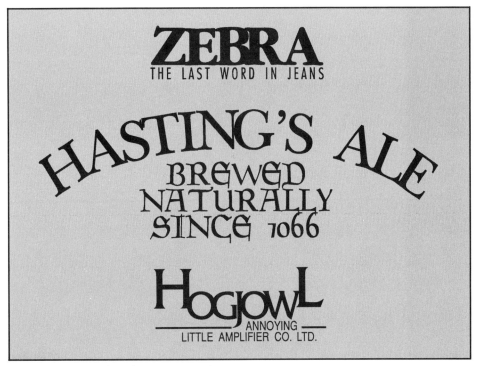

*Figure 10.2:* Running characters together.

There are a lot of things which Corel Draw can do to text to simply make it visually interesting. More to the point, some of the effects that are no trouble for Corel Draw would be very difficult to achieve through mechanical means and as such will not have been seen before. Figure 10.4 illustrates a number of hypothetical logos which are really nothing more than special effects.

While perhaps interesting, these logos are conceptually shallow. They say nothing, and like most other special effects they lose their magic and appeal quickly. The logo for a one-time-only trade show, a publication which will be produced once and never again, or an advertisement that's to run for only a short time can probably be treated in this way with acceptable results. Something which is to endure—a logo which will adorn a corporation that plans on being around for a while, for example—should have more substance to it.

*Figure 10.3:* Using nonalphabetic characters in logos.

## DESIGNING GRAPHIC LOGOS

The problem with designing graphic logos is that you very often have to actually draw the things. While people who call themselves artists probably wouldn't shy away from such an experience, drawing does take time.

The alternative to this is to work up a logo from clip art or a scanned image. This is cheap, odious, and not at all artistic, but it can be an effective way to produce quick results. One of the questions which people rarely ask about a successful logo design is "How did you do this?"

Coming up with visual icons to represent the intangible values and aspirations of a company can be a difficult undertaking. Some companies, such as Apple Computer, have obvious visual connections. However, one might well argue that Apple's logo doesn't really fulfill very many of the criteria of good logo design. It says nothing at all

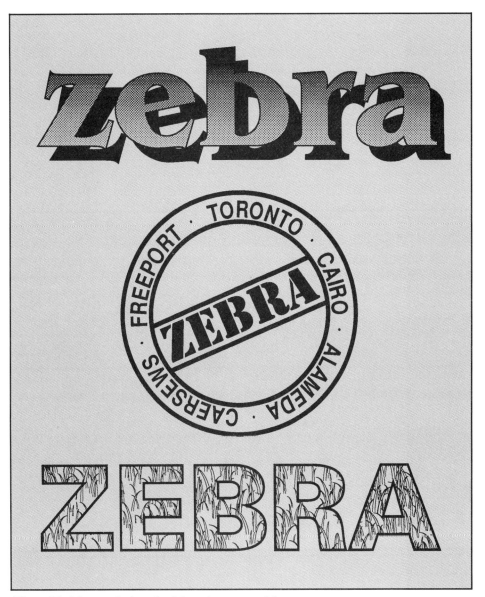

*Figure 10.4:* Logos designed solely to be eye-catching.

about the company it represents, save that Apple is successful enough to be able to afford four-color printing on virtually every document which bears its corporate symbol.

Figure 10.5 is a corporate logo. It's an interesting study in logo design. As an exercise in design you'll probably appreciate it better if you've not seen it previously, and don't know what it stands for.

This is a much beleaguered symbol. It has been given all sorts of disparaging names, including "the happy donut," "the exploding cabbage," "the self-destructing pizza," and "the nuclear basketball." It may or may not deserve them, but it's hard to differentiate between what people feel about the symbol and what they feel about the corporation. Canadians will unquestionably recognize this as being the symbol of the Canadian Broadcasting Corporation. When it first came out, a lot of people thought it was a new logo for the Continental Can Company.

The CBC logo might actually be quite clever. If you regard the big C as being a broadcast antenna and the curves emanating from it as being stylized radio waves, it's a very interesting depiction of the rather abstract process of broadcasting. I have never met anyone else

*Figure 10.5:* A genuine corporate logo.

who interpreted it this way, however, and most of the people to whom I've suggested this analysis had to scratch their heads for a while to regard it as such.

This logo is moderately eye-catching. It's usually printed in orange ink against a blue background, which certainly makes it more eye-catching still. It provokes a certain amount of curiosity, but its actual meaning—if the analogy of an antenna is actually what was in the mind of its designer—is so obscure as to make its message unlikely to be seen by most people.

It might well be argued that a logo whose meaning is subject to this degree of interpretation and uncertainty probably should go back to the drawing board—or be loaded back into Corel Draw—for one more set of revisions.

In general, a company which makes things should be a lot easier to design for than one which provides intangible services. The CBC logo, above, is a good example of someone trying to represent something intangible in a visual way.

Designing a graphic logo for a lawyer, a stockbroker, or an investment counselor would be a lot more difficult. You'll probably find yourself pressed into using some pretty well worn symbols if you're confronted with such a task. Consider how many of the logos used to represent medical products or services have a caduceus in them. The caduceus is a dreadful symbol—the actual connection it has to medicine is lost to most people—and it appears to be used only because of a kind of unwritten agreement that it might be appropriate, given the lack of anything better.

## USING ABSTRACT GRAPHICS

An awful lot of logos use graphics which are simply abstract and eye-catching, but say nothing. Consider the color fountain which runs through the Compaq computer logo. The message in this logo, as with most good logos designed this way, is in the general design and typography. The fountain is simply an attention-getting device.

One really elegant source of abstract graphics in Corel Draw is the PostScript Textures library. Figure 10.6 illustrates some potential uses for these.

*Figure 10.6:* Using PostScript textures as logo graphics.

Confronted with a design problem in which there are no obvious symbols available—or one in which the good symbols have already been used—this is not a bad way to approach your design. It implies that the company in question has a sense of originality and abstract thinking, which is better than saying nothing at all. An abstract graphic that looks abstract doesn't take a lot of time to appreciate.

At the other end of the spectrum, the Dover books of public-domain clip art may provide you with a limitless supply of potential symbols and adornments if your designs are destined for more traditional clients.

If you apply abstract thinking to your logo designs, you might well find that you can do some particularly clever things with them. Figure 10.7 is another well-known Canadian logo, that of the Canadian National railway. Many people who think consciously about these things regard this as being the most brilliant logo one could ever come up with for a railroad. They say you can almost hear the rattle of wheels on steel rails and the sound of a train's horn echoing in the mountains as you look at it.

*Figure 10.7:* The CN logo.

## WRAPPING UP

As was touched on briefly in the chapter on exporting graphics from Corel Draw, you can apply symbols—icons—to all sorts of designs. A well-chosen symbol can tie the pages of a publication together, reinforce the feeling of unity at a large trade show or seminar, or relate disparate products together.

In designing logos and other symbols with Corel Draw, you'll have the advantage of being able to try out new designs and variations quickly. One school of symbol design recommends that you create a logo by drawing what you think it should have in it and then removing everything you can take out without it becoming meaningless. Corel Draw allows you to undertake exercises like this easily and without a lot of redrawing and mechanical work.

*Using Color*

NE OF THE LESSER USED FACILITIES OF COREL
Draw is that of drawing in color. Although it handles color in a particularly elegant way, you might not have as much recourse to its talents in these areas simply because unlike color monitors, workable
and affordable color printers are a bit hard to find.

As we'll discuss in this chapter, Corel Draw offers some attractive
alternatives to buying a really expensive color hardcopy device. It
allows you to take advantage of some of the less expensive color
printers available at the moment—you needn't buy a $10,000
color PostScript device just to enjoy the color drawing capabilities of
Corel Draw. In fact, depending upon your applications, you might
not need a color printer at all.

Color art from Corel Draw can look superb. Because of the inher-
ently simple approach to color specification which Corel provides—
essentially an extension of the gray-level tools you're already familiar
with—you will probably find that it will not take you very long to
learn the mechanics of color using Corel Draw.

The color plates in this book were all created using Corel Draw.
Corel Draw not only did the art—it also output the printers' color
separations, something we'll discuss later in this chapter. As a result,
you are seeing these plates exactly the way I did, that is, as first-
generation art. There was no intermediate color print to be optically
separated, and no attendant loss of image quality. In many cases,
Corel Draw can create color film for printing which is of much higher
quality than anything you could manage using traditional optical
separation techniques.

If all this sounds a bit Martian at the moment, you might want to
ignore it until we get into the details of using separations.

## A PRINT HOUSE PRIMER

Later in this chapter we'll discuss stand-alone color printers, those
glorious little boxes which actually generate color art. However, even

the best of these machines doesn't really do justice to what Corel Draw can output. Its best work is handled by print houses.

The mechanics of printing in color are a bit involved, and will be dealt with as they crop up. However, there are a few terms with which you should probably familiarize yourself before you begin. These have to do with the way printing presses actually reproduce color art.

A printing press is a mechanical system which deposits ink on paper—analogous to a laser printer, which does so electronically. Modern printing presses, of the sort you're likely to encounter if you go somewhere to print your Corel Draw art, print with *photoresistive plates*. This is a metal plate coated with a photographic emulsion which, when processed, will cause the black areas of the plate to accept ink and the white areas not to. Ink spread across the plate will stick to the black areas, and from there will be transferred to paper.

While they look quite different, printing plates work in the same way that a roll of 35-millimeter film does. One notable difference is that it doesn't take two pressmen to lift a roll of 35-millimeter film into most cameras.

In most cases, printing is done in *signatures*. A signature is a single sheet of paper which holds a number of pages. The number of pages is usually an even power of two, as the signature will get folded some number of times before it is trimmed to produce the final pages. Signatures of eight and sixteen pages are common. Bearing in mind that a signature of sixteen pages requires that all sixteen pages get printed at once, you can imagine the size of the printing plate involved.

Printing plates are made by contact printing them from immense negatives. The negatives for each page are "stripped" together, such that they're positioned in the right order for printing. The order for a publication having multiple signatures can get quite intricate, since the page order has to come out correct after each signature has been folded, trimmed, and added to other signatures of the completed print job.

If your publication will be folded in half and stapled, what is called *saddle stitching*, half of each signature will appear at the back of the book and half at the front. Publications which are bound with square spines—such as this book—are referred to as being *perfect bound*. In this case, each signature is folded in half and all the signatures follow one after the other. Having said this, it's worth noting that figuring out the order of the pages is the responsibility of the print house. You need never concern yourself with it—although there is one particular situation in which you may want to, which we will discuss shortly.

In order to print color, each sheet of paper must run through one printing press, or "station," for each color. As we'll discuss shortly, a full-color photograph or piece of Corel Draw art usually requires four actual colors of ink.

In order to print color art, the color image has to be reduced to a number of monochrome negatives to produce monochrome plates. If you want to print a drawing which has black and red in it, there will ultimately be a black plate and a red plate. The black station of the press will have—predictably—black ink in it. The red one will have red ink. Even though your pages will come out with two colors of ink on them, no one station will have to lay down more than one color of ink.

The process of creating these individual monochrome negatives from a color original—whether the original is a sheet of paper or a drawing file—is called *color separation*. Traditional color separation, in which an optical scanner or separator filters the image into its component colors, has several drawbacks. Being an optical process, it's inexact—you always lose something in the separation process, so there's no assurance that your original art will be separated in such a way as to print exactly as the original did. Secondly, separations are among the most expensive parts of pre-press negative preparation. Finally, they're time-consuming, and the sooner you need them the more they cost.

Corel Draw allows you to generate color separations without the intermediate step of using an optical scanner or separator. It bypasses all three of the above problems, and the results are superb.

## COLOR PROCESSES

**Color Plate 1** is a typical Corel Draw color picture. It was created by loading up one of the black-and-white EPS files which comes with Corel Draw's clip art collection and "colorizing" it, that is, assigning different color fills to each of its objects. The colors are wholly arbitrary—if you prefer your parrots with different color schemes, you're free to paint them any way you like.

You can work with color by assigning arbitrary colors in this way and hoping for the best. If you can restrict your use of color to a few basic and predictable colors, simply knowing what to click and when will get you through basic color applications.

This isn't very adventurous, however. It denies you most of the power of Corel Draw's color facilities, and it also denies you the opportunity to understand the theory behind what you are doing.

Unlike monochrome art, which is just black ink—or black laser printer toner—on white paper, color is a process. In drawing with color, a lot of what you can do and much of the way you do it will be determined by the medium which ultimately will create the colors you use. Just as monochrome art is limited by the mechanical qualities of the printer it will be output on—the screen limitations of a 300-dot-per-inch laser, for example—so too are color processes at least partially a function of whatever it is that will be producing your drawings.

It's important to keep the color process you'll be using in mind, especially if your color art is ultimately to be reproduced at a print house. Poorly-thought-out color implementations can look bad and get really expensive.

Let's start with some of the theory of color.

There are two ways of creating color. They're called *subtractive color* and *additive color*. Each one relates to a particular medium.

A computer monitor uses additive color. In its quiescent state, a computer monitor is black, and emits no light. In order to make color appear on the screen of a monitor, colored light must be added to its blackness.

The three primary colors of additive color are red, green, and blue. The picture tube of a monitor contains three electron guns which excite spots of red, green, and blue phosphor on the inside face of your monitor, creating light. The relative intensities of the three dots for any given pixel on your screen determines the color you see for the pixel in question.

Printing on paper involves the use of subtractive color. A sheet of paper is initially white, that is, it reflects all colors of light equally. If

you put some blue ink in one area on the page, that area will be a
good reflector of blue light but a poor reflector of other colors of light.
The blue ink serves as a filter.

The three primary colors of subtractive printing are *cyan, magenta,*
and *yellow.* Cyan is a medium blue, and magenta is an electric purple-
red. Magenta is kind of ugly, and is rarely used by itself. If you have
an EGA card and a color monitor in your computer, you can see
pretty good approximations of these colors in Corel Draw.

**Color Plate 2** illustrates the primary additive and subtractive colors.

In theory, if you mix equal amounts of cyan, magenta, and yellow
ink you'll wind up with black. However, because the ink used by
printing presses is never absolutely pure—cyan ink, for example, is
never exactly cyan in color—the result of creating black in this way
usually comes up looking like a muddy brown. The eye may have a
hard time determining that a particular color of cyan is really cyan,
but it can certainly tell the difference between something which is
black and something which is not. For this reason, areas of a color
graphic which are supposed to have equal amounts of cyan,
magenta, and yellow are instead printed with percentages of black.

Color printing thus actually involves four colors of ink, these being
cyan, magenta, yellow, and black, and you will frequently hear full-
color printing referred to as four-color printing. The four colors are
often designated by the letters C,M,Y, and K, where K stands
for black.

You might be able to see the difference between three- and four-
color printing if you're interested. Many newspapers use only
three-color printing, as the color definition on newsprint frequently
does not justify using a black plate. Pretty well all other commercial
printing is done with four colors. If you can find the same color
advertisement in a newspaper and in a glossy magazine you will
probably be able to observe the difference from using a black plate.

It's possible to "create" any color you like with percentages of
these four colors of ink. Creating color in this way is called using *process colors.*

There are a number of potential pitfalls in using process color. For
example, if you specify a color which is composed of 90 percent of
each of the cyan, magenta, and yellow inks, the fill in question will

have a 270 percent ink density. Printing presses can certainly handle more than 100 percent ink density—the exact amount varies from press to press—but this is certainly excessive. As a rule, 240 percent is about the upper limit.

Optical separations deal with high ink densities through a process called *black removal.* If you specify a particular color as being 50 percent cyan, 60 percent magenta, and 40 percent yellow, some or all of the shared percentages of each of these three ink colors can be removed and transferred to black. This serves to reduce the overall amount of ink deposited on the page.

Corel Draw does not do black removal automatically. Therefore, in using process colors you must be careful not to create fills which will use an excessive amount of ink if the final destination of your art will be a printing press. The process-color selection facility of Corel Draw does not force you to include a black component in your process color specification, so you must do so yourself if you want to use colors which require a lot of ink.

In the preceding example, you could reduce this color:

```
50 cyan
60 magenta
40 yellow
```

to this color:

```
20 cyan
30 magenta
10 yellow
30 black
```

The two colors would print the same, but the amount of ink on your page would be 40 percent less in the second example. In practice, neither of these ink combinations would be really excessive for most printing presses, although as a rule the second one would look nicer, especially if it was being used to print a screened fill. High ink densities are more likely to bleed and run, especially on high-speed web presses, and this can be quite noticeable in a screened area.

## PANTONE COLORS

Process color has its limitations. Because of the potential impurities in color inks, it's impossible to specify a process color and know you'll get precisely that color in your final output, especially if you're planning to have your output mechanically printed. When exact colors are required, the printing industry uses a second way of specifying colors. This is called *spot color*. The most frequently used method of specifying spot color is through the use of the Pantone color matching system.

The Pantone system is incorporated into Corel Draw, something which you'll probably learn to love if you deal with color a lot.

The Pantone system simply assigns numbers—and in a few cases names—to specific mixed ink colors. The Pantone company creates books with color swatches for each of its numbered colors, such that if you specify a particular Pantone color your printer will be able to look at his or her Pantone book and see exactly that color.

For reasons which will become apparent in the very next section on color separations, it's not practical to specify a different Pantone color for each object in a complex drawing and plan to have them printed this way. Spot color is used mainly when you want to have an additional color in a drawing and you want that color to match a known color exactly.

One frequently finds, for example, that corporations or particular products are associated with certain colors which are defined by Pantone numbers—consider the blue in the IBM logo or the yellow which borders National Geographic magazine every month. If you wanted to create a drawing which contained an IBM logo using IBM's particular blue color, you might well use process colors for your drawing and a Pantone color for the logo. The Pantone color would become the fifth color in your drawing if there were four-color art in there as well.

## COLOR SEPARATIONS

As we discussed briefly at the beginning of this chapter, four-color printing is handled by, in effect, four separate single-color printing presses, one for each color of ink. In order to print a colored object, four separate plates must be created, one for each press. These are created from four film negatives.

If you wanted to print a color photograph, the photograph would first have to be made into color separations. Separations are actually four black-and-white negatives which represent the four color components of an original image. In creating separations—or "seps"—the photograph would be scanned first for its cyan component, then for its magenta component, and finally for its yellow component. The fourth piece of film would be created by finding any components the first three have in common and using black removal.

Color separation is both expensive and time-consuming. In the case of printing a photograph in color, there's no way around it. However, Corel Draw's artwork starts out in a digital form, and the program is capable of manipulating it in a lot of ways. One of these is to create color separations.

If you have a drawing which uses color, you can have Corel Draw output four sheets of paper for each page, one each for the four process colors. It can also output negatives. If you load your laser up with clear film rather than paper, the result will be usable separations—sort of.

We'll get to that "sort of" in a moment.

Color separations are usually accompanied by what is called a *color key* or *chroma key*. Because a separation is very hard to "read"—it consists of four pretty inscrutable negatives—a chroma key is pretty well indispensable. It is, simply, four sheets of film printed in the four process colors from the four negatives of the separation and taped together. The result is a *proof* or test image of the picture in the separations. Chroma keys are also kind of interesting, as you can remove one or more of the sheets of film from them to see what your picture would look like without some of its color components.

Printers can usually arrange to get chroma keys made for you from any separations you happen to generate. While modestly expensive—expect to spend twenty or thirty dollars to get a set of chroma keys made—this gives you the best indication of what your separated images will look like without going to the expense of actually printing them.

If you have a color printer available you can create instant color proofs, of course, but a chroma key will show not only the colors, but the potential separation effects as well.

This gets back to the "sort of" from a few paragraphs ago. Color separation is a very exacting process. If you specify an area in your drawing as being filled with a color composed of specific percentages of inks, the inks will be printed as screens—assuming that they aren't all 100 percent. As we mentioned earlier in the chapter on fills, printing screens one on top of another can cause them to interfere, producing aberrations in the final drawing. In order to get around this, separations are created with their screens at different angles and with spot shapes designed not to interact with each other.

In order for all this to work, the screens of the four layers of a color separation must be printed very accurately—in most cases, with more accuracy than can be managed by a 300-dot-per-inch laser printer. As a result, if you load your laser up with clear film and print separations on it you will get something to print with, but it may not produce particularly attractive results.

If your "seps" are going to be run through a web press onto news-print for the local shopping center throwaway, you might well be prepared to live with this lack of quality. If you're planning to print to glossy paper on a sheet-fed press—a combination which is capable of doing better things—you should consider using higher quality output.

If you print your Corel Draw files as separation negatives to disk files, you can have them output on a PostScript typesetter. The results of doing color separations this way rival anything that can can be done though optical separations. This is how the color plates in this book were created.

It's also worth noting that there is special laser printer film for applications which involve printing on film. If you use normal clear acetate, there's a good chance that the fuser of your laser printer will melt it, necessitating a trip to the shop for your printer.

## *SIGNATURES AND COLOR IMPOSITION*

The next section of this book will deal with a very arcane subject, one which you might want to avoid. You can, too. It might not even have any bearing on your applications of Corel Draw and color. If you choose to plow through it, however, you will understand a lot more about how print houses deal with color print jobs, and if you use a lot of color in multiple-page publications you'll consequently (probably) be able to prune your print bills substantially.

When you have a multiple-page document printed, it's handled in signatures, as we discussed earlier. For the sake of this discussion we will deal with a single sixteen-page signature, although these principles apply to any signature size.

A sixteen-page signature will result in eight actual pages, each page having two sides. If this signature will be part of a publication to be saddle stitched—folded in half and stapled in the middle—there will be four actual sheets of paper.

The press that prints your signature will do so with two massive plates, one for each side of the page. This is assuming that this signature will only be printed in black. If you want full color on both sides, there will be eight plates.

Print houses charge for color printing based on the number of plates they use. The efficient use of color will reduce the number of plates involved and, hence, what it costs you to get your printing done.

It's a lot more efficient to print color on one side of a signature than it is to do so on both. This reduces the number of plates from eight to five. In this case, you will be able to position color art on some pages and not on others. If you can arrange to do so, you will require less color and, as such, less of a budget.

Figuring out where the color will appear is a bit tricky at first. Figure 11.1 illustrates how the pages work out in a single signature of a saddle-stitched publication. If you have color on page 1, color will also be available on pages 8, 9, and 16. Depending on how your printer actually handles this signature, it might also appear on 4, 5, 12, and 13. Note that the numbering system your print shop uses may also differ from what is shown in Figure 11.1, which simply numbers *signature* pages.

The position of the color in a signature is called the *color imposition.* Most print houses have diagrams or tables of one sort or another to help you work this out for various signatures as it  relates to their

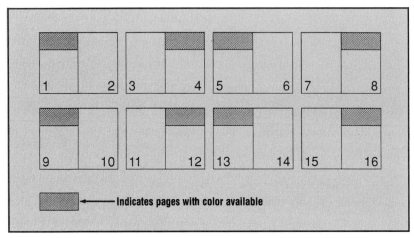

*Figure 11.1:* The color imposition for a sixteen-page signature.

presses. While it's important to consult with your print house before you start trying to figure out how best to use color, don't be dismayed if you can't make any sense of the charts they provide for you. These things are invariably drawn up by people who work with color impositions every day.

To further confuse the color imposition issue, consider that if you add the above signature to a completed publication, the page numbers will change. Figure 11.2 illustrates the above signature as the second signature of a 64-page saddle-stitched book.

Note that half the color has found its way—inconveniently—to the back of the book. One of the attractions of perfect binding is that if you open a color section, all the color stays in the same place.

In planning the use of color in a large publication, you can reduce your print costs by keeping the number of signatures having color in them down. Each time you introduce color into an otherwise black-and-white signature, your print house will have to use more press stations. If you need lots of color, consider using four-color in only some sections and spot color in the rest.

Secondly, you can effectively cut your color costs in half by arranging the pages which use color in a signature so they appear on only one side of the signature. They'll probably look like they've been used with great abandon when your publication is finally printed and read by someone,

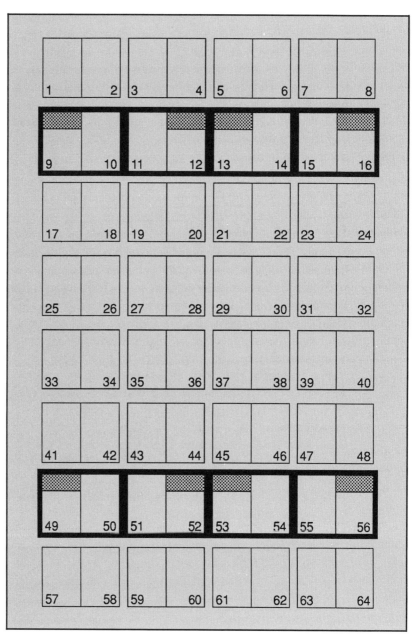

*Figure 11.2:* A multiple-signature publication.

since the color pages will appear at irregular intervals throughout a signature; however, the result, from your printers' point of view, will be a substantial reduction in cost.

Grappling with color imposition is tedious at first. If you ignore it and just put your color art where it looks like it should go, your print house will love you. They'll just open up color wherever it's needed, probably to the detriment of your final bill. Understanding how to juggle the positions of your color pictures, however, you can make a severe dent in that bill—if you use color with an eye to how it will be printed.

## USING COLOR SEPARATIONS

If you want to incorporate Corel Draw artwork into another document—a Ventura Publisher chapter, for example—you would normally just export it into a suitable file and import it into your final document. This is not quite as easy if your artwork is in color.

In most cases, if you plan to have your final document reproduced by a print house, you will have to provide the printer with the artwork for your document and then the color separations separately. The place where your color art is to go should have a black-and-white version of it to mark its place. It is traditional to scrawl ''Pos,'' or ''Position Only,'' over the picture so the printer knows it's not to be reproduced in black-and-white. To be completely traditional, you should use a light blue chinagraph pencil to mark your position-only pictures. This is done for more than just traditional reasons—the final printing film which a printer assembles is usually made up in a darkroom under red lights. Blue chinagraph pencil marks are fairly easy to read under these conditions.

### FILM STRIPPING

Print houses do not necessarily expect you to have all your separation art assembled, perfectly aligned, in a full-page negative ''sandwich'' when you give it to them. If your pages consist of some type, a spot-color overlay, and a few four-color separations, it's usually the case that you will provide all the elements separately—clearly labeled—along with a mockup to illustrate how everything is to be assembled. The film will then be "stripped" (taped) together.

Film work is not done for free—like everything else they do, printers will charge you for it, based in part or totally on the amount of time it takes them. If you can create a separation such that all the graphic elements are positioned properly and won't require cutting apart and repositioning, you'll save a bit on film stripping.

As most of the places that produce high-resolution PostScript output on film charge by the page, "ganging" (grouping) multiple images onto a single set of color separations will save you a bit on output charges, too.

## USING SPOT COLORS WITH SEPARATIONS

The most common use of spot colors is to add a second color to an otherwise black-and-white page. You might also want to add a fifth color to a four-color page to accommodate a specific Pantone color in artwork which requires it. However, in doing so, make sure that the print house you'll be dealing with actually has a five-station press to handle your work.

If you specify an object as being filled with a particular spot color, Corel Draw will produce two pieces of paper for your page if you ask it to, one for the black parts and one for the spot color parts. This might be useful if, for example, you wanted to have a mechanical drawing in which the drawing itself was black and the dimensions and other legends were printed in blue.

If you specify five different spot colors in addition to black you will get six sheets of output for your drawing (again, if you ask for separations when you print). Unless you happen to be dealing with a printer with a six-station press—they exist, but they're anything but common—this will be of no real use to you.

In situations where you need lots of different colors, specify the colors as process colors and use four-color printing.

You can usually have any Pantone color you want as a spot color. However, you should know that many print houses will charge you less if you choose one of the three primary process colors as your spot color. The next most favorable colors are usually warm red and reflex blue—Pantone colors 2 and 6 respectively—as these are commonly used colors of mixed ink which print houses tend to have on hand.

Many spot colors can yield several additional colors if you mix them with black. For example, if you print a 50 percent black screen over the usual warm red spot color—100 percent magenta and yellow—the result will be a warm brown, the exact color being determined by the percentage of red.

**Color Plate 5** illustrates, among other things, the effects of adding black to a spot color.

## WORKING WITH COLOR PRINTERS

The alternative to color print shops is color printers. Having your Corel Draw artwork printed on a printing press is great if you need ten thousand copies and can wait a week, but if you want fast results or a small print run, having a color output device in-house might be more attractive.

A color printer is also almost essential as a proofing device if you'll be doing a lot of color art with Corel Draw.

The most flexible color output available at the moment is afforded by the QMS ColorScript 100 using the Mitsubishi G650 color print engine, which manages print quality comparable to that of a laser printer. Versions are available to handle up to 11-by-17-inch paper. The ColorScript is an expensive machine, however, starting at about $10,000 as of this writing. It's also expensive to use (the cost of replacing its color ribbons must be considered), although it's still a lot cheaper to output a color proof from a ColorScript printer than it is to truck on down to your local print shop and get a chroma key made.

Several other high-end color printers have turned up of late too, all of them based on slightly exotic sounding technologies. The Howtek Pixelmaster, for example, produces 240-dpi output using an engine that shoots drops of melted plastic in the four primary process colors. The results are quite acceptable. However, this printer doesn't support PostScript directly. You can output to it from Corel Draw by treating it as a Hewlett-Packard LaserJet II printer—which limits some of the fill effects Corel Draw can manage—or you can print PostScript files to disk, get out of Corel Draw, and use a PostScript clone interpreter to send your pictures to the printer.

The Pixelmaster starts at about $8,500.

Seiko makes a thermal color printer called the CH-5504 which uses ink sheets to print its colors. It supports true 300-dpi resolution, but like the PixelMaster, it doesn't have onboard PostScript. Once again, you would have to save your PostScript output to disk from Corel Draw, get back to DOS, and run a PostScript clone interpreter, in this case the Freedom of Press package from CAI (Custom Applications Inc.). Freedom of Press enables all sorts of non-PostScript printers to deal with PostScript files by doing all the calculations on your computer rather than in the printer.

Unfortunately, compared to a PostScript printer's 68000-based engine, Freedom of Press can be very slow, especially if your computer lacks a math coprocessor. Freedom of Press ties up several megabytes of disk space.

Finally, the Tektronix Phaser CP costs about $13,000 and uses a wax transfer engine. This produces great colors, but the wax prints are a bit fragile. They're also fairly expensive as color output goes. The Phaser CP uses a PostScript interpreter which lives on a card in your computer. It ties up a slot, but it doesn't mean getting out of Corel Draw every time you need to print something.

If you want to step down in price quite a bit, the Hewlett-Packard PaintJet printers start at about $1,000. Their color facilities are not the equal of a ColorScript, but they're pretty impressive. They don't support PostScript, of course, but you can drive one directly from Corel Draw. At the moment, a PaintJet would be my choice for a color proofing device.

## DESIGNING WITH COLOR

Having the facility for using color can be a double-edged sword. You can produce some really nice looking graphics and excellent pages. You can also produce pictures which look like they were left out in the rain.

Designing effectively with color is an exercise in restraint. It's also a very good opportunity to consider what you're actually trying to achieve with your pages. It's all too easy to be blown away by the color tools in Corel Draw, slapping color onto anything that doesn't move or salute, but the results of the unbridled use of color rarely look attractive.

In many cases, the sparse use of color can do a lot more than having it all over a page.

## APPLYING COLOR TO BLACK-AND-WHITE PAGES

The simplest use of color in a conscious design is to ornament or otherwise enhance an intrinsically black-and-white graphic or page. This applies whether the design in question is for a stand-alone graphic or for a complete page. A small amount of dominant color on an otherwise monochrome page will, without exception, serve to focus the eye to the colored area.

**Color Plate 3** is a good example of this. In the monochrome version of this picture, the focus of the graphic is on the cherries. In the color version it's definitely on the lips, even though the cherries are foremost in the picture. This picture actually uses several colors—it's a full-color plate—although with some care and a color proof printer it probably could have been done with nothing but black and spot red.

It's extremely easy to go a bit wild when you start working with color, especially if you've already figured out how to pay for it. Having sprung for a color signature in your publications, you might well question the economy of using your color facilities only now and again.

If the purpose of adding color to a page is to make it more eye-catching, to serve as an additional method of focusing your readers' attention, there is a good argument for exercising restraint in the way you apply color. A colored headline, a single colored graphic, or a few spot-color rules or ornaments are all things which stand out from a page. A page which is littered with colored graphics and other regalia might as well have been left black-and-white. The focus of such a page will have been lost in the myriads of colored images.

**Color Plate 1**

Cyan

**Magenta**

Yellow

**Black**

**Red** 100% M 100% Y

**Green** 100% C 100% Y

**Blue** 100% C 100% M

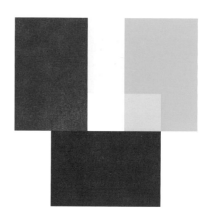

**Color Plate 2**

**Color Plate 3**

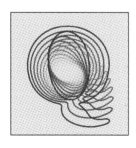

**Color Plate 4**

Fountain:
White to red
(100% Y 100% M)

Fountain:
Red to blue
(100% Y 100% M)
(100% C 100% M)

Fountain:
Yellow to black
(100% Y)
(100% Y 100% K)

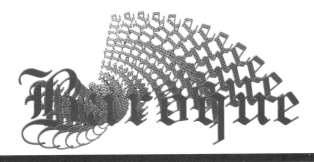

**Color Plate 5**

# Art of the Lute

# ROAD BLOCKS

This effect was created by duplicating the text eleven times, with the color ranging from 50% M 100% Y to 100% M 100% Y. The duplicates are offset by 1.25 points in both directions.

**Color Plate 6**

Ian Anderson · Barriemore Barlow · John Hammond · Jeffrey Hammond · Micheal Stephens

# The Blades

Ian Anderson · Barriemore Barlow · John Hammond · Jeffrey Hammond · Derek · Jim Skyrme · Martin · Chris Riley

# The John Evan Band

Barriemore Barlow · Ian Anderson · John Evan · Chick Murray · Tony · Neil Valentine · Glenn Cornick

# John Evan's Smash

McGregor Pyle · Pete Fenwick · Mick Abrahams · Clive Bunker — **McGregor's Engine**      Barriemore Barlow · Andy Trueman · Paul Greaves · Chris Riley — **All Jump Kangaroo Band**

Martin Barre · Bryan Stevens · Malcolm Corniknon · Mike Ketley — **Gethsemane**

Glenn Cornick · Ian Anderson · Mick Abrahams · Clive Bunker — **Jethro Tull #1**

Andy Pyle · Jack Lancaster · Mick Abrahams · Ron Berg — **Blodwyn Pig**      Glenn Cornick · Ian Anderson · Martin Barre · Clive Bunker — **Jethro Tull #2**

Glenn Cornick · Ian Anderson · Martin Barre · Clive Bunker · John Evan — **Jethro Tull #3**      Barriemore Barlow · Tony Williams · Mike Proctor — **Requiem**

Glenn Cornick · Mike Lewis · Jeff Blackmore · Jeff Jones · Gary Hopkins — **Wild Turkey**      Jeffrey Hammond · Ian Hammond · Martin Barre · Clive Bunker · John Evan — **Jethro Tull #4**

Frankie Miller · Robin Trower · James Dewar · Clive Bunker — **Jude**      Jeffrey Hammond · Ian Anderson · Martin Barre · Barriemore Barlow · John Evan — **Jethro Tull #5**      John Glascock · David Allen · Angela Allen · Roberto Amaral · Paul Fenton — **Carmen**

John Glascock · Ian Anderson · Martin Barre · Barriemore Barlow · John Evan — **Jethro Tull #6**

Simon Nicol · Dave Swarbrick · Dave Pegg · Bruce Rowland — **Fairport Convention #15**      John Glascock · Ian Anderson · Martin Barre · Barriemore Barlow · John Evan · David Palmer · Tony Williams — **Jethro Tull #7**

Allan Holdsworth · Bill Bruford · Terry Bozzio · John Wetton · Eddie Jobson — **U.K.**      Dave Pegg · Ian Anderson · Martin Barre · Barriemore Barlow · John Evan · David Palmer — **Jethro Tull #8**

Dave Pegg · Ian Anderson · Martin Barre · Mark Craney · Eddie Jobson — **Jethro Tull #9**      Peter Vittese · Dave Bogle · David Valentine · Billy McGhee · Tam McTavish — **The R.A.F.**

Jon Anderson · Chris Squire · Alan White · Trevor Rabin · Eddie Jobson — **Yes #8**      Dave Pegg · Ian Anderson · Martin Barre · Paul Conway · Burgess · Peter Vetesse — **Jethro Tull #10**      Barriemore Barlow · Zal Cleminson · Charlie Tumahai · Ronnie Leahy — **Tandoori Castle**

Simon Nicol · Dave Swarbrick · Dave Pegg · Dave Mattacks — **Fairport Cnvntn #16**      Dave Pegg · Ian Anderson · Martin Barre · Doane Perry · Peter Vetesse — **Jethro Tull #11**      Mickey Barker · Bill Worrall · David Bristow · John Evan · David Palmer — **Tallis**

Simon Nicol · Martin Allcock · Dave Pegg · Dave Mattacks · Ric Sanders — **Fairport Cnvntn #17**      Dave Pegg · Ian Anderson · Martin Barre · Doane Perry · Don Riley · Gerry Conway — **Jethro Tull #12**

Gerry Conway · Doane Perry · Dave Pegg · Martin Allcock · Martin Barre · Ian Anderson — **Jethro Tull #13**

# The History of Jethro Tull

Color Plate 8

Color drop caps can be exceedingly effective, and there are a lot of really interesting things you can do with color and single characters. Just as a large or ornate drop cap serves to focus the attention of someone looking at a black-and-white page, a colored one can be even more eye-catching, especially if it's the only object with color on the page.

**Color Plate 4** illustrates some four-color display caps that could be used quite effectively as drop caps. Obviously, these are a small fraction of what you can dream up. As these examples use several Post-Script effects which would not export into GEM files without a fuss, they would have to be created as separations and stripped into a final document by your print house.

If your publication lends itself to having icons, symbols, or logos in it, these also make ideal applications for color.

## COLOR GRADIENTS AND FOUNTAINS

One of the things which plagues magazines and other multiple-page publications is that white paper is, well, so white. You can make a particular page stand out by changing this. One way to do so is simply to instruct your print house to lay a screen of some fairly muted color behind whatever's on your page. However, a still more interesting way to do so is to have Corel Draw produce a large fountain in such a color. This will not only make the background of your page something other than white, but it will also make it more visually interesting, as it won't simply be a constant tone.

You can also fill specific areas of the page or individual elements with color fountains and other effects in which you blend colors or change their density. **Color Plate 5** illustrates several examples of graphics which change color.

Color fountains are no more difficult to do than black-and-white ones. They were discussed earlier, in Chapter 4. However, there are a few things worth noting about fountains and color.

To begin with, Corel Draw's fountains take a moderately long time to output. This is true whether you're sending them to a 300-dpi laser printer or a Linotron PostScript typesetter. Bearing in mind that most typesetting house add to their charges for each minute

Linotron output takes, graphics with lots of fountains in them may get expensive.

Secondly, keep in mind how your color will be printed. A fountain which blends between two Pantone colors, for example, is not a very effective use of spot colors, because it requires you to output separations (as it will have lots of intermediate spot colors in the fountain). If you're using spot colors, make sure your fountains work with single colors. They can blend between varying densities of a single color. In order to blend between two colors, you must work with process colors and be planning on full-color printing.

A further complication in the use of color fountains is that they don't show up in color in Corel Draw's preview. No matter what colors you specify for a fountain, they'll be drawn in gray in the preview window. This can make judging the effect of your work a little difficult. Sadly, there's no way around it at present.

Repeating "macro" graphics, such as the one in Color Plate 5, are another obvious use of varying density color fills. Creating the repeating elements of the graphic itself is quite easy, and has been discussed previously (in Chapter 3). Unfortunately, Corel Draw does not provide any easy way to include repetitive color changes in a macro—you can't, for example, create a macro which decrements the color density by 5 percent with each consecutive iteration. As a result, in order to do things like this you'll have to create the graphics and then set up each colored element by hand, a moderately tedious procedure.

Once again, bear in mind that the greater the number of colored elements, the longer it will take to output. If you're running with a budget, a macro graphic which seems too tedious to color by hand might also be too expensive to output to a Linotron.

## COLOR TEXT EFFECTS

Adding color to text—especially for use as eye-catching exported headlines—is an ideal application for Corel Draw. There are all sorts of things you can do in this area. **Color Plate 6** illustrates some possible examples.

Simply setting type in color isn't all that exciting and you can usually manage this without Corel Draw's help at all. Setting text with a color fountain running through it is a lot more interesting, and is effective because it isn't seen all that often.

Colored text often looks a lot more interesting against black or some other dark color than it does against white, largely because people are used to seeing white pages. If your document will be handled by a print shop, you can have your desktop publishing type ''reversed out'' of a black background. In this case, a colored headline graphic against a black background can be stripped into your black page and look really striking. If you do try this effect, bear in mind that large black areas will tend to bleed into small white ones when your work finally gets printed. If you have small type on your page, consider setting it in a bold face rather than a medium one to give it a better chance of surviving the printing process.

## *WORKING WITH CONTRAST*

The nice thing about sticking a color photograph on a page is that all the color has been handled for you by nature, which has been working with color for some time now. In a color graphic, you will be forced to specify all the colors yourself. This can be a much more difficult task than you might think, especially if you lack a color proof printer to see the results of your work.

Figure 11.3 is a chart which illustrates the effective use of contrasting colors—or rather, the need for the effective use of contrasting colors. You will note that it's somewhat unreadable in its monochrome form. Reproduced in Color Plate 7, however, it's quite easy to read.

In working with color, you should keep in mind that you can often do things which aren't possible in black-and-white because objects with the same density can stand out from each other by virtue of having different colors. **Color Plate 7** is a rather extreme example of this—its colors contrast markedly from each other. Of course, you can be a lot more subtle in your designs and still use contrasting colors effectively.

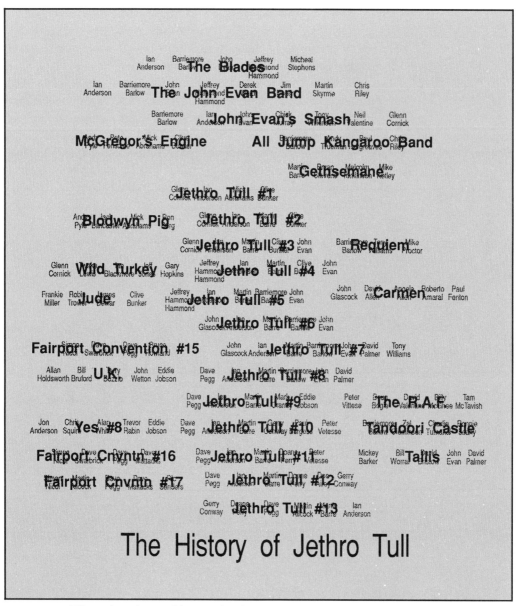

*Figure 11.3:* The rather obscure history of Jethro Tull. See Color Plate 7 for the less obscure version.

## *COLORING CLIP ART*

Adding color to some of the monochrome clip art which accompanies Corel Draw can be a quick, painless way to generate color graphics. Be warned, however—it's not as easy as it looks. Many of the pictures in the Corel Draw clip art sampler are really designed to be reproduced in black-and-white, and will take a bit of cunning to colorize effectively.

Human subjects are the most difficult ones to color. The contours of a human face are hard to represent in objects, and a solid color fill seems to emphasize the lack of details far more than a white one does.

It's also hard to see what you're doing in coloring clip art if the clip art in question uses fountain fills, because the fountains won't be visible in your preview.

**Color Plate 8** illustrates some examples of Corel Draw's clip art with color added to them.

## *WRAPPING UP*

Most experienced graphics artists are a bit nervous about experimenting with color, as the results can be embarrassingly costly if they don't work out. Print houses generally print what you give them—whether or not it's actually what you wanted.

Corel Draw, especially when it's coupled with a color proofing device like a PaintJet printer, is a much friendlier way to learn about color. You can try out color effects and just get some experience with the nuances of color applications, all without incurring any excessive print bills or nasty surprises.

Weighed against the cost of a couple of print jobs which don't work out, you might find that you can justify the cost of a PaintJet pretty easily.

# *appendix* A

*Hardware, Software,
and Using Microsoft Windows*

**Y**OU CAN GET AWAY WITH KNOWING VERY LITTLE about Microsoft Windows if all you're interested in is running Corel Draw. However, there are a number of things about Windows which you might have to know in order to optimize its operation, and the operation of Corel Draw, for your specific system. Knowing how to work with Windows will make Corel Draw a much more useful tool.

In addition, Windows is a very useful package in its own right. It incorporates a powerful, consistent user interface, and if you learn its basic set of dialogs, menus, and other phenomena you'll be most of the way towards knowing how to run any Windows-based application.

This appendix will discuss Windows and the hardware it needs to operate. It will be especially useful if you're still shopping for a computer to run Corel Draw on, as it includes information about the various levels of performance you can expect from Windows and Corel Draw for various sorts of computers.

## *HARDWARE AND SOFTWARE REQUIREMENTS OF COREL DRAW*

Defining the hardware you'll need to make Corel Draw work for you might be a difficult task. Much of the question is somewhat subjective, predicated on such things as the likely complexity of the drawings you're going to create, the time you'll have to create them, the quality of the results you expect and, most important, who you can lean on to foot the bill for equipment.

With the exception of the last point, all of this is intimately tied to one of the popular catch-22's of computers. You won't really know what level of hardware you need until you're well into learning about Corel Draw, and by then it will be too late to take any of the equipment back if it isn't what you need.

We can look at a few guidelines for hardware, but ultimately you'll be forced to take your best shot. In all cases—especially if someone else is paying the bills—it's a lot better to buy computer hardware which is more powerful than your application requires than hardware which can't really do the job.

You can run Corel Draw on any PC compatible computer, but you probably would not want to. Corel Draw is amazingly fast considering all the work it does, but in a relative sense it's a very processor-intensive program: it needs a lot of computer power to make it go at a decent speed.

The minimum hardware upon which Corel Draw will run at an acceptable clip is an AT compatible, or a "286 machine." This latter designation refers to the microprocessor which drives an AT compatible computer, the 80286. There are very fast AT-class machines available now. In fact, ATs haven't been the state of the art for some time, and for this reason even the really impressive ones are not terribly expensive.

The successors to AT-class computers are the 80386 based systems, or "386 machines." These computers are typically faster than comparable ATs. They also have a lot of sophisticated memory options and other things which are very slick, but which don't really affect Corel Draw. If you can afford a 386 machine by all means spring for one. All of the example drawings in this book were done on a 386 system, and while it's clearly overkill I'd buy it again if I had to.

However, at least inasmuch as it affects the operation of Corel Draw, a fast 286 system will make a better place to work than will a middle-level 386.

## MEMORY CONSIDERATIONS

For historical reasons, the memory situation on AT- and 386-class machines is a bit fragmented. There are several sorts of memory, each of which does something just a little different.

The basic memory that programs run in is usually called system memory or DOS memory. There can be as much as 640 kilobytes of it. This used to be a lot of memory—now it's an extremely tight fit for many applications, Corel Draw among them. A no-frills AT machine will probably come with this memory and nothing more.

One common variation on this is an AT with one megabyte of memory. There is an extra 384 kilobytes of memory in such a machine, but you can't use it directly. The upper part of it resides in the same place that a lot of the inner workings of the computer live. For example, it overlies the same memory space as the video board that drives the system monitor. While there are some side benefits to a 1-megabyte AT—primarily in that it lets some of the low-level system software run a bit faster—such a computer would not make any additional memory beyond 640 kilobytes available for use with applications like Corel Draw.

There are two forms of memory which exist beyond the limits of DOS memory, called *expanded* and *extended* memory. These two words are enough alike that it's often hard to remember which is which.

An AT compatible machine can actually address memory beyond 1 megabyte, the official end of the road for the earlier PC compatible computers. This extra memory is called extended memory. Unfortunately, an AT can't just make this extra memory appear on the end of the basic 640 kilobytes of DOS memory. Extended memory is useful for storing data under software which knows how to access it, but it does not expand the basic memory of a computer which has some installed.

As you know, Corel Draw runs under Microsoft Windows. How well it is able to use extended memory is a function of how well the version of Windows it's running under supports it. As of this writing, the current version of Windows, Version 2.0 and its derivatives, made some use of extended memory, with substantial room for improvement. Microsoft has announced an impending vastly improved Windows package (Version 3.0) which should ease the memory pinch Corel Draw often experiences.

You should have some extended memory in the machine which you choose to run Corel Draw on. It will help you out to some extent now and—hopefully—a lot more when you acquire the new version of Windows.

The second sort of extra memory is expanded memory, also called LIM memory. LIM stands for Lotus, Intel, and Microsoft, the three companies which ''pioneered'' the standard of expanded memory. Unlike extended memory, expanded memory does not require any additional addressing capability of the machine it's installed in. It is applicable to old-style PC compatible machines, which is really what it was designed for; it's not really needed in an AT environment. In fact, expanded memory is slow and funky in comparison with extended memory.

If you spring for an AT-class machine, make sure that you get an *extended* memory board.

A 386 machine can do some very clever tricks with memory. For example, if you buy a 1-megabyte 386 machine, you can make the hitherto useless upper 384 kilobytes appear as extended memory. The 80386 processor is able to tell its memory where to show up and how to act when it gets there.

With the diminishing price gap between 286 and 386 machines—to some extent due to the approach of 486 machines—the memory-juggling facilities of the 80386 are well worth considering if you plan to run applications in addition to Corel Draw, ones which have potentially conflicting memory requirements.

## DISPLAY CARDS

Part of the issue of speed in a computer running Corel Draw is tied up in how fast the screen updates. Part of the usefulness of Corel Draw in the long term will therefore be governed by your choice of display cards and monitors.

Some of the considerations affecting your choice of a display card will be tied up with characteristics of Microsoft Windows. If you're not too clear about where Windows fits into the picture yet, you might want to skip ahead to the section which explains it and return to this page once you understand what Windows is all about.

There are many specialized monitors and display cards which can run Windows and, hence, Corel Draw. However, the common ones fall into three groups. These are as follows:

- *Hercules or "monochrome graphics" cards.* These are very simple display cards which drive an inexpensive kind of monitor called a TTL monitor, which only does black-and-white, or, more often, black-and-amber. Because good TTL monitors are quite inexpensive, it's easy to afford one that's kind to your eyes. However, color is a useful asset under Windows, and while the lack of it doesn't disable Corel Draw, it does diminish the package.

The simple monochrome display of a Hercules card is quick to update, making this the snappiest sort of display.

- *EGA cards.* These are 16-color graphics cards which drive special EGA-style monitors. (EGA stands for Enhanced Graphic Adapter.) This is probably the optimum sort of card to run Corel Draw with. A good EGA monitor is not all that expensive, so your eyes needn't suffer with a cheap one. EGA cards are not blindingly fast to update, but they aren't bad. Color makes a world of difference to Corel Draw.

- *VGA cards.* There are lots of enhanced VGA (Video Graphics Array) cards that offer drivers for Windows capable of putting an 800-by-600-pixel display on your screen in 16 colors. Some can do even better than this. The results are quite impressive to look at. However, a good VGA compatible multisync monitor is an expensive tube. Because there's a lot more data on an 800-by-600-pixel VGA screen than there is on a 640-by-350-pixel EGA screen, updating one takes longer and Corel Draw will not seem to run as quickly, all other things being equal. For this reason, VGA cards should not be used with Windows on slower AT machines.

  VGA cards have EGA cards within them. Thus, if you start off with a VGA card and decide you don't like it, you can just reinstall Windows for an EGA display and carry on. Of course, you will have bought a very expensive card and monitor, much of the power of which will not be used.

VGA cards come with many modes. Most of the VGA cards one encounters have what are called super-VGA modes. These allow you to get still more pixels on the screen. More pixels allow for a much nicer looking display for Corel Draw to work with, but at the price of slower screen updating. In addition, the fact that a particular VGA card can display a very high density screen in its demonstration program does not mean that it will work with Windows. A super-VGA card is unusable unless it comes with its own Windows driver.

The super-VGA modes of enhanced VGA cards differ widely from manufacturer to manufacturer. Microsoft does not offer Windows drivers for them—getting a Windows driver working is the responsibility of the card manufacturer who cooked up the oddball mode in question. Hence, not all super-VGA cards have Windows drivers available for them. Further, super-VGA drivers are not interchangeable. The Windows driver for a Paradise Professional VGA card, for example, will not drive a Tatung VGA card.

Think carefully about which screen mode you want to use. If you have a machine which is only moderately fast you might well be better off with an EGA card. The somewhat lower resolution of an EGA display won't affect the *final* results of Corel Draw, which are independent of the resolution of your screen. It will, however, speed up the process of working with Corel Draw over what you might experience with a super VGA display.

## *MICE*

Windows and Corel Draw are both virtually useless without a mouse. Mice are the unthought-of extra element in any computer which uses Windows.

Mice long ago replaced modems as the cheapest peripheral device available for microcomputers. They come in all sorts of permutations and levels of compatibility. A good mouse is a joy to use. A bad one is a first-class pig.

In order to work well with Corel Draw, a mouse must be able to track movement accurately and it must be compatible with Windows. Both of these things are relative qualities.

The basic mechanism of a mouse is so simple that anyone with an injection molding machine and a few transistors can knock off working mice without having to undergo lengthy and unpleasant night-school engineering courses. For this reason, a lot of questionable mice exist. The difference between these mice and good mice will become apparent once you've used a cheap mouse for a while.

Cheap mice often track badly, that is, they don't translate movements of your hand to movements of the cursor very accurately. Still more annoying, most cheap mice have fairly coarse resolution. This means that you must move the mouse over a large distance relative to the movement of the cursor on your screen. On a normal-size desk with a normal amount of desk clutter, this usually means picking up the mouse frequently when you come to the peripheries of the clear space you've set aside for a rodent run.

Good mice feature accurate tracking, tight resolution, reliable buttons, and case designs that don't require you to contort your hand into a Vulcan salute every time you want to grasp the mouse.

A second consideration is the *driver* with which the mouse and Windows interface. Every mouse works differently, and the common element which makes it possible for all these diverse mice to communicate with Windows is a memory-resident program called a driver. As with VGA cards, the driver for one brand of mice probably won't work—or won't work very well—with another brand.

A driver which refuses to communicate with Windows changes an otherwise great mouse into something that is useful only as a cat toy.

Rodents such as the Microsoft and Logitech mice are good reliable choices for use with Corel Draw. There are many other very good mice as well, but if you are unable to try a potential mouse out with Corel Draw before you whip out your charge card, make sure you know you are buying one which will work.

The difference in price between a good mouse and a bad one is minimal, especially in comparison to the cost of the rest of your system hardware, so there is little sense in having anything less than the best.

## HARD DRIVE SPACE

While it might just be possible to squeeze a stripped-down version of Corel Draw onto a single quad-density floppy, the results of doing so would be too horrible to contemplate. Windows, and hence Windows-based applications, requires hard drives to be used effectively.

The amount of hard-drive space needed to run Corel Draw without its getting cramped will be determined by how you expect to use it. Windows itself will take about 2 megabytes to sprawl out and get comfortable. This will vary a bit with the number of fonts you have installed in Windows itself, which printer drivers you use, and so on. You can pare it down a bit from this level, but the resulting Windows package would be somewhat short of features.

Aside from serving as a platform from which to launch Corel Draw, you'll probably find that Windows is a nice place to work. It's handy to be able to step out of Corel Draw and write a letter or edit a bitmap file and then step right back to where you left off. This sort of convenience doesn't cost extra—Windows comes with a very well engineered word processor and many versions include a Windows-based implementation of Z-Soft's PC Paintbrush package—but it ties up disk space. The word processor alone needs about 200 kilobytes.

Corel Draw also requires about 2 megabytes of disk space, for a total of 4 so far. This includes lots of fonts and other accessories, and not even any drawing files as yet. You'll need room for drawing files. Plan to load the 6 megabytes worth of free sample clip art onto your hard drive; much of it is very good, and it would be a shame not to have it on tap.

In addition to all this, Windows frequently likes to write temporary files in the course of managing its memory and spooling print jobs. These files never stick around after a Windows session is over, but you will require enough free disk space to accommodate them for what little time they do exist. Plan on a megabyte for the temporaries, and you'll be looking at 11 or 12 megabytes of hard-drive space for the package in total.

Obviously you can get away with a 20- or 30-megabyte hard drive if Corel Draw will be the only thing running on your machine. However, most users run several applications at various times. In most cases you'll need a much larger hard drive to accommodate Corel Draw and everything else you'll be doing with your computer.

Having Windows on hand makes it easy to add additional Windows-based applications. For example, Corel Draw has superb text facilities—it can do wonders with a few outline fonts and a couple of hundred kilobytes of memory. Z-Soft's Type Foundry package for Windows, which lets you create outline fonts suitable for use with Corel Draw, is a natural accessory. It takes up the better part of a megabyte of hard-drive space. You will undoubtedly find other things with similar appetites to add to Windows.

## *PRINTERS AND COREL DRAW*

The ultimate destination of everything Corel Draw handles will be a printer of some sort. Corel Draw pictures can pass through a few hands along the way—you might import a Corel Draw picture into a desktop-publishing document before it finally finds its way to hard copy, for example—but printers are a primary concern in using Corel Draw.

As with any well-behaved Windows application, Corel Draw prints through Windows. In other words, it actually tells Windows where the picture is and lets Windows handle the printing. In this way, Corel Draw can be somewhat printer-independent.

This starts to unravel a bit because different printers have different capabilities, and Corel Draw has been written to take advantage of everything that high-end printers can muster. As a result, once you've gotten into using Corel Draw you'll see that some of its more innovative tricks and features rely on special characteristics of specific printers. We'll discuss this point further in the upcoming discussions of different printers.

Windows deals with printers through the use of printer drivers, which contain the specialized code to handle the details of individual printer protocols. With the appropriate drivers, Corel Draw can print the same picture through Windows to a dot-matrix printer or to a quarter-million-dollar PostScript RIP typesetter and in most cases will get the best output each of these devices can provide.

Windows comes with a rich selection of printer drivers. Most of the popular dot-matrix printers are supported, as well as a host of plotters. Both LaserJet compatible and PostScript laser printers are also supported by Windows. It's this latter group of devices which Corel Draw really likes to deal with.

Quite a few third-party Windows printer drivers also exist to support specialized printers for which Windows itself does not provide drivers.

Adding a printer driver is covered in the Windows documentation. As with most Windows features, it's all handled with a couple of mouse clicks and a brief pause.

The printer or other output device you choose to create hard copy from your Corel Draw pictures will probably be at least partially an economic decision. Laser printers are expensive. The 24-pin dot-matrix printers, such as the latest generation of Toshiba and Panasonic machines, do pretty creditable work. They don't produce reproduction-quality output and they aren't all that fast in comparison to lasers; however, they also won't set you back a couple thousand dollars.

### *LaserJet Printers*

The most commonly found type of laser printers suitable for use with Corel Draw are LaserJet Plus compatible printers. The LaserJet Plus itself is a product of Hewlett-Packard. (Actually, it has been superseded by the LaserJet II, but this fact doesn't essentially change the following discussion.) It incorporates a fairly simple "page description language," a protocol by which software can describe the text and images it wants the printer to output. This language is usually referred to as PCL, for *printer control language.* Corel Draw speaks PCL when you tell it to print to a LaserJet.

Being a very simple language, PCL has been rewritten for quite a few other laser printers. These printers are said to emulate the LaserJet Plus, and because PCL is quite uncomplicated to write, most PCL emulations are flawless.

A LaserJet compatible printer is a very simple machine as laser printers go. It represents relatively little research and development on the part of the company which makes the printer, and as a result these printers are usually pretty inexpensive. Some of the rather slow ones are available for as little as a thousand dollars.

LaserJet compatible printers can turn out first-class work when they're driven by Corel Draw. In fact, for reasons which we will discuss in a moment, a LaserJet Plus can do some things that a PostScript printer—the expensive sort of laser—cannot.

LaserJet Plus compatible printers are limited to a resolution of 300 dots per inch, which is not quite reproduction quality, but it is extremely close. In order to handle the graphics which Corel Draw sends to a LaserJet Plus, such a printer requires a minimum of one and a half megabytes of memory. This latter feature is important to keep in mind. The LaserJet Plus and many of its compatibles come with half a megabyte of memory installed. These printers look pretty competitive in price until you go to add the cost of extra memory required to make them do anything more than basic text.

### *PostScript Printers*

PostScript is a page description language which performs the same function PCL does on a LaserJet compatible printer. PostScript, however, does it with a lot more class and rather better facilities. The PostScript language makes it possible for Corel Draw to do a number of things which aren't possible on a LaserJet.

In order to print a simple Corel Draw drawing to a LaserJet Plus printer, Corel Draw would have to create an enormous bitmapped picture on the PC which created the drawing—for enormous, read about 1 megabyte of data—and then port this information to the printer. This requires a lot of time to make up the picture and a lot more to send it out through the printer port. It also requires a lot of free memory and disk space.

In printing the same drawing to a PostScript device, Corel Draw would wind up doing a great deal less work. PostScript printers define pictures as objects, just like Corel Draw does, and PostScript printers can use all of the path types and so on which are fundamental to the workings of Corel Draw. Printing an image to a PostScript printer simply involves Corel Draw translating the internal notation it uses to represent objects into the PostScript language and sending the resulting PostScript code to the printer.

The same PostScript program which is sent to a 300-dot-per-inch LaserWriter can also be sent to a 2500-dot-per-inch Linotronic Post-Script typesetter for typeset-quality output. Thus, you can create drawings under Corel Draw with the help of a PostScript laser and then take your files to a typesetting shop with a PostScript typesetter for final output.

A PostScript printer has a very sophisticated graphics library inside it, along with a fast computer to drive it. PostScript printers are usually based on the 68000 series processors which are found in Apple Macintosh machines. For this reason, a PostScript printer is able to handle graphics operations which Corel Draw itself cannot. One example of these is filling an object with a complex pattern. Figure A.1 illustrates some examples of this. These patterns are referred to in Corel Draw as *PostScript textures*. They're defined in the Post-Script language and can only be printed on a PostScript printer.

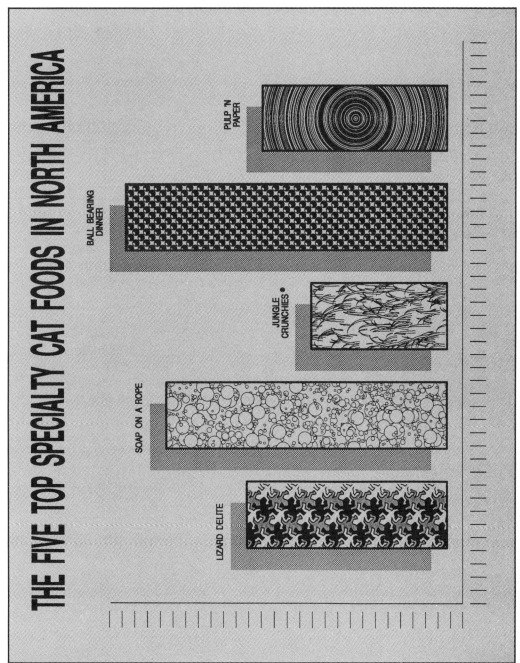

*Figure A.1:* PostScript textures used in a drawing.

As was noted in the section on LaserJet Plus printers, there are a few things that LaserJets can do which PostScript printers cannot. In PostScript there is a fixed upper limit to the number of paths an object can contain. The actual value varies from printer to printer and with the particular revision level of PostScript which your printer uses. If you exceed this limit, the object—or the whole drawing—will not print.

The maximum number of paths PostScript will accept is extremely high, and you'd have to create a fairly complex drawing to exceed it. Corel Draw, however, is more than capable of doing this. In fact, it does so now and again without half trying. Figure A.2 is an example of a Corel Draw document which will not print on a PostScript printer. The problem is in the fountain in the word Violin. Corel Draw creates fountains like this as myriads of individual paths, and the myriads have proven too complex for the printer.

Because a LaserJet Plus is just sent a bitmap when it prints, it has no limitations of this sort. This should explain how I printed the unprintable violin.

You can have the best of both worlds in laser printers. This will be discussed momentarily.

*PostScript Clones*   The biggest drawback to PostScript is that it costs so much. A large part of the price of a PostScript printer is the licensing fee which the printer manufacturer must pay to Adobe, the creator of PostScript, for the use of the language.

The high cost of PostScript has prompted a number of printer manufacturers to do with PostScript what was done earlier with PCL, and a number of laser printers are now available with PostScript compatible languages, or "PostScript clones." However, cloning PostScript is not anywhere near as simple as cloning PCL was.

As of this writing, none of the PostScript clone printers emulate PostScript perfectly. In addition, none of them are all that much less expensive than comparable printers which support real PostScript. Moreover, if you don't know laser printers extremely well, a PostScript clone can cause you some problems if you run into one of the imperfect areas of its emulation. Should you not get the output you expected you will be confronted with the question of whether the fault is in your drawing, in Corel Draw, or in the printer.

*Figure A.2:* A Corel Draw drawing which will not print on a PostScript device.

PostScript clones are unquestionably improving. Microsoft and Apple recently announced a joint effort to develop a PostScript-like page creation language, largely in response to Adobe's refusal to provide detailed descriptions of the inner workings of PostScript. Further, the existence of the clones has driven the prices of real PostScript printers down, and probably will continue to do so as the competition gets hotter. You can have it both ways in this respect. However, despite these bright prospects, you should know that Corel Draw makes sufficiently exacting demands on its output devices as to make a PostScript clone printer inadvisable.

The solution to all of these problems, however, may be in the form of a multiple-mode laser printer, to be discussed next.

### Multiple-Mode Laser Printers

PostScript is a programming language. It's quite possible to write an emulation of PCL in PostScript. If you downloaded such a program to a PostScript printer, the printer would turn into a LaserJet Plus temporarily, accepting LaserJet graphics and page description commands rather than PostScript.

In fact, pretty well all of the latest generation of PostScript printers incorporate a feature which handles this automatically. At the touch of a switch or with a couple of stabs at a front panel menu, you can choose between LaserJet Plus emulation or PostScript. This allows you to have things all ways—you can use PostScript to get the most of what Corel Draw offers in the way of features and PCL when you encounter a drawing with too many drawing paths.

This facility is available on such printers as the Apple LaserWriter IINTX and the NEC LC890, among others. It's not a particularly expensive feature to implement—the LC890, for example, is one of the lower priced PostScript printers at about $3,500—and well worth having.

## USING MICROSOFT WINDOWS

When you first start your computer, DOS loads into memory from your hard disk and starts to run. DOS is a special program called a *disk operating system*. It provides certain kinds of help for applications software which you will subsequently load or run from disks. Applications include things like WordStar, Lotus 1-2-3, AutoCAD, and Space Invaders.

The basic functions of DOS—and of any other operating system—are as follows:

- to provide you with a way to run programs
- to provide your programs with basic services, such as reading the keyboard, writing text to the screen, opening disk files, and so on
- to handle the computer's housekeeping functions, such as coping with disk errors or managing the printer ports
- to provide some fundamental file functions, such as displaying a disk directory or typing a file

Purists will note that not all of these things are done by DOS per se—some are handled by the BIOS in your computer. For the sake of this discussion let's allow that all these things are handled by the operating system, of which DOS is the visible component.

A PC is a ''text-based'' computer. This means that it defaults to working with characters rather than pictures as does, for example, a Macintosh or an Amiga. This is not to say that a PC can't do first-class graphics for use with programs like Corel Draw. However, its native language is text. DOS, insofar as it deals with the outside world, likes to think of things in terms of text. If a program asks DOS to go fetch a character from the keyboard, DOS will be able to cope with the request handsomely. Asked to draw a picture on the screen, however, DOS will be confused at best. It provides no graphics facilities at all. Likewise, it cannot manage a mouse.

You can think of Microsoft Windows as being a sort of DOS-extension environment. It bolts onto DOS and makes it into a graphic operating system. With Windows running, commands can be entered by clicking on pull-down menu items, applications can run in dedicated areas of the screen (not surprisingly, these areas are referred to as *windows*), and so on.

Applications such as Corel Draw are written with the assumption that Windows will be in place before you run the application—and with the ability to complain if this is not so. As such, when Corel Draw wants to refresh a drawing on your screen, for example, it does so by calling a part of Windows. Windows handles all the graphic functions of Corel Draw, among other things.

The power of Windows is that it does all the hard parts involved in maintaining a friendly user interface, leaving Corel Draw to handle the actual tasks of manipulating paths and objects and such. In addition, Windows is more or less a *multitasking* operating system, which means that you can run Corel Draw and then run a second application such as PC Paintbrush or the Windows Write word processor without having to exit from Corel Draw.

There are a number of drawbacks to Windows. For one thing, it's somewhat memory hungry. Applications like Corel Draw, which do a lot, are also memory hungry. Running several big applications often requires more memory than Windows currently knows how to address.

Windows gets around this memory problem in various ways. None of them are completely effective, and Windows Version 3 is expected to improve on this considerably. However, for Windows to be as effective as possible in its management of memory it should have at least a small amount of extended memory available to it. Extended memory was discussed earlier in this appendix.

As a rule, starving Windows for memory doesn't make it crash and, much to its credit, rarely keeps it from ultimately performing a task. It just slows it down a great deal as it investigates alternatives to stashing things in memory it doesn't have.

## *THE ART OF THE MOUSE*

In moving around Windows and using the functions of Corel Draw, you will need to know a bit of the terminology of mice. Being a very simple device, there aren't too many ways to do the things you can do with it, so this section will be pretty short.

When you move your mouse around on your desk, a *mouse cursor* will move on the screen. This defaults to looking like an arrow pointing to the upper left corner of your screen, but it may change its shape under Corel Draw and other applications when the program wants to indicate that something out of the ordinary is happening. For example, when an action is taking place which does not permit your computer to do anything else until it's done—such as saving a file—the mouse cursor will turn into an hourglass, the "wait cursor." It will turn back into whatever it was previously when the wait's over.

Most mice for the PC come with two or three buttons. Corel Draw recognizes only the leftmost button of the mouse, so when you're instructed to click the mouse button you should always use the left button. On a single-button mouse, of course, you would use that button.

*Clicking* on something under Windows involves moving the mouse cursor to the thing you're to click on and pushing and releasing the mouse button very quickly. *Double-clicking* involves doing the same thing but clicking twice in rapid succession. You may find that this doesn't work very well as Windows first comes out of the box; however, the Windows control panel allows you to adjust the "double-click time" to suit your mouse and your fingers.

*Dragging* (or "grabbing") something involves placing the mouse cursor on the thing to be dragged, holding down the mouse button, and pulling the thing to someplace else on the screen. When it gets there, release the mouse button.

*Selecting an area* of the screen—something which is done frequently under Corel Draw—involves dragging the mouse cursor over an area such that a "selector box" is drawn. A selector box, or "rubber band box," is just a rectangle drawn with broken lines which indicates the area traversed by the mouse.

You should make sure you understand these ideas, as they're pivotal to the operation of Windows and, hence, of Corel Draw.

## WALKING THROUGH WINDOWS

It's beyond the scope of this book to provide a detailed explanation of Windows and its operation. Chances are you wouldn't need one if it was provided, actually. Windows is a very intuitive system and you'll probably find that you're able to pick it up without much study.

We will not get into the installation of Windows or of Corel Draw either, as both of these procedures are explained quite adequately in the documentation for these two packages. As a matter of fact, in both cases all you need do is run the installation programs provided with Windows and Corel Draw respectively and answer the questions.

This section will explain those aspects of Windows which are relevant to the operation of Corel Draw. In these examples we'll assume that you have installed the two packages such that Windows itself lives in a subdirectory called C:\WINDOWS and that Corel Draw lives in a subdirectory called C:\WINDOWS\CORELDRW.

In order to run Windows you must issue the command WIN, which runs WIN.COM. This will display the Microsoft logo and, a while later, the main screen of Windows. If you have a less than stellar computer the Windows logo will become annoying after a while—consult Appendix C of this book for a procedure to disable the Windows logo.

Figure A.3 illustrates the Windows main screen.

The Windows screen resembles many of the file managers which have been developed for use with DOS, although it does so using a

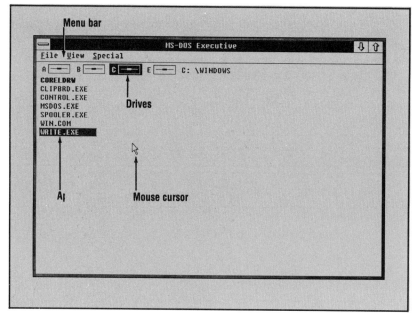

*Figure A.3:* The main screen of Windows.

graphics display rather than a text mode screen. Initially it will show you all the files in your \WINDOWS directory.

If you move your mouse cursor to the listing of a file which is named with a .COM or .EXE extension and double-click on the name, Windows will run it. If the application was written for Windows—the WRITE.EXE program which comes with Windows is such an application, as of course is Corel Draw—it will come up in a window on the screen.

Windows itself is a Windows application. The main screen which comes up when you first run Windows behaves just like any other Windows application in the way it uses its menus, controls, dialogs, and so forth. Once you understand how to use it—it will be presented in the following section on Working with Controls—Corel Draw will be a great deal easier to master.

Many applications have specific file name extensions associated with them. Corel Draw, for example, names its drawing files with the extension .CDR. Windows knows that the .CDR extension has to do with Corel Draw—the Corel Draw installation package tells it so. As such, if you click on a file name with the extension .CDR, Corel Draw will automatically boot up and load the drawing file you've selected.

Non-Windows applications can also be run from within Windows, although they typically force you to give up most of Windows' more advanced features, such as its multitasking abilities, during the time the application in question is running.

### Working with Controls

One of the really powerful aspects of Windows is its consistency. All Windows applications are constrained to behave themselves according to certain guidelines. Thus, if you know how to work the controls and menus and whatnot of one Windows application you're well on your way to knowing how to run any other one.

Once an application has opened a window for itself you can change the size and position of the window with the mouse. If you grab the top bar of the window you can drag the window to a new location. Grab the lower right corner of the window and you'll be able to make it larger or smaller.

There are two boxes in the upper right corner of any Windows application. One has a downward facing arrow and the other an upward facing arrow. The downward facing arrow is the *minimize button* and the upward facing arrow is the *maximize button.* These are examples of Windows *controls.*

If you double-click in the minimize box the window for the application will vanish. A small icon representing the application will appear somewhere along the bottom of your screen.

A minimized application is still running, and if you minimized it in the middle of a task it will continue executing the task even though you can no longer see it. When you go to print a picture from within Corel Draw, Corel Draw basically hands the picture to another Windows application called Spooler, which does all the work. Spooler comes "pre-minimized"—when it's running all you'll see is its icon.

You can return a minimized window to its former state by double-clicking on its icon.

The maximize control causes the window of an application to grow from whatever its current size is to the maximum size the screen allows.

You can have lots of open windows on the screen at once, and you needn't minimize the ones you aren't using just to get at the one you want to use. You can bring any window to the front of the screen by clicking in some part of it. Having done this, anything you type will be received by the application in this window. This is referred to as the *active window.* Figure A.4 illustrates a stack of windows and the result of clicking in one of the more rearward ones.

### Working with Menus

The minimize and maximize controls are really shortcuts. Windows provides a lot of shortcuts like this. The "long way" to minimize and maximize an application's window is to use the appropriate *menu items.*

Most Windows applications have some menus. Corel Draw has quite a few. The names of the menus are displayed along the top of the application's window in what is called the *menu bar.* If you click on a menu name and hold the mouse button a menu will drop down. Drag the mouse down the screen and the various menu items will be

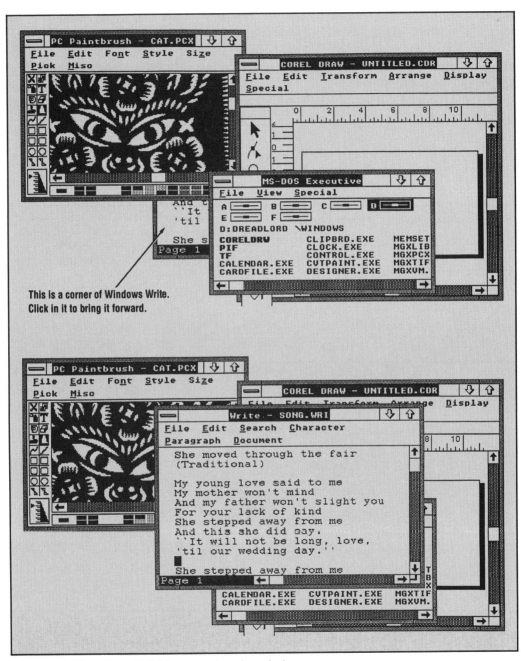

*Figure A.4:* The effect of clicking in an inactive window.

highlighted as the mouse cursor passes over them. If you release the mouse button when an item is highlighted that item will be selected.

The inside covers of this book display the various Corel Draw menus and their corresponding "dialog boxes." Dialog boxes will be discussed shortly.

Some items in a menu may appear dim relative to the rest of the items in the menu. These are "inactive" items, and cannot be selected. There is usually some logical reason for an item to be inactive. In this case, the Close item is inactive because there's nothing to close. Once a file has been opened this item will become active.

To a large extent, becoming proficient in the use of any Windows application is a matter of learning what's in each of its menus and what each item actually does.

Every Windows application has one more menu than appears in its menu bar. This is called the *system menu,* and it is available by clicking in the box in the extreme upper left of an application's window. The location of this box and the appearance of a typical system menu are illustrated in Figure A.5.

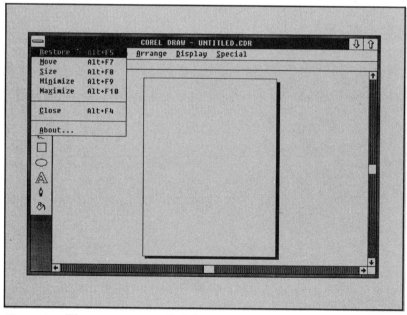

*Figure A.5:* The system menu of a Windows application.

The system menu has items which, among other things, will minimize and maximize an application's window just like the two controls we discussed a few minutes ago did. It also has a Close item, which is used to terminate the application.

Most system menus feature an About item. If you click on the About item of an application you should see a box which tells you the name of the company which wrote the program, possibly the names of the programmers involved in its creation, and usually a version number. The version number will be important if you have to contact the application's manufacturer for help. Figure A.6 illustrates the About box of Corel Draw.

There's a very important shortcut involved in the system menu. If you double-click on the control that brings up the system menu you'll terminate the application. This is a handy way to exit in a hurry. If you double-click on this box in the main screen of Windows you'll end your Windows session and return to DOS.

Corel Draw also uses this feature to close up auxiliary menus and windows within the application. Figure A.7 illustrates a Corel Draw

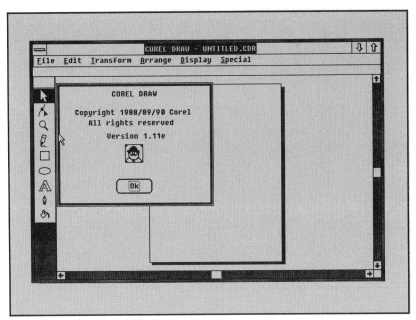

*Figure A.6:* The About box of Corel Draw.

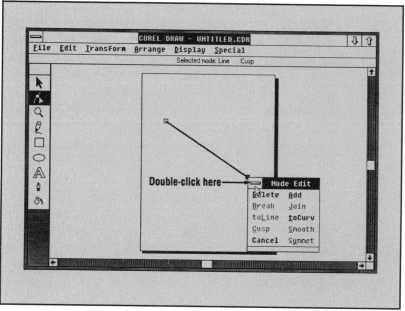

*Figure A.7:* Disposing of a Corel Draw pop-up menu.

pop-up menu (in this case the Node Edit popup) and how to dispose of it quickly. You'll want to remember this shortcut.

### Working with Dialogs

Windows applications usually communicate with you through dialog boxes, or *dialogs* for short. A dialog is any box which pops up to tell you something, to wait for a reply, or to ask a question.

There's a lot of rather involved terminology relating to dialog boxes under Windows, much of it only of interest to Windows gurus and Windows programmers. You don't really need to know any of it: dialogs are designed to be self-explanatory, and the ones under Corel Draw are even better than usual in this respect.

Any dialog which wants a reply will contain one or more *controls*. The most common sort of control is a *button*. A button contains some text—usually a word or two—which defines what clicking on that control will do. Many dialogs will have one default button, indicated by the extra thickness of its outline. If you hit the Enter key on your keyboard while such a dialog is active, the default action will be selected and whatever would have happened had you explicitly clicked on the default button will transpire.

Many dialogs contain *radio buttons*. These are analogous to the buttons on a mechanical car-radio station selector. If you click on one of a set of radio buttons, that button will be selected and all the others will be deselected. Radio buttons are used to select one action from a list of several in cases where only one of them can be performed at a time. When you may select more than one action (or set more than one condition) at a time, you will be presented with another group of controls known as *check boxes*.

Figure A.8 illustrates a *scroll bar* control. This device allows you to scroll a list of text or other material which is too long to fit in the available space all at once. Clicking on the arrows at the top or bottom of a vertical scroll bar will bring additional lines of text into the list box one line at a time. Clicking in the gray area of the scroll bar will scroll larger increments. The ''thumb''—the box in the gray area—shows

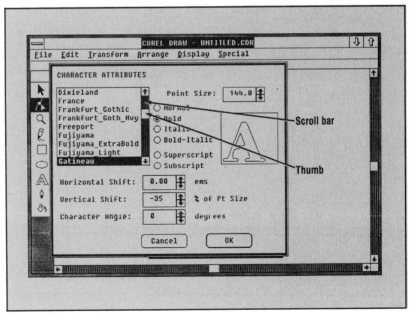

*Figure A.8:* A scroll bar.

your relative position within the list. When it is close to the top of the scroll bar, the contents you see are close to the top of the list; when it is closer to the bottom, the contents you see are closer to the end of the list. If you drag the thumb down the scroll bar, the contents of the list will change in relation to the thumb's location. Horizontal scroll bars work in a similar fashion.

*File Dialogs*    The file dialog is a special dialog for opening and saving files. Figure A.9 illustrates what one looks like in Corel Draw. Other Windows applications may use slight variations on this dialog, although all the important elements of it will be present in some form no matter where it turns up. In this case the dialog is being used to open a file, but the same box would be used if you try to save one.

The narrow horizontal text box close to the top of the dialog, next to the word Path, indicates the DOS path to the directory where the file will be saved. It also indicates the file specification for the file names which are visible in the Files list box directly below it. If the path said C:\WINDOWS\CORELDRW\*.CDR, all the files with

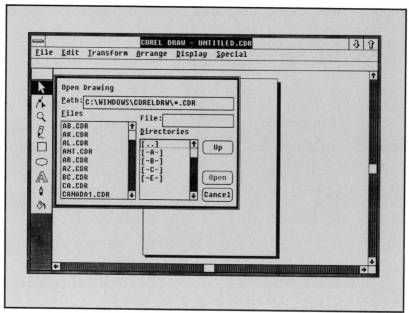

*Figure A.9:* A file dialog as it appears in Corel Draw.

the extension .CDR in the the subdirectory called C:\WINDOWS \CORELDRW\ would be shown in the list.

The path can be edited by clicking on it to place a text-editing cursor in the text and then using the keyboard to change it.

The Files list box in this dialog is normally used when you're opening files. It will show you all the appropriate file names and allow you to choose one. You can select a file name by clicking on it. The scroll bar to the right of the box allows you to scroll through the list of names if there are too many to fit in the window all at once.

The drive and directory selection box is the smaller list box to the right of the Files list box (under the word Directories). It will show you the names of any subdirectories present in the directory specified by the path. For example, in Figure A.9, if there were a subdirectory called EPS-FILES in the directory C:\WINDOWS\CORELDRW, its name would appear in the list. Double-clicking on it would change the path and file specification to C:\WINDOWS\CORELDRW\EPS-FILES\*.CDR. The Files list box is updated automatically if you change directories.

If the path points to something other than the root directory, the Directories list box will contain, in addition to any subdirectory names, a file name which is just two dots. Double-clicking on this will cause the path to "back up" to the previous directory. For example, if the current path were

C:\WINDOWS\CORELDRW\EPS-FILES\*.CDR

double-clicking on the [..] entry would change the path to

C:\WINDOWS\CORELDRW\*.CDR

Clicking on the Up text button does the same thing.

The Directories box will also contain the letters of all the valid disk drives on your system. Double-clicking on one of these will allow you to load or save files to a different drive.

### Keyboard Shortcuts

Corel Draw offers keyboard equivalents for just about everything. Virtually all of the menu items, the choices in dialog boxes, and so on can be selected using the keyboard.

Keyboard shortcuts are handy because once you get used to Corel Draw you'll find that in many cases the keyboard is a much more convenient way to perform some operations than mousing around is. For example, an action which might take several drags and clicks can often be repeated in Corel Draw simply by hitting Ctrl-R.

All menu options can be handled by using two keyboard commands. The first activates the menu and the second selects a specific option from the menu. The first command is always an Alt combination, which means it's entered by holding down the Alt key on your keyboard and hitting a letter key. The second key is a normal letter.

One commonly used keyboard equivalent is Alt-F to activate the File menu and then O to select the Open option. This will open a file; that is, it will bring up the File dialog to allow you to load a drawing file into Corel Draw.

In Corel Draw there are a number of frequently used menu options which can be handled with single Control-key equivalents. To use one, such as Ctrl-R described above, you would hold down the Control key and hit the appropriate letter key.

The keyboard equivalents for every menu item are listed in the menus themselves. Figure A.10 illustrates the File menu of Corel Draw. You will notice that in the menu bar, the F in File is underlined. This indicates that the key to access the File menu is Alt-F. If you hit Alt-F when Corel Draw is running, the File menu will drop down and stay visible until you hit a second key to select an option or do something to banish the menu. The screen in Figure A.10 was captured immediately after hitting Alt-F.

Looking down the list of menu items in Figure A.10, you'll note than each one has an underlined letter. For example, the O in Open is underlined. The underlined letters tell you the second letter for each two-letter keyboard equivalent.

You will also note that there is something on the same line as the Open menu item, this being ^O (a caret character and the letter O). The caret represents the Control key. What this tells you is that there are actually two keyboard equivalents for opening a file. You can use Alt-F O or you can use Control-O. Obviously, the latter requires one less keystroke.

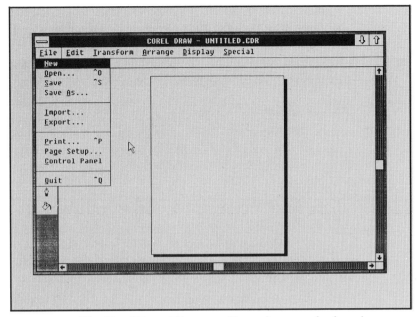

*Figure A.10:* The Corel Draw File menu illustrating some keyboard
equivalents for its items.

There is no printed list of keyboard equivalents in Corel Draw, nor
is one needed. The menus themselves will tell you what they are. You
will find that over time you'll learn the ones which help you out.

Note that keyboard shortcut commands are always sent to the
application whose window is foremost on your screen, that is, to
the active window. If the application in your active window doesn't
recognize a particular keyboard shortcut, it will beep and ignore it.

## WINDOWS MEMORY TIPS

Windows is a very easy environment to learn and work in. You
don't have to know very much about it to start using Corel Draw,
and most of what you do need will prove almost self-explanatory after
you've started working with Windows. However, there are a few
useful things to know about the internal workings of Windows which
will help you to make the best use of it and its resources.

As has been mentioned before, Windows has a limited amount of memory to work with. Large applications, such as Corel Draw, run more efficiently if they have lots of memory. You will improve the performance of Windows and of Corel Draw if you free up all the memory you can. The following are guidelines for accomplishing this:

- Avoid resident programs. Programs which provide pop-up utilities, such as SideKick, tie up memory when they're loaded. Most of them can't be used under Windows in any case, so make sure they haven't been run before you go to run Windows.

- Avoid Windows gadgets. There is an increasing library of interesting programs which you can run under Windows concurrent with Corel Draw. These provide things like a screen clock, a free-memory display, a fancy screen blanker, and so on. All of these programs occupy memory.

- Avoid running other "serious" Windows applications when you're working with large drawings under Corel Draw. If you have Windows Write in memory along with Corel Draw, Corel Draw will have less memory for itself and, as a result, will probably slow down quite a bit.

- Simplify your CONFIG.SYS file. If you really want to free up the last bit of available memory for use with Windows, have a quick look at your CONFIG.SYS file. The DOS manual which came with your system will aid you in interpreting its contents. Some users will have extravagant numbers of files and buffers allocated, which tie up lots of memory. You might also have device drivers in there which are not needed under Windows. If you have a network driver in your CONFIG.SYS file, for example, you'll probably find that removing it frees a lot of memory. Note that Windows does not even need ANSI.SYS.

Obviously, some of the above suggestions may interfere with other operations of your computer—those which do not involve Windows. What many Windows users do is to create a Windows "boot floppy." This is a disk you can boot your system from when you plan to use Windows without having to boot from your hard drive. The AUTOEXEC.BAT and CONFIG.SYS files on the boot floppy can be set up so as not to load any resident programs, to leave out any unnecessary device drivers, and so on.

If you want to create a boot floppy, format a blank floppy disk using the /S option after the FORMAT command to transfer your system files to it. Create the appropriate AUTOEXEC.BAT and CONFIG.SYS files on it—if you use the HIMEM.SYS file supplied by Windows, this must be included in the CONFIG.SYS file on your boot floppy. Now, whenever you want to use Windows, place the boot floppy in drive A, close the drive door, and reboot your computer by holding down the Ctrl and Alt keys and hitting the Del key.

### Squeezing in a Bit More Memory

If you have some extended memory in your machine you can make Windows use it, as we've discussed. One of the best ways the current version of Windows can use extended memory is for the storage of its temporary files. This will not only speed up your system— the files will effectively be stored in fast memory rather than on a much slower hard drive—but it will greatly reduce the amount of overhead you must maintain on your hard drive as well.

Windows creates temporary files for many reasons. The print spooler, for example, uses them to store jobs to be printed. When Corel Draw asks Windows for some memory and there's no memory to be had, Windows "pages out" some presently unused data or code into temporaries. This means that it temporarily moves the code or data out of memory into a file and declares the memory it was occupying as free. It will retrieve the code later if it's needed.

If you have extended memory in your system you can make it into a RAM (Random Access Memory) disk. A RAM disk will appear to be a disk drive—it will have a drive letter and all the characteristics of a real disk drive—but the files on it will be stored in memory. Reading and writing files to a RAM disk takes almost no time at all.

When you bought DOS for your computer you got the software to implement a RAM disk in extended memory for free. Depending on your version of DOS, you will have either VDISK.SYS or RAM-DRIVE.SYS. Your DOS manual will explain how to install one of these files in your CONFIG.SYS file.

There are a few things to note about these programs.

- VDISK.SYS is the older of the two RAM disk programs, and has some drawbacks in that it's reluctant to share extended memory with other programs that use it. Install RAMDRIVE.SYS if you have a choice.

- Both of these programs are smart enough to figure out how much extended memory you have and "adjust" the size of the RAM disk you ask for if you've asked for more space than is really available.

- Both RAM disks default to using DOS memory for their memory requirements. You must tell them that you want to use extended memory by including the /E switch in your CONFIG.SYS file.

- The RAM disk will default to using the next unused drive letter. If you have a system with two floppies called drives A: and B: and a hard drive called drive C:, your RAM drive will appear as drive D:.

- A RAM drive's contents will exist only until the next time you reboot or switch off your computer. An unexpected crash will wipe out your RAM drive. Never store anything important in one.

Having created a RAM disk, you must tell Windows and Corel Draw that it's available for use as a temporary file stash. This is done by adding a line like the following to your AUTOEXEC.BAT file:

```
SET TEMP = D:\
```

The part after the equal sign must point to the root directory of your RAM drive.

Here's another useful thing to know about Windows and Corel Draw. Whenever you run Windows in order to subsequently run Corel Draw, you'll be giving up a fair bit of memory to Windows. This is a necessary expense if you want to actually use Windows—for example, to run additional concurrent tasks—but a dead waste if your entire session is to be done wholly within Corel Draw.

You can instruct Windows to load up only those parts of itself which are actually needed by Corel Draw and then to run Corel Draw itself. The main screen of Windows, all its menus and the functions which they contain, will remain behind on the disk. This frees up a lot of extra memory for Corel Draw to use. The following command will do this, loading Corel Draw directly from DOS, bypassing the Windows main screen and saving some memory in the process.

WIN :C:\WINDOWS\CORELDRW\CORELDRW

Note the colon before the drive letter. This tells Windows that it's to run a program—CORELDRW.EXE in this case—rather than itself.

# appendix

# B

*Dublin*

*Claudius*

*Bauhaus*

*Charac*

## Using WFNBOSS and WIN.INI

**T**HE TYPOGRAPHIC FACILITIES OF COREL DRAW have been discussed at length in this book. One of the things which makes Corel Draw so attractive in comparison to other drawing packages is its vast supply of typefaces. It might seem, when you first uncrate the software, that any font not already part of Corel Draw must not be worth having.

In fact, once you get into using Corel Draw you'll probably find that the fonts provided with the package are not adequate for all the typography you want to do. This isn't really the fault of Corel Draw, but rather an aspect of the nature of type. Having a lot of fonts usually just makes one want a lot more fonts.

As of version 1.1 Corel Draw comes with an ancillary program called WFNBOSS which allows you to add third-party fonts to Corel Draw. The process is painless, is not unduly slow, and will give you access to all sorts of additional typefaces at a nominal cost. Figure B.1 illustrates some of the typefaces I've added to Corel Draw with WFNBOSS. (WFNBOSS, I am told, stands for Waldo Fonts Boss. Waldo was the development name for Corel Draw, and is also the name of the mustachioed man appearing in the program's About box.)

Third-party typefaces can come from a number of sources. We'll discuss these shortly.

A related issue in using the fonts in Corel Draw involves renaming them. The font names which Corel Draw uses are effectively fictitious, because Corel does not have licenses for the real copyrighted names. However, to make your understanding of type more in keeping with the way it's really used, you should probably change the names in the Corel Draw text window to their real counterparts. This appendix will discuss how to do this.

## *USING WFNBOSS*

In order to use WFNBOSS, you must run Windows and then double-click on WFNBOSS.EXE. (It should be in your Corel Draw directory.) A screen like the one in Figure B.2 will appear.

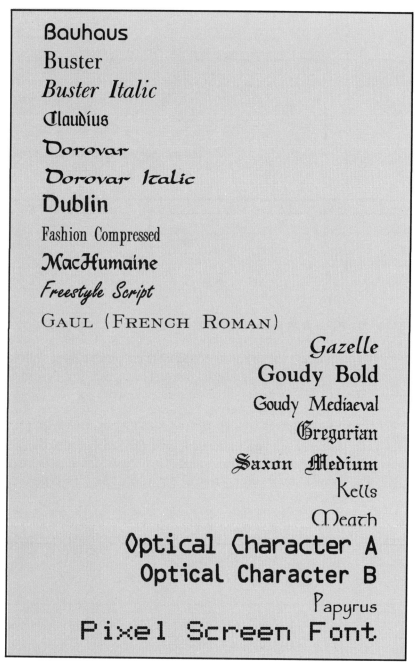

*Figure B.1:* Some third-party fonts.

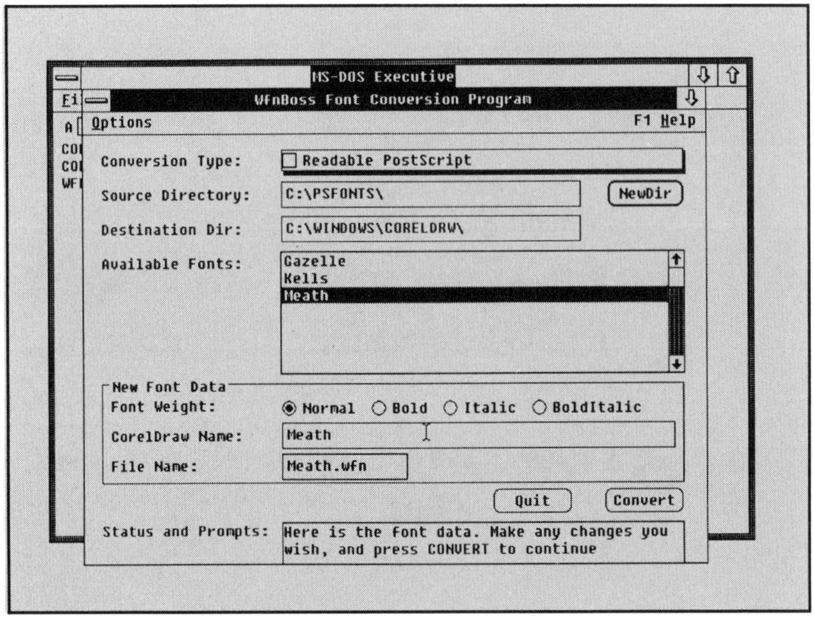

*Figure B.2:* The WFNBOSS screen.

The actual purpose of WFNBOSS might seem a little vague. It does two things. First, it converts foreign font files into Corel Draw font files. Second, it creates name entries for the Corel Draw text window.

WFNBOSS can work with most outline-font files designed for laser printer applications. It will not convert the Hewlett-Packard LaserJet's style of bitmapped soft fonts, which are not in a form Corel Draw would know what to do with. The font types supported at present are:

- Adobe type-1 PFB fonts

- Agfa/Compugraphic FF fonts

- Bitstream TDF, BCO and BEZ outline fonts

- DigiFont DFI fonts

- Fonts created by the OTLEDIT program in Z-Soft's Type Foundry package

- Third-party PostScript fonts, such as those from Casady & Greene, Image Club, and so on. These are fonts created using the Fontographer package on the Macintosh. Also included in this group are fonts created by the Bitstream FontWare package.

Given fonts in one of these categories, WFNBOSS will inhale them and create corresponding Corel Draw fonts. It will also generate a file called WFNBOSS.INI, which will contain some data for Corel Draw to use when it adds the fonts to its text window. We'll discuss this process shortly.

WFNBOSS does not modify the source files of the fonts it converts. However, certain sets of font data relating to a technique called "hinting" (available with Adobe oblique fonts) are unusable by Corel Draw itself. If you try to convert files containing such data, WFNBOSS will display a message notifying you of the presence of more than one set of data in the font file, and ask whether you want to use the "next set" or the "previous set." Corel Draw can use only the so-called "previous set," which you select by answering No. If answering No calls up further messages, answer No to those as well.

For the sake of this discussion, we'll look at the process of converting the Casady & Greene PostScript font *Meath* for use with Corel Draw. It lives in two files called MEATH.PFA and MEATH.AFM, and I keep it in a subdirectory called \PSFONTS, which allows it to be accessed by Ventura Publisher as well.

WFNBOSS only needs to get at the font to be converted for a short while—once converted, the original font file is no longer needed as far as Corel Draw is concerned. For this reason, you can easily convert font files directly from a floppy disk if you like.

The first thing to do is to tell WFNBOSS where Meath has come from. Start by clicking in the box to the right of the Conversion Type item at the top of the screen until "Readable PostScript" appears. Next, click into the Source Directory field and change it to the directory where MEATH.PFA resides. Alternatively, you can click in the NewDir control and use the file dialog box that pops up to move around in your directory tree.

You probably will not have to alter the Destination Dir field, as the default entry points to the CORELDRW directory, which is where your Corel Draw fonts are supposed to reside.

If you have selected the font type and source directory correctly, one or more font names will appear in the WFNBOSS Available Fonts window. Select the fonts you want to add to Corel Draw by clicking on them and then clicking in the Convert button. Alternately, select Convert All from the Options menu if you want to convert all the fonts in your source directory.

The conversion process can be a little time-consuming, but you probably won't have to do it very often. As a rule of thumb, Corel Draw fonts converted from readable PostScript fonts will be a little less than half the size of the original file. This usually comes out to between 10 and 20 kilobytes per font. Corel Draw fonts converted from most of the other font types will have files of about the same size as the original source files.

## FONTS AND WHERE TO FIND THEM

There is a growing number of third-party font suppliers. Some, such as Agfa/Compugraphic, provide pretty pedestrian, conventional faces. You would probably use one of these if you had to match the typeface in an existing document originally set with a Compugraphic font. In most cases, you will want to add fonts to Corel Draw to give yourself access to a wider range of display faces. Although Corel Draw comes with lots of display faces, you will probably find that you occasionally need additional unusual or very specialized fonts.

The faces in Figure B.1, at the beginning of this appendix, came from several sources. The Meath, Kells, Gazelle, Dorovar and Gregorian faces were done by Casady & Greene. You may recognize this name, as Casady & Greene also provided some of the example clip art which comes with Corel Draw. Casady & Greene typefaces are certainly among the best of the available third-party display faces. They're interesting, they set well as type, and they come with Ventura width tables and Windows installation procedures as well, making the same face applicable to quite a few applications.

Casady & Greene also has arguably the most interesting variety of display faces. In addition to the ones just discussed, for example, there's a cat face, examples of which can be found in the Corel Draw clip art book. This is a caps-only face in which all the characters are formed from cats.

With one exception, the rest of the typefaces in Figure B.1 are DigiFonts. DigiFonts have the advantage of being wonderfully cheap—as of this writing you could have the whole DigiFont library, 264 fonts, for about $400. The drawback to this is that DigiFonts are not always very well executed. Some are a bit crunchy, they don't always set well, and they frequently get erratic at small point sizes. Furthermore, many of the faces are incomplete.

The secret of using DigiFonts with Corel Draw is to select faces for which these limitations don't matter. Fonts such as Goudy Mediaeval, Papyrus, Dublin, Claudius, and French Roman—all of which are intended to look hand-set and a bit funky—don't suffer much for the relatively poor quality of DigiFonts. In fact, the rough edges which characterize DigiFonts probably improve the appearance of these sorts of typefaces.

The third source of fonts in the list in Figure B.1 is the public domain. The MacHumaine face, by Zachary Miller, was found on a bulletin board. Created with Fontographer, it turned out to be wholly digestible by WFNBOSS, and quite an attractive font when set. It's a bit ornate for some applications, but there are already dignified fonts in Corel Draw for those situations in which you must exercise restraint.

Obviously, finding fonts such as MacHumaine takes a bit of looking. If you're not familiar with modems, bulletin boards, and the vagaries of public-domain software, it might not be worth the effort. On the other hand, MacHumaine—at least as I found it—didn't even come with a request for donations from its creator. I couldn't beat the price.

## MODIFYING WIN.INI

There is a file in your Windows directory called WIN.INI. This is a text file, and you can edit it with any text editor or with a word processor such as WordStar in its non-document mode. The Windows Notepad application will also suffice.

The WIN.INI file is a catch-all for default settings and other basic information used by Windows itself and by other Windows applications, including Corel Draw. Corel Draw uses it to store the names and some other information about its fonts.

In modifying WIN.INI, you should start by making a copy of your original WIN.INI file so that if you mangle it in the process you will be able to revert to your previous version. Secondly, as you work through it be sure to leave anything you don't understand alone.

The part of the WIN.INI file you'll be meddling with here is the Corel Draw font list. If you haven't modified WIN.INI previously and you have installed Corel Draw, this will begin with the following lines.

```
[CORELDrwFonts]
Avalon = 15 avalon.wfn 3
Aardvark = 2 aardvark.wfn 0
Banff = 1 banff.wfn 0
Bangkok = 3 bangkok.wfn 0
```

The first thing on each line is the name of the font as it will appear in the Corel Draw text window. The fonts will appear in the order they occur in the WIN.INI file. When you rename the fonts—we'll get to that in a moment— you will also have to move the lines around if you want them to continue to appear in alphabetical order.

The font names can be anything you like, although we'll discuss the "official" names in a moment. The only restrictions are that they be 25 characters or less in length and that they not contain any spaces. If you want a space to appear in a typeface name, replace it with an underscore. Thus, if you wanted to use Times Roman, you would make the WIN.INI entry:

```
Times_Roman = 15 toronto.wfn 1
```

The file name is the actual file in which the Corel Draw font in question resides. This name doesn't have to look anything like the font name you use, since it only matters to Corel Draw.

Finally, the number at the end of the entry tells Corel Draw about how the font is likely to be handled by your PostScript printer— assuming you will be printing to one. It's ignored if you'll be outputting your Corel Draw art to a different sort of printer, such as a LaserJet.

Some typefaces, such as Times Roman, are resident in all Post-Script printers. If Corel Draw knows that a face is resident, it will in some cases attempt to use it. This will make drawings using these faces print faster, and frequently will produce somewhat better type, especially at small point sizes.

If the face is not resident Corel Draw will draw each character as paths.

Older PostScript printers had very few resident faces—usually only Helvetica, Times, Courier, and a symbol set. The newer machines typically come with 35 to 40 resident faces.

If the resident font code in a Corel Draw WIN.INI entry is 0, Corel Draw will assume that the face in question is not resident in any PostScript printers. If it's 1, it will assume that it's resident in all PostScript printers. If it's 3, Corel Draw will assume that it's resident in recent PostScript printers.

If you have an old or unusual PostScript printer—usually indicated by Corel Draw printing things in Courier rather than in the face you want—you might have to change some of the resident font codes in WIN.INI to reflect the resident fonts you really have.

Some PostScript printers, such as the latest generation of Apple LaserWriters, support dedicated hard drives upon which you can store PostScript fonts. If you were to add the Meath font to Corel Draw and place it on the hard drive of such a printer, Corel could treat it as a resident font.

In most cases, the fonts added to Corel Draw should be set up as non-resident. Obviously, it's better to err this way if you're not quite sure what's happening. If you tell Corel Draw that a font is not resident when it really is, your drawings may take longer to print, but nothing really nasty will happen. On the other hand, if you say that a font is resident when it really isn't, your drawings will emerge from your printer with huge, ugly Courier type splashed across them, or they might not print at all—something you probably want to avoid.

## *RENAMING COREL DRAW'S FONTS*

By this time, you should have figured out what's involved in changing the default Corel Draw font names to their real, commonly used names. All you need to do is locate the font names in WIN.INI and replace them with their corresponding proper names. Figure B.3 illustrates what the modified section of WIN.INI should look like. Of

```
[CORELDrwFonts]
Aachen=2 aardvark.wfn 0
American_Typwrtr=3 memorand.wfn 0
AvanteGarde=15 avalon.wfn 3
Benguiat=3 bangkok.wfn 0
Bodoni Poster=1 bodnoff.wfn 0
Bookman=15 brooklyn.wfn 3
Brush_Script=1 banff.wfn 0
Caslon=15 casablca.wfn 0
CenturyOldStyle=7 centold.wfn 0
CooperBlack=5 cuprtino.wfn 0
Friz_Quadrata=3 france.wfn 0
Franklin_Gothic=15 frankgo.wfn 0
Franklin_Goth_Hvy=5 frankgoh.wfn 0
FreestyleScript=1 freeport.wfn 0
Futura=15 fuji.wfn 0
Futura_ExtraBold=5 fujibold.wfn 0
Futura_Light=5 fujilite.wfn 0
Garamond=15 gatineau.wfn 0
Geographic_Symbols=1 geograph.wfn 0
Helvetica=15 swz.wfn 1
Helvetica-Black=5 swzblack.wfn 0
Helvetica-Light=5 swzlight.wfn 0
Helvetica-Narrow=15 swznarrw.wfn 3
Hobo=1 homeward.wfn 0
Machine=1 motor.wfn 0
Musical_Symbols=1 musical.wfn 0
New_Baskerville=15 nebraska.wfn 0
NewCenturySchlbk=15 brunswik.wfn 3
Optima=15 ottawa.wfn 0
Palatino=15 palmsprn.wfn 3
Park_Avenue=1 paradise.wfn 0
Review=1 renfrew.wfn 0
Souvenir=15 southern.wfn 0
Stencil=1 stamp.wfn 0
Symbols=1 symbols.wfn 1
TimesRoman=15 toronto.wfn 1
Tiffany=15 timpani.wfn 0
Tiffany_Heavy=5 timpanih.wfn 0
University_Roman=1 unicorn.wfn 0
Univers-Black=5 usablack.wfn 0
Univers-Light=5 usalight.wfn 0
Zapf_Chancery=4 zurich.wfn 3
Zapf_Dingbats=1 dixiland.wfn 3
```

*Figure B.3:* The modified WIN.INI file showing the proper font names.

course, you don't have to duplicate exactly my style of abbreviating the longer names. However, do make sure you don't inadvertently include any spaces in the font names or exceed 25 characters per entry.

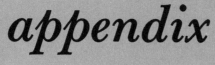

# appendix C

*Disabling the
Windows Logo*

THE ANIMATED MICROSOFT LOGO WHICH APPEARS every time you run Windows is amusing for a while, but it gets annoying quite quickly. It's hardly necessary—few users of Windows need to be reminded who created the software. If you usually run Corel Draw from Windows, rather than directly from the command line as discussed in Appendix A, you might well long for a way to dispense with the Microsoft logo.

In order to disable the display of the logo, you must modify the WIN.COM program, which can be found in your \WINDOWS directory. This program is called a "bootstrap" or "loader." It's the first stage in the process of waking up Windows and getting it going. Among other things, it's responsible for placing your screen in its graphics mode and displaying the logo.

Modifying WIN.COM involves what is called *patching*. This is a rather tricky procedure, as it involves making a slight change to the actual machine-language code of WIN.COM. If you have never done anything like this and don't feel adventurous, you might want to skip this appendix entirely, or at least seek out someone with a bit more experience in these matters.

The first thing to do in modifying WIN.COM is to make a copy of this file so that if you damage WIN.COM beyond repair you can simply revert to your original file and try again.

The patch to be discussed in this appendix may be a bit version-dependent, and there might well be versions of Windows upon which it will not work. If, as you work through the following instructions, you don't get the appropriate results, *stop what you're doing* and abandon your patched version of WIN.COM.

In order to patch WIN.COM, you will need the DEBUG program supplied with your DOS disks. You can load WIN.COM into DEBUG by typing the following line at the DOS prompt:

```
DEBUG WIN.COM
```

When WIN.COM is loaded and DEBUG is ready for action, it will display a dash prompt.

WIN.COM determines whether or not to display its logo by looking at a particular memory location for the string "LOGO". If it finds something else at this location, it skips the logo and goes on to run the main part of Windows immediately. All you have to do to disable the logo, then, is to find this string and change it somewhat. We will change it by making the uppercase L in LOGO lowercase.

To begin with, you must find the string. Enter the following command at the dash prompt:

S100,FFFF,'LOGO'

DEBUG should respond with something like

1A00:09F0

If no number appears, and DEBUG returns you to the dash prompt immediately, it has been unable to locate the LOGO string. Your version of Windows probably handles the display of its logo in a different way. In this case, simply type Q and hit Enter to quit—this patch won't work for your version of WIN.COM.

Assuming that you do get a number, you now know the address in memory where the LOGO string lives. The D (for Display) command will display it. In this case, you would type

D1A00:09F0

and DEBUG would show you something like the lines shown in Figure C.1. Note that the string "LOGO" is visible on the first line.

```
1A00:09F0  4C 4F 47 4F E9 C2 00 33-C0 8E C0 A0 19 00 26 A2   LOGOiB.3@.@ ..&"
1A00:0A00  10 04 A0 18 00 CD 10 CB-00 00 FC 8B D7 BB 07 00   ....M.K..|.W;..
1A00:0A10  B4 02 CD 10 AC 0A C0 74-06 B4 0E CD 10 EB F5 C3   4.M.,.@t.4.M.kuC
1A00:0A20  FC 51 57 32 D2 26 8B 05-86 C4 D1 D8 D0 D2 D1 D8   |QW2R&...DQXPRQX
1A00:0A30  D0 DA 86 C4 AB E2 EE 5F-59 83 C7 50 FE CE 75 E1   PZ.D+bn_Y.GP~Nua
1A00:0A40  C3 FD 51 57 32 D2 26 8B-05 86 C4 D1 D0 D0 D2 D1   C}QW2R&...DQPPRQ
1A00:0A50  D0 D0 DA 86 C4 AB E2 EE-5F 59 83 C7 50 FE CE 75   PPZ.D+bn_Y.GP~Nu
1A00:0A60  E1 FC C3 33 C9 8A CA D1-E9 F3 A5 73 01 A4 03 F8   a|C3I.JQis%s.$.x
```

*Figure C.1:* The sort of listing you will see when you use DEBUG to display a memory address.

To actually perform the patch, you would do the following, substituting the address DEBUG gave you for the LOGO string for the one I've used here:

E1A00:09F0

DEBUG would print

4C

and you would type in 6C, which is the code for a lowercase l. (In fact, any code other than 4C will do.)

You must now save your modified version of WIN.COM. Type W at the dash prompt and hit Enter. Then type Q and hit Enter to quit and return to DOS.

If you run Windows by typing WIN at the DOS prompt and hitting Enter, the Microsoft logo should be gone. If something untoward happens—such as Windows failing to run or your system crashing—reboot your machine and revert to the old copy of WIN-.COM which you saved before you started patching.

# *Index*

# L

labels
    connecting lines for, 84–86
    for pie charts, 81–84
landscape orientation, 68, 73
laser printer film, 322
laser printers, 164, 165, 346
    fills using, 162
    functioning of, 174
    minimum margins on, 70, 234
    multiple-mode, 352
    small point sizes on, 122
laser typesetters, 104
LaserJet printers, 347
    EPS files to, 249
    exporting files for, 248
    screens for, 168
layers
    colors as, 177–180
    of objects, 79–80
leading, 105, 124
legal aspects of clip art, 20–21
Letraset, 108
ligatures, 155, 158–159
LIM (Lotus, Intel, and Microsoft)
    memory, 340
line art files, exporting, 245–248
line cap settings, 130
line drawing, 38–99
linear fountains, 180
lines of type, spacing between, 105
lines, 28–30
    attributes of, 85
    complex curved, 10
    curved from straight, 60–63
    duplicating, 55–57, 65
    length of, 93
    as paths, 5
    removing, 96–97
    spacing between, 124
    straight, 44–45
    thickness of, 32, 44, 80, 98
Linotronic typesetter, 167, 175, 241,
    348
Linotype machine, 103

Logitech mouse, 344
logos, 157
    abstract graphics for, 309–311
    approach to, 300–303
    color in, 331
    disabling Microsoft Windows logo,
        386–388
    graphic, 306–311
    requirements of, 301
    type, 303–305
Lotus, Intel, and Microsoft (LIM)
    memory, 340
Lotus PIC files, importing, 192
lute, 86–99

# M

Macintosh system, 353
    exporting EPS files for, 202
    type on, 282
macros, 133–135, 332
magenta, 318
magnifying glass icon, 28
margins
    justified text and, 105
    on laser printers, 70
marks, rotation and skew, 68–70
marquee, 26. *See also* area (selec-
    tion by)
math symbols, 110, 139
maximize button, in Windows, 358
measurement of distance, on
    screen, 93
measurement units, 40
    Ruler display (Display menu), 43
mechanical drawing, 177
mechanical typesetting, 272
medium type, 108
Meidinger, Max, 273
Memorandum typeface, 8, 145,
    286–287
memory
    Corel requirements for, 339–341
    for laser printers, 347
    maximizing in Windows, 367–371

# Selections from The SYBEX Library

## DESKTOP PUBLISHING

### The ABC's of Ventura
**Robert Cowart/Steve Cummings**
390pp. Ref. 537-9

Created especially for new desktop publishers, this is an easy introduction to a complex program. Cowart provides details on using the mouse, the Ventura side bar, and page layout, with careful explanations of publishing terminology. The new Ventura menus are all carefully explained. For Version 2.

### Mastering PageMaker on the IBM PC (Second Edition)
**Antonia Stacy Jolles**
384pp. Ref. 521-2

A guide to every aspect of desktop publishing with PageMaker: the vocabulary and basics of page design, layout, graphics and typography, plus instructions for creating finished typeset publications of all kinds.

### Mastering Ready, Set, Go!
**David A. Kater**
482pp. Ref. 536-0

This hands-on introduction to the popular desktop publishing package for the Macintosh allows readers to produce professional-looking reports, brochures, and flyers. Written for Version 4, this title has been endorsed by Letraset, the Ready, Set, Go! software publisher.

### Mastering Ventura (Second Edition)
**Matthew Holtz**
613pp. Ref. 581-6

A complete, step-by-step guide to IBM PC desktop publishing with Xerox Ventura Publisher. Practical examples show how to use style sheets, format pages, cut and paste, enhance layouts, import material from other programs, and more. For Version 2.

### Understanding PFS: First Publisher
**Gerry Litton**
310pp. Ref. 616-2

This complete guide takes users from the basics all the way through the most complex features available. Discusses working with text and graphics, columns, clip art, and add-on software enhancements. Many page layout suggestions are introduced. Includes Fast Track speed notes.

### Understanding PostScript Programming (Second Edition)
**David A. Holzgang**
472pp. Ref. 566-2

In-depth treatment of PostScript for programmers and advanced users working on custom desktop publishing tasks. Hands-on development of programs for font creation, integrating graphics, printer implementations and more.

## Understanding
## Professional Write
**Gerry Litton**
400pp. Ref. 656-1

A complete guide to Professional Write that takes you from creating your first simple document, into a detailed description of all major aspects of the software. Special features place an emphasis on the use of different typestyles to create attractive documents as well as potential problems and suggestions on how to get around them.

## Ventura Instant Reference
## SYBEX Prompter Series
**Matthew Holtz**
320pp. Ref. 544-1, 4 ¾" × 8"

This compact volume offers easy access to the complex details of Ventura modes and options, commands, side-bars, file management, output device configuration, and control. Written for versions through Ventura 2, it also includes standard procedures for project and job control.

## Ventura Power Tools
**Rick Altman**
318pp. Ref. 592-1

Renowned Ventura expert, Rick Altman, presents strategies and techniques for the most efficient use of Ventura Publisher 2. This includes a power disk with DOS utilities which is specially designed for optimizing Ventura use. Learn how to soup up Ventura, edit CHP files, avoid design tragedies, handle very large documents, and improve form.

## Ventura Tips and Techniques
**Carl Townsend/Sandy Townsend**
424pp. Ref. 559-X

Packed with an experienced Ventura user's tips and tricks, this volume is a time saver and design booster. From crop marks to file management to using special fonts, this book is for serious Ventura users. Covers Ventura 2.

## Your HP LaserJet Handbook
**Alan R. Neibauer**
564pp. Ref. 618-9

Get the most from your printer with this step-by-step instruction book for using LaserJet text and graphics features such as cartridge and soft fonts, type selection, memory and processor enhancements, PCL programming, and PostScript solutions. This hands-on guide provides specific instructions for working with a variety of software.

# DESKTOP PRESENTATION

## Mastering Harvard Graphics
**Glenn H. Larsen**
318pp. Ref. 585-9

Here is a solid course in computer graphing and chart building with the popular software package. Readers can create the perfect presentation using text, pie, line, bar, map, and pert charts. Customizing and automating graphics is easy with these step-by-step instructions. For Version 2.1.

# APPLE/MACINTOSH

## The ABC's of Excel
## on the Macintosh
**Douglas Hergert**
314pp. Ref. 562-X

This title is written for users who want a quick way to get started with this highly-acclaimed spreadsheet program. The ABC's offers a rich collection of hands-on examples and step-by-step instructions for working with worksheets, charts, databases, and macros. Covers Excel through Version 1.5.

## AppleWorks Tips and
## Techniques
## (Second Edition)
**Robert Ericson**
462pp. Ref. 480-1

An indispensible collection of timesaving techniques, practical solutions, and tips on undocumented problems for every AppleWorks user. This expanded new edition covers all versions through 2.0, and includes in-depth treatment of macros.

## TO JOIN THE SYBEX MAILING LIST OR ORDER BOOKS PLEASE COMPLETE THIS FORM

NAME _____ COMPANY _____

STREET _____ CITY _____

STATE _____ ZIP _____

☐ PLEASE MAIL ME MORE INFORMATION ABOUT **SYBEX** TITLES

ORDER FORM (There is no obligation to order)

PLEASE SEND ME THE FOLLOWING:

| TITLE | QTY | PRICE |
|-------|-----|-------|
| _____ | ___ | ___ |
| _____ | ___ | ___ |
| _____ | ___ | ___ |
| _____ | ___ | ___ |

TOTAL BOOK ORDER _____ $_____

CUSTOMER SIGNATURE _____

SHIPPING AND HANDLING PLEASE ADD $2.00 PER BOOK VIA UPS _____

FOR OVERSEAS SURFACE ADD $5.25 PER BOOK PLUS $4.40 REGISTRATION FEE _____

FOR OVERSEAS AIRMAIL ADD $18.25 PER BOOK PLUS $4.40 REGISTRATION FEE _____

CALIFORNIA RESIDENTS PLEASE ADD APPLICABLE SALES TAX _____

TOTAL AMOUNT PAYABLE _____

☐ CHECK ENCLOSED    ☐ VISA
☐ MASTERCARD    ☐ AMERICAN EXPRESS

ACCOUNT NUMBER _____

EXPIR. DATE _____ DAYTIME PHONE _____

CHECK AREA OF COMPUTER INTEREST:

☐ BUSINESS SOFTWARE

☐ TECHNICAL PROGRAMMING

☐ OTHER: _____

THE FACTOR THAT WAS MOST IMPORTANT IN YOUR SELECTION:

☐ THE SYBEX NAME

☐ QUALITY

☐ PRICE

☐ EXTRA FEATURES

☐ COMPREHENSIVENESS

☐ CLEAR WRITING

☐ OTHER _____

OTHER COMPUTER TITLES YOU WOULD LIKE TO SEE IN PRINT:

_____

_____

OCCUPATION

☐ PROGRAMMER          ☐ TEACHER

☐ SENIOR EXECUTIVE     ☐ HOMEMAKER

☐ COMPUTER CONSULTANT  ☐ RETIRED

☐ SUPERVISOR           ☐ STUDENT

☐ MIDDLE MANAGEMENT    ☐ OTHER:

☐ ENGINEER/TECHNICAL   _____

☐ CLERICAL/SERVICE

☐ BUSINESS OWNER/SELF EMPLOYED

CHECK YOUR LEVEL OF COMPUTER USE

☐ NEW TO COMPUTERS

☐ INFREQUENT COMPUTER USER

☐ FREQUENT USER OF ONE SOFTWARE

  PACKAGE:

  NAME _____

☐ FREQUENT USER OF MANY SOFTWARE

  PACKAGES

☐ PROFESSIONAL PROGRAMMER

OTHER COMMENTS:

_____
_____
_____
_____
_____
_____
_____

PLEASE FOLD, SEAL, AND MAIL TO SYBEX

**SYBEX, INC.**
2021 CHALLENGER DR. #100
ALAMEDA, CALIFORNIA  USA
94501

SEAL

# SYBEX Computer Books are different.

---

# Here is why . . .

At SYBEX, each book is designed with you in mind. Every manuscript is carefully selected and supervised by our editors, who are themselves computer experts. We publish the best authors, whose technical expertise is matched by an ability to write clearly and to communicate effectively. Programs are thoroughly tested for accuracy by our technical staff. Our computerized production department goes to great lengths to make sure that each book is well-designed.

In the pursuit of timeliness, SYBEX has achieved many publishing firsts. SYBEX was among the first to integrate personal computers used by authors and staff into the publishing process. SYBEX was the first to publish books on the CP/M operating system, microprocessor interfacing techniques, word processing, and many more topics.

Expertise in computers and dedication to the highest quality product have made SYBEX a world leader in computer book publishing. Translated into fourteen languages, SYBEX books have helped millions of people around the world to get the most from their computers. We hope we have helped you, too.

## For a complete catalog of our publications:

---

SYBEX, Inc. 2021 Challenger Drive, #100, Alameda, CA 94501
Tel: (415) 523-8233/(800) 227-2346   Telex: 336311
Fax: (415) 523-2373

# Principal Dialog Boxes
## from the Corel Draw Menus

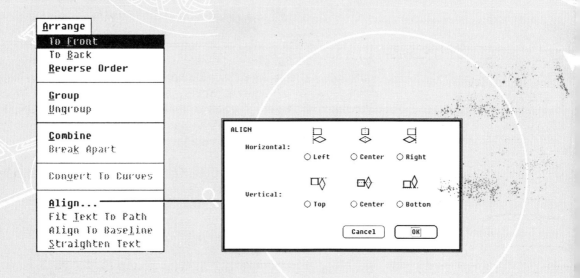

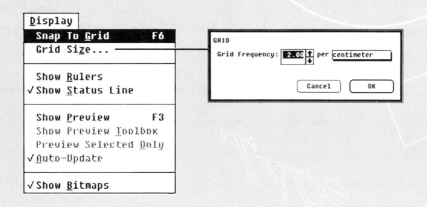